INTERNATIONAL ECONOMICS
Analysis and Issues

CHARLES E. STALEY
State University of New York at Stony Brook

PRENTICE-HALL, INC.
Englewood Cliffs, New Jersey

© 1970
by PRENTICE-HALL, INC.
Englewood Cliffs, New Jersey

13–471672–8
LIBRARY OF CONGRESS
CATALOG CARD NUMBER: 78–113043

Current printing (last digit):

10   9   8   7   6   5   4   3   2   1

Prentice-Hall International, Inc., *London*
Prentice-Hall of Australia, Pty. Ltd., *Sydney*
Prentice-Hall of Canada, Ltd., *Toronto*
Prentice-Hall of India Private Limited, *New Delhi*
Prentice-Hall of Japan, Inc., *Tokyo*

Printed in the United States of America

To Rhoda and the children

PREFACE

I ventured into this writing to help organize my thoughts about the large amounts of research in international economics which have been appearing in recent years. The organizing principle for the book itself is to present the subject on the basis of what is done by international economists. Such a presentation should provide the background for the reader's simultaneous or subsequent plunge into the literature, and it should help him to appreciate the applications, changes, and improvements in the tools of his craft which he will encounter.

In these pages the reader will find, if he does not already know what international economists do, that the field includes the concoction of models of international trade and finance, extending, revising, and replacing previous models; there is also the study of patterns of trade and finance, sometimes explicitly to test models, sometimes rather to learn something about the facts; finally, there is comment on the policies followed by governments and suggestions about desirable alternative policies. Each of these forms of intellectual action finds a place in the book, not necessarily in the proportions actually undertaken by the profession.

I wish to thank the following for their encouragement, assistance, and advice, all of it good but not always followed: Professor Egon Neuberger, State University of New York at Stony Brook; Professor David E. Bond, The University of British Columbia; Dr. Ewan Clague, Senior Associate, Leon Kramer, Inc., Washington, D.C.; Professor H. Robert Heller, University of California, Los Angeles; Professor Leo Spier, The Pennsylvania State University.

The sins of omission and commission are of course my own.

Charles E. Staley

CONTENTS

Part One

INTERNATIONAL TRADE

CHAPTER 1

INTRODUCTION TO INTERNATIONAL ECONOMICS

INTERNATIONAL ECONOMICS, as part of the branch of knowledge under the special concern of economists, is related to the other fields of economics. But it does have some distinctions of its own that have given it a tradition of separate study. One of the first concerns of an introduction to the subject is to inquire into just what it is that distinguishes international economics.

Like the other specialties—public finance, labor economics, agricultural economics, and so on—international economics draws on the central body of economic theory, both microeconomics and macroeconomics. The usual techniques of statistics and econometrics are widely used in statistical studies of trade problems. On occasion, too, the skills of economic historians are called for.

But these various tools are used, first of all, to analyze situations with a rather different institutional background than is common in other economic subjects. In studying economic contacts between countries, the usual economic theory would do very well if trade between the United States and France, for example, were trade among 250 million people. But it is not. Both countries are sovereign; both may regulate trade, migration, and the exchange of money. And these regulations have to be studied explicitly, for they have enormous influence on the course of events. It is then a matter of the division of labor, along good Adam Smith lines, to have specialists whose concern is problems such as these.

In addition, problems that are often studied from the point of view of a single country (the closed economy) take on new dimensions that sometimes require attention to international economics. For example, for many years it was almost unnecessary that the theory and practice of fiscal and monetary policy in the United States be concerned with international repercussions. But then, a series of years during which foreign countries accumulated a large volume of dollar holdings forced American policy into concerning itself with the effects of different actions on foreign countries. (This concern, by the way, goes under the name of the balance-of-payments constraint on domestic policy.) For another example, labor economics may be concerned with the international migration of people into such labor-scarce economies as Switzerland and other European countries. These "inter-sub-disciplinary" problems need the insights of international economics in order to make progress toward understanding the implications of new developments in the world.

Furthermore, the esoteric doctrines of welfare economics may be viewed from strictly a domestic angle, but they have important applications in the study of international economics as well. It is also true that international economics has led to some innovations in welfare economics, notably in the propositions dealing with the theory of the second-best (a subject that we come to later).[1]

Within the limits of economic problems that have special relevance to economic relations among nations, the approaches and the problems still have a broad range. With dozens of countries and currencies, thousands of commodities, and millions of dollars of investments and intergovernmental loans, there is no end of current raw material, to say nothing of the riches of historical research. Over the years the variety of trade patterns, the evolution of monetary systems, and the continuous rise of new problems have led to a correspondingly impressive body of theoretical work designed to help one understand the workings of the international economy. This book is basically built around the theoretical work that has been done in recent years. It attempts to make the theory more accessible, as well as to illustrate the applications of theory by drawing on the voluminous storehouse of empirical work and the wide range of current policy problems.

The beginning point is the theory of trade, ranging from classical notions of comparative advantage through the modern formulations of general equilibrium. The initial development is based on very severe abstractions, but gradually the important problems presented by transportation costs, monopoly, intermediate goods, tariffs, and economic development are introduced.

The second part of the book is concerned with the thorny problems of balance-of-payments equilibrium and its related aspects of exchange systems

---

[1] Apart from that example, it is generally agreed that international economics has not pioneered in new directions in theory. See W. M. Corden, *Recent Developments in the Theory of International Trade*, Special Papers in International Economics No. 7 (Princeton, N.J.: International Finance Section, Princeton University, 1965); and Charles P. Kindleberger, "Trends in International Economics," *Annals of the American Academy*, CCCLVIII (March 1965), 170–79.

and exchange rates, international monetary arrangements, and the like. These problems rank high on the list of unsolved issues facing the governments of the world today, and they occupy a correspondingly large share of the attention of international economics.

And now, on to international trade.

CHAPTER 2

THE THEORY
OF COMPARATIVE
ADVANTAGE

INTERNATIONAL ECONOMICS may be thought of as two parallel roads with occasional crossovers between them. One road is international monetary theory, whose concern is balance-of-payments equilibrium. Can it be achieved? Can it be maintained? What are the implications of various types of international monetary arrangements? The second half of the book is devoted to these questions. The other is often called the "pure" theory of trade. This simply means that concern with monetary issues is avoided by the twin assumptions of balance-of-payments equilibrium (external balance) and full employment (internal balance). Instead, the focus is on the "real" side of such questions as the gains from trade, the pattern and volume of trade, relative prices, and the effects of trade on the internal economies of the trading countries.

It is obvious that if a country wishes to consume something that it cannot produce because of climate or lack of resources, it will have to import it. For a century and a half economists have emphasized a much less obvious factor in trade, the idea of comparative advantage. International commerce is not a matter of shipping goods from nations that can make them to those that cannot; it does not even depend on the exporter being a more efficient producer than the importer. According to the English classical economists, it rests on the much more subtle principle that even if one country is more efficient than its trading partner in producing all goods, beneficial trade can be carried on with each concentrating on producing and exporting the items in which it is *relatively* most efficient. This theory was the basis of the international economics writings of the classical school; its elaboration and refinement took them a century. Even today researchers find that it helps in the understanding and explanation of trade flows. Accordingly, it is worthwhile to analyze comparative advantage in some detail.

6

RICARDO'S MODEL OF COMPARATIVE ADVANTAGE

Perhaps the most famous and influential exposition is that of David Ricardo (Chapter VII of his 1817 book, *The Principles of Political Economy and Taxation*). He set up a very simple and abstract model to explain the working of comparative advantage. Suppose, Ricardo says, that in England 100 men work for one year to produce a unit of cloth, and 120 men for one year to produce a unit of wine. In Portugal, assume the requirements are 80 man-years for the same amount of wine and 90 man-years for cloth. Labor inputs per unit of output do not vary, no matter how much or little is produced. Portugal has an absolute advantage, since it requires a smaller amount of resources for each commodity, and if resources moved freely, entrepreneurs would set up their plants in Portugal rather than England. But if capital and labor are reluctant to move overseas, production will take place in England in spite of its high costs. (We will not be far wrong in regarding the quantity of labor as the cost; Professor Stigler has remarked that Ricardo had a 93 per cent labor theory of value with the returns on capital accounting for the rest. However, in his trade chapter Ricardo used labor time for his illustration of the principle of comparative advantage.)

Suppose no foreign trade is possible. Then wine is relatively expensive in England. In competitive markets the price ratio will be determined by the cost ratio; in this case the cost of wine is 120 and the cost of cloth is 100, so the ratio is

$$C_w/C_c = P_w/P_c = 120/100 = 6/5. \qquad \text{(2-1)}$$

Here C_w means the cost of wine, P_w the price of wine, and so on. In the same way it can be seen that wine is relatively cheap in Portugal, where $P_w/P_c = 8/9$.[1]

Now assume that the two nations may trade with one another and, as is customary, leave transportation costs aside at the first approximation. England would find it cheaper to buy wine in Portugal because at Portuguese prices 1 unit of cloth exchanges for 9/8 units of wine. England could use 100 men to produce a unit of cloth, ship it to Portugal, and obtain a quantity of wine that would have cost the labor of 135 men (9/8 × 120 men) if made at home. Portugal, finding cloth relatively cheap in England, could make 1 unit of wine, ship it to England, and exchange it at British prices for 6/5 units of cloth. In this way it could acquire for the labor of 80 men as much cloth as 108 men (6/5 × 90) could make at home.

Of course the additional demand for wine raises P_w/P_c in Portugal,

---

[1] Notice that these price ratios are the reciprocal of the ratios of the quantities of goods exchanged. In England, $\frac{5}{6}$ unit of wine will exchange for 1 unit of cloth, since each will cost the labor of 100 men and therefore will have equal value. The reciprocal relation between price and quantity ratios is important and we shall exploit it often.

and the new demand for British cloth by raising P_c lowers P_w/P_c in England. This process will continue until the relative prices become equal in the two countries. However, we would need to know the demand schedules to be able to say what the final equilibrium price would be and to make sure that peculiar demand structures do not render cost conditions powerless to affect trade. (For an illustration of this, refer to the article by Bhagwati cited in footnote 2.) It is interesting to note that while competition in the Ricardian model forces prices to equal (labor) costs when there is no international trade, the same forces of competition serve to make prices diverge from labor costs with trade. For equilibrium to exist, the same relative prices must prevail in both countries. (Labor costs serve to set the limits within which this price ratio may fall, of course.)

If we define the *gains from trade* as acquiring goods at a smaller expenditure of resources, the gains in the final equilibrium will be less than the amount each would gain if it could trade at the other's relative prices. But each will gain something and each will have an incentive to trade as long as the international P_w/P_c ratio is higher than in isolated Portugal and lower than in isolated England. Since Portugal would not trade if the international price ratio fell below her own, and England would refuse to buy internationally if the P_w/P_c ratio rose above her own, at the very worst no country would lose by trade.[2]

Once the foundation is laid and the principle established, it is not necessary to repeat this elaborate analysis for each separate case. What is needed to predict trade flows is the information that a certain good is relatively cheapest in a certain country. This may be simply established by comparing labor cost ratios. For example, in Ricardo's example we have

$$\frac{C_w^P}{C_c^P} = \frac{80}{90} < \frac{C_w^E}{C_c^E} = \frac{120}{100}, \tag{2-2}$$

where the superscripts refer to countries and the subscripts to commodities. By inverting the ratios, you may show that England has the lowest relative cost in cloth.

MONEY WAGES AND EXCHANGE RATES

The Ricardian approach is very abstract and stark, which often bothers students. Traders make decisions on the basis of comparing money costs and prices, not ratios of amounts of resources used. Money costs are

[2] Jagdish Bhagwati, "The Proofs of the Theorems on Comparative Advantage," *Economic Journal*, LXXVII, No. 305 (March 1967), 75–83, deals with the case where labor is equally productive in both goods in both countries, leading to the same price ratios in the absence of trade. In that case consumption is governed by demand but there is no need for production to correspond to consumption when transportation is costless. If production quantities and consumption quantities differ, trade will take place at the common pretrade price.

influenced by wage rates and by exchange rates when one purchases abroad. By ignoring these, might we not have left out something important? How do we know that we come out with the correct answers if we consider only comparative costs? To answer these questions, it is necessary to recast Ricardo's data into monetary form. Suppose that in Portugal the wage rate is 2,000 escudos per year and in England it is 1,000 pounds sterling per year. We can easily compile a table showing the prices of the goods, as in Table 2-1.

Table 2-1

	Price in Portugal (escudos)	Price in England (pounds)
Wine	160,000	120,000
Cloth	180,000	100,000

Before a trader can decide whether to export or import wine, he must be able to compare British and Portuguese prices. He can do this if he knows the rate of exchange between escudos and pounds. We shall denote the rate by R and define it as the number of escudos necessary to buy 1 pound.

For trade to be possible, R must be fixed within certain limits. If it is too low, the price of local Portuguese wine would be higher than the price of British wine bought with cheap pounds. For example, if $R = 1$ escudo/pound, British wine would cost 120,000 escudos in Portugal, far below the local price of 160,000 escudos. At this rate Portugal would import the good in which it has a comparative advantage as well as the one in which it has a comparative disadvantage. To buy these goods it would demand sterling, but since it does not sell anything to England, there would be no supply of sterling. The price of the pound would rise until the Portuguese wine-grower could compete with the British price converted into escudos. That is to say, the minimum feasible exchange rate is given by

$$P_w^P = P_w^E \cdot R. \tag{2-3}$$

Therefore,

$$R \geq \frac{P_w^P}{P_w^E} = \frac{160,000 \text{ escudos}}{120,000 \text{ pounds}} = \frac{4/3 \text{ escudos}}{\text{pound}}. \tag{2-4}$$

The upper limit is determined by the consideration that Portugal must not export everything. This event would happen if

$$180,000 \text{ escudos} \leq 100,000 \text{ pounds} \cdot R. \tag{2-5}$$

If that were the case, Portuguese cloth would have a lower money price in England than would British cloth (and, of course, Portuguese wine would be very cheap). The prevention of such a circumstance requires

$$P_c^P > P_c^E \cdot R \tag{2-6}$$

or, what is the same thing,

$$R < \frac{P_c^P}{P_c^E} = \frac{180,000 \text{ escudos}}{100,000 \text{ pounds}} = \frac{1.8 \text{ escudos}}{\text{pound}}. \tag{2-7}$$

At the limit, R could equal this ratio.

Combining the two limits, it appears that $1.33 \cdots \le R \le 1.8$, but remember, this holds only for the assumed wage rates.[3]

For the sake of a concrete numerical example, suppose that the forces of supply and demand for the pound set the rate at 1.4 escudos/pound.[4] Then the price of British cloth in Portugal is 1.4(100,000) = 140,000 escudos, so Portugal imports cloth. Furthermore, the price of foreign wine in England is $160,000/1.4 = £114,285\frac{5}{7}$. The foreign wine is cheaper and England imports wine just as the comparative cost ratios indicated. You may check to see that you get the same trade pattern for any R in the 1.33–1.8 range. Abstracting from money wages and costs was obviously justified as long as we are interested only in the real forces behind trade. Of course, when we turn to international finance, we must work with the broader model.[5]

THE TERMS OF TRADE

As one by-product of working with prices and exchange rates, we may compute the terms of trade and get an alternative view of the gains from trade.[6] The terms of trade are the international price ratio of the commodities, which of course have to be expressed in a common currency. In terms of escudos we found $P_w = 160,000$ and $P_c = 140,000$, when $R = 1.4$ escudos/pound. If we denote the terms of trade by T, we obtain

[3] See Paul A. Samuelson, "Theoretical Notes on Trade Problems," *Review of Economics and Statistics*, XLVI, No. 2 (May 1964), 145–54, for a more detailed treatment.

[4] If this is to be the equilibrium rate, the necessary condition is that the value of Portuguese exports equals the value of Portuguese imports.

[5] The illustration assumed that the exchange rate was flexible and could vary within the limits determined by relative prices. But in the contemporary world it is more common for the rate to be fixed and for wages or prices or productivities to be required to adjust to the rate. A nice exercise is to try setting the limits on wages in, for example, Portugal, given R, wages in England, and Ricardo's labor data. *Hint:* Since $P_w^P = \text{wages}^P \cdot 80$, one limit can be found by substituting this product in Eq. (2-3). This yields

$$\text{wages}^P \cdot 80 = P_w^E \cdot R. \tag{2-8}$$

If $R = 1$ escudo/pound, with British wages as before,

$$\text{wages}^P = 120,000/80 = 1,500 \text{ escudos} \tag{2-9}$$

as one limit. The section on international finance will investigate such problems in more detail.

[6] Remember that the gains from trade were treated as obtaining commodities for a smaller expenditure of labor than previously. The process of finding the equilibrium terms of trade will be examined shortly; at this point it is convenient to illustrate the concept.

$T = P_w/P_c = 8/7$.[7] A comparison of this number with the price ratios in the absence of trade shows the benefits of trade to each economy. In Portugal the pretrade price ratio of 8/9 fundamentally meant that $\frac{8}{9}$ unit of cloth exchanged for 1 unit of wine; with trade, remembering the reciprocal relation between price and quantity ratios, 1 unit of wine will exchange for $1\frac{1}{7}$ units of cloth. Hence, by trading, the sacrifice of 1 unit of wine will yield more cloth in return than could be acquired by cutting wine production at home in order to shift labor into cloth production. Similarly, in pretrade England the P_w/P_c ratio of 6/5 meant $1\frac{1}{5}$ units of cloth exchanged for 1 unit of wine; with trade, only $1\frac{1}{7}$ units of cloth are required. England gains by procuring wine at a smaller cloth expenditure. Both countries gain by trading, even though one is a more efficient producer of both commodities.[8]

A GEOMETRICAL VERSION
OF COMPARATIVE ADVANTAGE

Before leaving the theoretical discussion of Ricardo's model, a translation into geometry will help clarify the subject and prepare the way for subsequent work.

Suppose Portugal's labor force consists of 720 men. Then if all the men work in the cloth industry, 8 units of cloth can be produced; or if all work in the vineyards, 9 units of wine. These numbers appear on the axes of the diagram in Fig. 2-1(a), and they are connected by a solid line. The line is straight, reflecting the standard Ricardian assumption of constant cost: Whether a few workers or many are transferred from the textile to the liquor business, the decrease in cloth and the increase in wine will be in the ratio 8/9. No increase in cost results from increasing the output of either commodity. Notice that the absolute value of the slope of this line is the same as the price ratio P_w/P_c, which we saw was 8/9.[9] Since we are assuming full employment, we know that the Portuguese economy will be able to produce and consume any desired combination along the transformation curve.

[7] Note that T is the same in pounds: $114,285\frac{5}{7}/100,000 = \frac{8}{7}$. This must be the case, since the terms of trade in Portugal are $P_w^P/(P_c^E \cdot R)$, and in England $T = [P_w^P \cdot (1/R)]/P_c^E$, which is the same ratio.

[8] Both nineteenth-century classical writers and contemporary developments of classical models of comparative advantage are reviewed in John S. Chipman, "A Survey of the Theory of International Trade: Part 1, The Classical Theory," *Econometrica*, XXXIII, No. 3 (July 1965), 477–519. Although the article concentrates on mathematical aspects of the theory, becoming fairly advanced at times, Chipman does such an excellent job of placing the developments in their context in the history of thought and of stating assumptions and conclusions clearly that those with modest mathematical knowledge may profit from it.

[9] The line is given various names: transformation curve, production-possibilities curve, or opportunity-cost curve. The names all stem from the idea of converting one good into another by the process of shifting resources from one industry to the other.

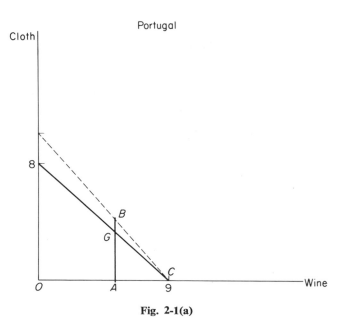

Fig. 2-1(a)

England's transformation curve in Fig. 2-1(b) is derived from the assumption of 600 workers; hence England's production options range between 6 units of cloth and 5 units of wine, with the absolute value of the slope of the transformation curve, 6/5, equal to P_w/P_c.

How can we show foreign trade in these diagrams? That is easy; we draw in the international terms-of-trade line. In each diagram the dashed

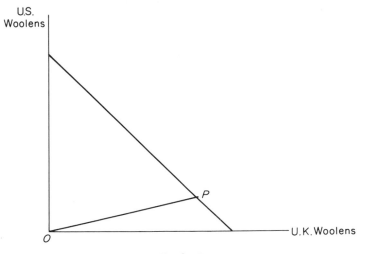

Fig. 2-1(b)

line shows the terms of trade, drawn so that $P_w/P_c = 8/7$, in accordance with the previous example. Portugal, with its comparative advantage in wine, specializes completely in wine production and trades for cloth along the terms-of-trade line. England specializes in cloth and trades along a line with exactly the same $-8/7$ slope. For this to be the equilibrium terms of trade, the desired exports of wine must equal the desired imports, and the same is true for cloth; otherwise, the divergence between supply and demand will force a price change. In the diagrams the exports and imports are equal: Portugal exports AC of wine, and England imports DF; while Portugal imports AB of cloth, which is equal to England's exports of DE.

Notice in particular that the terms-of-trade line lies above and to the right of the transformation curve for each country. For any given consumption of the export good, it is possible for each to consume more of its import good than would have been feasible without trade. (This statement excludes the intercepts C and E, of course.) Portugal can consume GB more of cloth than would be possible with a wine production of OA in isolation, and England can consume HF more of wine than a cloth production of OD would allow without trade. Both gain.

It is possible that the terms-of-trade line will coincide with the transformation curve of one or the other country. For example, this would be the case if Portugal were so small that its supplies of wine and demand for cloth made no perceptible difference in British prices. In that case, only Portugal would specialize and receive the benefits of a posttrade price ratio, which differs from the pretrade ratio. From our previous analysis we know that in any case the terms of trade will lie between (in the limit, be equal to one of) the transformation curves.

We have come a long way on the basis of some remarkably simple assumptions. We have shown how trade arises from a difference in comparative costs, how we may concentrate on real factors rather than monetary aspects, and how the gains from trade arise. These points, so clearly shown in the model, are fundamental but are often overlooked in debates on the tariff and on economic development. Like any economic model, the Ricardian theory allows us to examine in detail the workings of part of the economic system. The abstractions from reality are made to prevent cluttering up the reasoning with what is for the purpose at hand taken to be extraneous aspects of the world. But it must be admitted that the comparative cost model makes extremely large demands on one's willingness to abstract. Surely the demand side was given very short shrift. And on the supply side, what about the effects of the large amounts of capital in developed countries compared to the capital scarcity of underdeveloped countries? Or the existence of large amounts of fertile land in temperate-zone countries compared to the easily depleted soils of the tropics? Or the constant cost assumption? Modern international trade theory deals with these and other considerations; but before surveying it, some recent applications of the Ricardian approach are worth our attention.[10]

EMPIRICAL STUDIES BASED ON CLASSICAL TRADE THEORY

In common with other fields of economics, much empirical work in international economics currently takes the form of the testing of hypotheses by means of statistical procedures such as regression analysis. Empirical studies as such are by no means a novelty, but the sophisticated techniques employed stand in great contrast to the historical survey, informed judgment, and tabular presentation of data employed by the great earlier writers such as Taussig.[11] The Ricardian model has recently stimulated several studies designed to investigate its explanatory value in determining trade patterns. These studies provide good examples of empirical research as well as helping us to understand the role of comparative advantage in trade theory.

Before the model can be used, some of the glaring oversimplifications have to be remedied. One of these is that trade involves thousands of commodities, not just two. This complication may be easily handled, however, by a development of the cost ratio comparisons used in the two-goods case. In Eq.(2-2) we expressed Portugal's comparative advantage by the inequality

$$\frac{C_w^P}{C_c^P} < \frac{C_w^E}{C_c^E}.$$

This may be rearranged to read

$$\frac{C_w^P}{C_w^E} < \frac{C_c^P}{C_c^E}. \qquad \text{(2-10)}$$

Now, if there are many commodities, for example, n of them,

$$\frac{C_i^P}{C_i^E} \qquad (i = 1, 2, \ldots, n), \qquad \text{(2-11)}$$

list the ratios in order, with the lowest ratio first and the highest ratio last. Then we may be sure that Portugal's imports all appear at the bottom of the list and her exports at the top, for the first of the list consists of the goods that are relatively cheap to produce at home. The dividing line in the list between imports and exports will depend on the strength of each country's

---

[10] There is a case for the position that Ricardo's theory should properly be construed as a welfare model whose purpose was to make the case for free trade rather than as a positive model designed to explain the facts of trade. See J. Bhagwati, "The Theory of International Trade," *Indian Economic Journal*, VIII, No. 160 (July 1960), 1–17.

[11] See, for example, Frank Taussig, *Some Aspects of the Tariff Question* (Cambridge, Mass.: Harvard University Press, 1915), or his famous *International Trade* (New York: The Macmillan Company, 1927).

demand for the other's products. The higher Portugal's demand for British goods, other things equal, the more exports will be necessary to pay for them, and the further down the line the division between exports and imports will fall. Suppose the dividing line falls so that product m is the end of the export list. Symbolically, we would have

$$\frac{C_i^P}{C_i^E} < \frac{C_j^P}{C_j^E} \qquad (i = 1, \ldots, m; j = m + 1, \ldots, n). \qquad \text{(2-12)}$$

Another complication in reformulating the hypothesis more in accordance with reality is that wage rates are not uniform within a country, as we assumed in dealing with wages in the example on p. 9. Actually, wages vary among industries, reflecting various strengths of labor unions, lags in adjustments to changed supply and demand conditions, regional variations, and so on. It is then possible for a lower labor input ratio for product i to be offset by relatively higher wages at home than abroad in the same industry, so that we would import the commodity in spite of its labor cost advantage. It is, however, easy to rewrite the hypothesis in terms of comparative money wage costs:

$$\frac{C_i^P}{C_i^E} \cdot \frac{w_i^P}{w_i^E} < \frac{C_j^P}{C_j^E} \cdot \frac{w_j^P}{w_j^E} \qquad (i = 1, \ldots, m; j = m + 1, \ldots, n), \qquad \text{(2-13)}$$

where w_i is the wage rate for the industry in question. This inequality says that all of Portugal's exports have a lower money labor cost relative to England than any of Portugal's imports.[12]

A third important factor in world trade, ignored by the Ricardian approach, is that actual imports and exports are greatly influenced by tariffs and a variety of other trade restrictions. The authors of the studies on comparative costs have avoided the necessity of estimating the effects of tariffs by a neat device: They compare the export performance of the two countries in a third market, assuming that the trade restrictions will affect the exporters equally. Differences in export patterns would then not be the result of tariffs, but of comparative costs, if the model is correct.

These ideas have been applied in three major studies.[13] The researchers

[12] Jagdish Bhagwati, "The Pure Theory of International Trade," *Economic Journal*, LXXIV, No. 293 (March 1964), 7–8, develops the Ricardian testable hypotheses in this way, with some additional details. This article has been reprinted in American Economic Association–Royal Economic Society, *Surveys of Economic Theory* (London: Macmillan & Co. Ltd., 1965), II, 156–239.

[13] G. D. A. MacDougall, "British and American Exports: A Study Suggested by the Theory of Comparative Costs," *Economic Journal*, LXI, No. 244 (December 1951), 697–724, and LXII, No. 247 (September 1952), 487–521; Robert Stern, "British and American Productivity and Comparative Costs in International Trade," *Oxford Economic Papers*, XIV, No. 3 (October 1962), 275–96; G. D. A. MacDougall, M. Dowley, P. Fox, and S. Pugh, "British and American Productivity, Prices, and Exports: An Addendum," *Oxford Economic Papers*, XIV, No. 3 (October 1962), 297–304; Bela Balassa, "An Empirical Demonstration of Classical Comparative Cost Theory," *Review of Economics and Statistics*, XLV, No. 3 (August 1963), 231–38.

all compared the United States and the United Kingdom because of the ready availability of productivity data.[14] Data exist for both countries for the years 1937 and 1950, and the studies have employed both years.

The simplest hypothesis that can be derived from the Ricardian model is that the United States will capture the biggest share of third markets when its labor productivity is higher than the United Kingdom, because then its labor costs are lower and it will have a comparative advantage. If we call the ratio of U.S. exports to U.K. exports y, and let x stand for the ratio of U.S. to U.K. labor productivity, the hypothesis is that a higher x leads to a higher y. The researchers found that in general that was true. For example, Stern computed the relationship[15]

$$y = -0.68 + 1.27x, \qquad r = 0.44. \qquad \text{(2-14)}$$
$$(0.43)$$

It may help those who have forgotten their statistics if we interpret the results. What has been done, in effect, is to plot the data on a diagram with y on the vertical axis and x on the horizontal axis. Then a line that fits the data best (by the least-squares criterion) has been computed. In Stern's case the regression line intersects the vertical axis at -0.68 and it has a slope of 1.27. That is, if the log of the ratio of U.S. to U.K. productivity increases by 1, the log of the ratio of U.S. to U.K. exports will increase by about 1.3. The figure in parentheses under the slope value is the standard error of estimate, which measures the dispersion of the actual values of y about the regression line. Since the standard error of estimate is considerably less than the slope, apparently the line fits the data pretty well. The symbol r stands for the coefficient of correlation. $r = 0.44$ means that the two variables are positively correlated, so that relatively higher productivity leads to relatively higher exports. It also means that the variables are not very highly correlated. In another test of the Ricardian model, MacDougall found $y = -2.19 + 1.89x, r = 0.61$.

These tests should be supplemented by investigation of the effects of money wages to see if the influence of productivity has been submerged by wage differences between industries. One way to handle wages was devised by MacDougall. He suggested that since U.S. wages were twice as high in 1937 as U.K. wages on the average, U.S. exports could not be competitive

[14] The Ricardian theory can be approached from the point of view of average labor productivity instead of labor requirements per unit of output, since labor/output (the ratio that we used) is just the reciprocal of output/labor, which is what is meant by labor productivity.

[15] Stern (as well as MacDougall) used 1950 export data, and they used ratios of quantities of exports. The industries in each sample varied. Note particularly that in the Stern and the subsequent MacDougall regressions y and x are the logarithms of the ratios, not the ratios themselves. By using logarithms one should be able to obtain a line that fits the data better, because in effect a curved line rather than a straight line is obtained. This follows from the fact that $\log y = \log a + b \log x$ is really $y = ax^b$.

(according to the Ricardian approach) unless the United States required less than half as much labor. That means that for the United States to be the major exporter its productivity must be more than twice as great. He found that out of 25 industries investigated, 20 fit the following pattern: The United States had the bulk of the exports when its productivity was at least twice the U.K. productivity and otherwise had only a small share. Similarly, Stern found that in 1950 U.S. wages were 3.4 times U.K. wages. He observed that his sample of 24 industries yielded 20 that matched the prediction that U.S. exports would predominate if its productivity was 3.4 times that of the United Kingdom and otherwise would not. From a larger sample of 39 industries, 34 met the prediction. When wages for individual industries rather than average wages were used, the results were about the same. These results indicate that perhaps the low export-productivity correlations were the result of wage differences.

The trouble is that life is not all that easy for the empirical worker. It is possible to make a direct test of the influence of wages, and this test shows rather poor results. Stern tried relating the U.S./U.K. export ratio to the ratio of the money labor costs in the two countries and found that $y = 0.01 - 1.40x$, $r = -0.43$.[16] The slope and the coefficient of correlation have the proper sign, because relatively higher labor costs in the United States should go along with lower export shares. But the coefficient itself is too low to be persuasive.

What may we properly conclude from these various tests? A judiciously cautious evaluation is that the Ricardian model has explanatory value. Enough of the tests showed good results to make the model worth exploring further. True enough, it did not pass all the tests. Perhaps this was because 1950 was an abnormal year, as Balassa suggested, and perhaps repeating the tests when new productivity data become available will allow us to evaluate the model with more confidence. As matters now stand, Professor Caves' remark that "The classical theory of international trade may earn its place today because of its empirical relevance" summarizes it neatly.[17]

There is one point suggested by theory that has not been satisfactorily handled by the empirical research. The tests are based on the notion that importers' purchases depend on relative prices, and relative prices depend on labor productivities and wages. We expect that a fall in the relative U.S. price in one industry would raise its relative share of exports. But the

---

[16] y is the log of the ratio of U.S. to U.K. export quantities in third markets; x is the log of the ratio of U.S. to U.K. money labor costs. This ratio was expressed in inequality **(2-13)** in the form

$$\frac{C_i^{US}}{C_i^{UK}} \cdot \frac{w_i^{US}}{w_i^{UK}}.$$

[17] Richard E. Caves, *Trade and Economic Structure* (Cambridge, Mass.: Harvard University Press, 1960), p. 281.

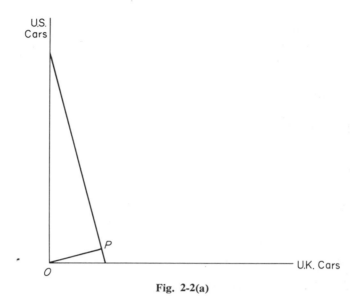

Fig. 2-2(a)

statistical tests are cross-section tests, covering several industries at a given point in time, not relative prices at two points of time. In a cross section it is quite possible for the situation illustrated in Figs. 2-2(a) and 2-2(b) to prevail. These diagrams show the choices available to a third country in purchasing woolens and cars from the United States and the United Kingdom. The United Kingdom has a comparative advantage in the production of woolens, and the United States in cars. But it does not follow that a larger

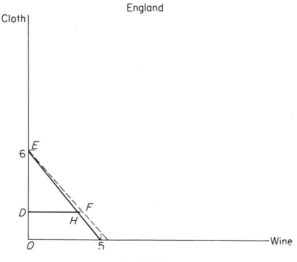

Fig. 2-2(b)

share of U.S. cars will be purchased and a smaller share of U.S. woolens. If we assume that demands are such that P indicates the quantities purchased in each figure, the U.S. share is low whether it has a comparative advantage or disadvantage.[18] This situation would fail the Stern–MacDougall correlation tests, but that is not relevant. The relevant question is whether a change—for example, a rise in labor productivity in U.S. cars—would lead to an increase in the share of U.S. cars sold. This question has not yet been answered. Until it is, we should not discard the Ricardian model on the basis of low correlations between productivities and export shares. The diagrams show that that is a perfectly respectable theoretical possibility.[19]

[18] The shares are measured by the slope of the line OP, because the slope of this line is the ratio U.S. cars/U.K. cars or U.S. woolens/U.K. woolens.

[19] Notice that we have assumed that it is possible for each country to continue selling in the third country even though it has a comparative disadvantage. This is possible when such aspects of monopolistic competition as product differentiation, quality differences, and commercial leadership are present.

Some writers make use of the concept of "the elasticity of substitution" to explain the phenomenon shown in Fig. 2-2. This elasticity is designed to measure the extent to which the relative export shares change when prices change. In Fig. 2-2 the assumption is that woolens have a high elasticity of substitution and cars have a low elasticity. It is known that elasticities of substitution in international trade vary greatly; see Arnold Harbeger, "Some Evidence on the International Price Mechanism," *Journal of Political Economy*, LXV, No. 6 (December 1957), 506–21. The advanced student who wishes to investigate a criticism of the tests of the classical model in terms of the elasticity of substitution may consult Bhagwati, *Economic Journal*, LXXIV, 11.

CHAPTER 3

THE
TRANSFORMATION
CURVE

THE THEORY OF COMPARATIVE ADVANTAGE did not long remain in the simple form presented by Ricardo. It had neglected many important elements, and some of these were added to the theory by the members of the nineteenth-century classical writers. John Stuart Mill showed how to handle demand. J. E. Cairns destroyed the idea of a homogeneous labor force by introducing the concept of "noncompeting groups". These and other refinements are traced out in detail in Jacob Viner's great book, *Studies in the Theory of International Trade* (New York: Harper & Row, Publishers, 1937). But this story now belongs to the history of economic thought. Today the theory of international trade is based on standard economic theory rather than the analysis of comparative labor costs.

THE BASIC STRUCTURE
OF THE TRANSFORMATION CURVE

To make the matter as simple as possible and still be able to make statements with relevance, it is convenient to keep Ricardo's assumption of two countries (perhaps ours and the rest of the world) and two commodities. We part company with Ricardo by assuming that production requires factors in addition to labor. The tastes of the citizens and the production functions of the industries are taken as given. A particularly handy assumption about production is that constant returns to scale prevail—double all inputs and output will exactly double. The markets for commodities and for factors of production are competitive. The basic theory of trade is built up from these assumptions. Then we can show how other conditions, such as monopoly, affect the course of trade.

The first tool we need is a revised version of the transformation curve used in Chap. 2. This requires another assumption for a simple development. We shall assume that there are only two factors of production and that the supply of each is perfectly inelastic. No matter what happens to wages, the same amount of labor will be supplied. Then we can draw a transformation curve between X and Y, as in Fig. 3-1. T is the maximum amount of good Y that could be produced in one country if all its resources were employed

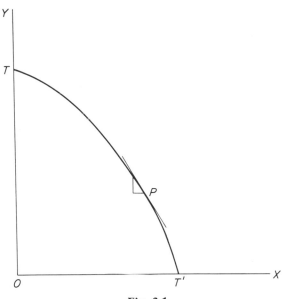

Fig. 3-1

in that industry. Alternatively, if all resources shifted over to industry X, an amount T' could be produced. Or various amounts of X and Y could be produced in combination along the curve. The difference between this diagram and Fig. 2-1 is that now the transformation curve is a curved line rather than a straight one. The slope becomes steeper as more X is produced. The economic meaning of this is that at larger outputs of X a bigger sacrifice of Y is required to produce another unit of X. If we define the cost of another unit of X as the foregone opportunity to produce some amount of Y, the diagram shows increasing cost. Ricardo assumed constant cost, which was the basis for the straight-line transformation curve of Chap. 2. Increasing cost is no doubt a more realistic picture of actual production conditions.

Increasing opportunity cost arises from differences among industries in their use of the factors of production; more specifically, from different proportions of factor inputs used. This point will be elaborated in the next section.

Since the slope of the transformation curve shows the amount of X sacrificed to produce more Y, it can be said to show the marginal cost of one commodity in terms of the other. Using the familiar equality of price and marginal cost under competitive conditions, and the reciprocal nature of price ratios and real ratios developed in Chap. 2, it follows that for any point on the transformation curve

$$dY/dX = -MC_X/MC_Y = -P_X/P_Y. \qquad \text{(3-1)}$$

The transformation curve can be regarded as a generalization of the Ricardo model. It gives us a theory that can handle a great number of cost and price ratios instead of just one. But Ricardo took it for granted that labor had different productivity in different countries and hence that each country had a different transformation curve. Today we ask, why might the transformation curves be different? For some commodities in some countries nature is niggardly—for example, bananas in Alaska and musk-ox in the Amazon. Some countries are backward technologically. The amount of capital per person and of arable land per person varies widely around the world. It would be nice to be able to systematize these and other factors that influence the shape and size of the transformation curve. One way to do so is by means of the production functions that lie behind transformation curves.

PRODUCTION FUNCTIONS AND BOX DIAGRAMS

The isoquant approach to production functions is typically used in international trade theory. Figure 3-2 shows the output of Y as a function of the inputs of labor and capital. A given output of Y, for example, $Y = 100$, can be produced with a great amount of labor and a small amount of capital. For example, rice may be planted by peasants wading in paddies and it may be harvested with a sickle. Or the same amount may be produced with much capital and a small amount of labor if it is sowed from an airplane and harvested with combines. The marginal products of capital and labor are essential parts of an isoquant diagram because they govern the slope of each isoquant. Suppose that from point P a small reduction in the quantity of capital is made. The change in the output of Y is

$$dY = MP_K \, dK.^1 \qquad \text{(3-2)}$$

To remain on the isoquant, more labor must be used until the same change in output is achieved:

$$dY = MP_L \, dL. \qquad \text{(3-3)}$$

---

[1] This follows easily from the definition of the marginal product of capital:

$$MP_K = dY/dK.$$

We may therefore equate the right-hand sides of **(3-2)** and **(3-3)**, but since dY in **(3-2)** is a fall and dY in **(3-3)** is a rise, one of them must first be multiplied by -1:

$$MP_K \ dK = -MP_L \ dL. \qquad (3\text{-}4)$$

From this it is easy to see that the slope of the isoquant depends on the ratio of marginal products:

$$dL/dK = -MP_K/MP_L. \qquad (3\text{-}5)$$

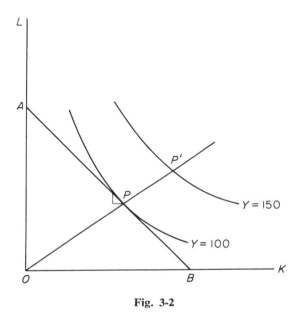

Fig. 3-2

There are some aspects of the isoquant diagram that we need to have in mind before attempting to relate the production function and the transformation curve. One important point is that the slope of the isoquant shows the ratio of factor prices as well as the ratio of marginal products. The theory of competition tells us that labor's wage equals its marginal product and that the return to capital equals its marginal product. By a simple substitution in Eq. **(3-5)** we derive

$$dL/dK = -P_K/P_L. \qquad (3\text{-}6)$$

The next point is not so obvious. If the production function is of the constant-returns-to-scale variety, the marginal products depend only on the ratios of the inputs. All isoquants then have the same slope along a line such as OPP'^2. The slope of the line OP gives the input proportions, L/K, which fixes all the marginal products (and hence the isoquant slopes) all along the line.

Finally, notice how technology affects the production function. A technological improvement that raises the marginal product of either input changes the slope of the isoquants. For example, if an innovation increased MP_K, leaving MP_L unchanged, the slope of the isoquant at P (or any other point) would be made steeper, according to Eq. (3-5). It also changes their position, because the same output can be obtained with a lower input of either or both resources. Alternatively, we could change the labor and capital units on the axes to show the reduction in inputs for the given outputs.

Since the minimum-size international trade model is two countries, each producing two goods, we might have as many as four production functions to handle. Sometimes it is assumed that each country produces the same goods in the same way as the other one, which reduces the number of production functions to two. A simple device, really a work of genius, is often used to make it easy to work with two production functions at once. This tool is called the Edgeworth–Bowley box diagram; an example is shown in Fig. 3-3.

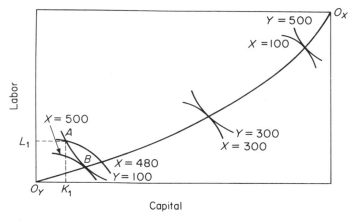

Fig. 3-3

The sides of the box have as dimensions the total amount of labor and capital available in the economy. The isoquants of good Y are drawn using the lower left-hand corner of the box as the origin; good X isoquants

---

[2] A standard example of a constant-returns-to-scale production function is the Cobb–Douglas function, $Y = AL^aK^{1-a}$, where A is some positive constant and a lies between zero and 1. The marginal product of labor is $\partial Y/\partial L = aA(K/L)^{1-a}$, and the marginal product of capital is $\partial Y/\partial K = (1-a)A(L/K)^a$. In this case it is obvious that the marginal products depend on the ratios of the factors of production. The same is true for all constant-returns-to-scale production functions, but we shall not prove it here.

originate from the upper right-hand corner. In effect, the isoquant diagram for X has been rotated through a half-circle and superimposed on the Y isoquants. Now, from any point in the box, such as point A, we can read off the production of X (480) and of Y (100). L_1 is the amount of labor used in making Y, and K_1 is the capital employed in industry Y. Since full employment is assumed, we know that the rest of the labor and capital goes into X. Furthermore, we know the relative marginal products in each industry from the slopes of the isoquants. Clearly a large amount of information is packed into the box diagram.

Still more information may be derived from it. Point A is a full-employment point, but it is not an efficient one. What would happen if labor were transferred from Y to X while capital moved from X to Y? We could increase the production of X while holding Y output constant. For example, at point B the production of X has gone up by 20 units while Y production has not fallen. Continuing the resource transfers past point B would result in a lower output for X, so the efficient point is at B. This is one of the points on the transformation curve, since it shows the most possible X for a given Y. All the points on the transformation curve are found in a similar fashion. Notice that the most X for a given Y is found by locating the X isoquant that is tangent to the given Y isoquant. This means that whenever we are on the transformation curve we know that a pair of isoquants are tangent. Since their slopes are equal at a point of tangency, an equivalent statement is that whenever we are on the transformation curve we know that the ratio MP_K/MP_L is the same in each industry.

The locus of all such points of tangency defines the transformation curve. In Fig. 3-3 this locus is the curved line running between O_Y and O_X. The locus is drawn so that in equilibrium commodity Y uses less labor per unit of capital than does X. X is said to be "labor-intensive."[3]

The purpose of the box diagram is to show how resource supplies and the technology embodied in the production functions determine the transformation curve. The box diagram, however, can also be used to show that under competition and full employment the economy *must* be on its transformation curve. Why? Because in competition the rewards to each factor in each industry are equal. Equation **(3-6)** assures us that the isoquants in each industry will have the same slope in that case. But this is the same thing as saying that the isoquants are tangent, so production must take place on the transformation curve.[4]

---

[3] One of the findings of the empirical work on modern theory is that some commodities vary from labor-intensive to capital-intensive, depending on factor costs. This is a refinement that we shall not bother with until the foundations of trade theory have been laid.

[4] One major shortcoming of this approach is clearly its reliance on fixed factor supplies. A general equilibrium system is needed to treat variable factor supplies fully; see Murray Kemp, *The Pure Theory of International Trade* (Englewood Cliffs, N.J.: Prentice-Hall, Inc., 1964), Chap. 7. A brief glimpse of the consequence of allowing the labor supply to vary can be obtained from Fig. 3-4. In this diagram, the X and the Y axes

INTERNATIONAL TRADE EQUILIBRIUM

The transformation curve is a basic and extremely versatile tool. In the first place, it can be used to analyze the course of international trade in a simple way. As an illustration, suppose there are two countries with very different production possibilities, as in Fig. 3-5. If trade were not possible, each country would find an equilibrium price ratio such as line B. Production and consumption would be at point P', where the price line is tangent to the transformation curve. Since P_X/P_Y is greater in country 1 than in country 2, we can predict what will happen when trade is opened up. Country 1 will buy X abroad, where it is cheaper. It will produce less X

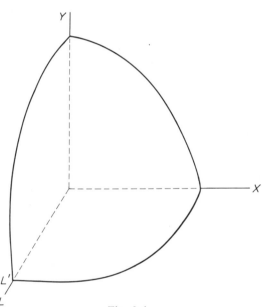

Fig. 3-4

show the output of commodities, as before. The L axis represents the community's consumption of leisure time. At the origin, with leisure at zero and the input of labor at a maximum, the outputs are at their maximum. At L', leisure is at its maximum; there is no labor input and consequently no outputs. A transformation curve for any given supply of labor is obtained by a slice through the surface parallel to the YX plane. Equilibrium is obtained at the point of tangency of the surface and a plane relating the wage rate and the prices of X and Y. All this is worked out in detail in V. C. Walsh, "Leisure and International Trade," *Economica*, XXIII, No. 3 (August 1956), 253–60; in Jaroslav Vanek, "An Afterthought on the 'Real Cost—Opportunity Cost' Dispute and Some Aspects of General Equilibrium under Conditions of Variable Factor Supplies," *Review of Economic Studies*, XXVI, No. 3 (June 1959), 198–208; and in Kemp's book. Figure 3-4 is taken from Murray C. Kemp, *The Pure Theory of International Trade*, pp. 104–7, 1964. Reprinted by permission of Prentice-Hall, Inc., Englewood Cliffs, N.J.

and transfer the resources to industry Y. Country 2 would produce more X for the expanding export markets and would have to reduce Y output. Country 1 moves up its transformation curve while country 2 moves down its curve. Finally, when the prices become equal in the two countries, equilibrium has been established.

In Fig. 3-5, line A is the equilibrium-terms-of-trade line. Several conditions are necessary to ensure that this is really the equilibrium. On the side of production, marginal cost must equal price in each country; this is shown by the tangency of A to the transformation curve at P. Consumption

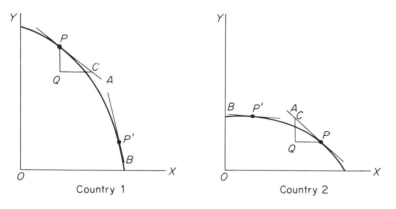

Country 1   Country 2

Fig. 3-5

must also be in equilibrium. We assume that at prices shown by A the demands in each country will be at point C. Finally, the balance of payments must be in equilibrium. In this model that requires the equality of desired imports from one country with desired exports from the other. PQ, country 1's exports of Y, equals QC, country 2's imports. Similarly, an equal amount of imports of X (QC in 1) and exports of X (QP in 2) must be desired.

One carryover from the Ricardian model is the notion of the gains from trade. In both countries, consumption point C lies outside the transformation curve. National income is increased by trade, because it simply would not be possible to produce the amounts of X and Y represented by C in isolation. Unlike the Ricardian case, specialization is incomplete. Both countries continue producing both commodities after trade.[5] This is a consequence of the assumption of increasing marginal cost. As long as marginal cost is below price, the country will produce; it begins to import only when marginal cost rises above price. In Fig. 3-5 we have moved so far away from Ricardo that specialization is less after trade than it was

[5] What international terms of trade would be necessary to induce country 1, for example, to specialize completely in industry Y?

before. The production patterns have moved from the extremes shown before trade to patterns more like the other country.

So far it may seem that we have built an imposing foundation for what turned out to be a brief exposition of international trade. The fact of the matter is that the presentation could be brief only because the groundwork had been carefully prepared. Furthermore, the tools are used to handle many problems in addition to the statement of the trading position. There is a very rich body of theory that can be understood only with the help of the transformation curve and the box diagram. We shall conclude the chapter with two illustrations that demonstrate the usefulness of the theory.

TARIFFS AND THE TRANSFORMATION CURVE

The first example is the problem of a tariff. Since this is an introductory example rather than a full-scale analysis, we can simplify by thinking of a country that is so small that its tariff policy does not affect the international terms of trade. Accordingly, in Fig. 3-6 we have country 1 facing the international price ratio given by the slope of line A. Point P is again its production equilibrium, and C its consumption equilibrium. Suppose country 1 decides to protect its import-competing industry by imposing a tariff on good X. The tariff rate is $100t$ per cent ad valorem, which means that the international price (P_X) appears to importers as $(1 + t)P_X$. For example, if P_X is \$10 and the tariff is 50 per cent, the domestic price would be $(1 + .5)$ \$10 $=$ \$15. The slope of the price line, $-P_X/P_Y$, is changed to $-(1 + t)P_X/P_Y$ as far as the decisions of producers and consumers in country 1 are concerned. The new after-tariff price ratio is shown by the broken line A' through P. But now prices are not equal to marginal costs. The price ratio is higher than the marginal cost ratio, so production of X is encouraged. This is usually called the *protective effect* of the tariff. The new equilibrium is at P', where equality between prices and marginal costs has been reestablished. Of course, consumption decisions are affected also, and the volume of exports and imports has been reduced.

Because the transformation curve is linked to the box diagram, we can use the box to explore the *redistribution effect* on incomes. Suppose the transformation curve were derived from the box diagram of Fig. 3-3. Point P corresponds to the tangency of the isoquants $Y = 500$, $X = 100$, we assume, and P' corresponds to $Y = 300$, $X = 300$. It is obvious that the change from P to P' lowers the ratio of labor to capital in both industries. Since this box diagram is based on constant-returns-to-scale production functions, when the L/K ratio falls, MP_L rises and MP_K falls. In a competitive economy this is equivalent to saying that wages rise while the return on capital is reduced. By protecting industry X, the tariff has really had the effect of protecting the domestic labor force. The old-fashioned pauper labor argument for the tariff said that a country should "protect domestic labor against cheap foreign labor that works for a bowl of rice a day." Our diagrams have shown that indeed a tariff can raise domestic wages under the circumstances we have posited.[6]

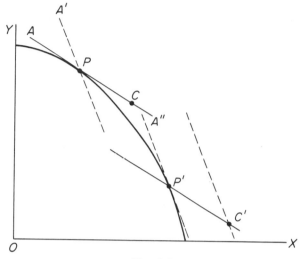

Fig. 3-6

Professor Kindleberger suggests that this result is illuminating for tariff history. If we think of a box diagram with wheat land on one axis and capital on the other, we have an abstract picture of the U.K. economy of the 1830's and 1840's. The tariff on wheat (quaintly referred to as the Corn Laws) raised the domestic production of wheat and benefitted the landlords, just as the tariff raised the return to labor in the previous example. The Corn Laws were repealed after a political struggle between the landed gentry and the rising industrial groups. As a result of the changed trade patterns following tariff repeal, the distribution of income shifted against the landlords.

By way of contrast, in the nineteenth century U.S. capital favored high tariffs in order to push the distribution of income in its favor. United States and U.K. capitalists took opposite positions on the tariff issue because

[6] This is not a general conclusion that applies to all tariffs, as we shall see later. And notice that the country is really impoverished by the tariff even though wages have risen. Since point C is chosen by consumers in preference to any point on line A above and to the right of C, it follows that a higher consumption of one or both goods could be achieved under free-trade than with the tariff. The example is derived from Wolfgang Stolper and Paul A. Samuelson, "Protection and Real Wages," *Review of Economic Studies*, IX, No. 1 (November 1941), 58–73, reprinted in the American Economic Association's valuable collection of articles, *Readings in the Theory of International Trade* (Homewood, Ill., Richard D. Irwin, Inc. 1949).

U.S. imports were capital-intensive while U.K. imports were land-intensive. The tariff in the United States protected industry and therefore raised the demand for capital, while in the United Kingdom it raised the demand for land.[7]

THE RYBCZYNSKI THEOREM

The second illustration is a problem in the comparative statics of economic growth. Suppose we are dealing with a country such as, for

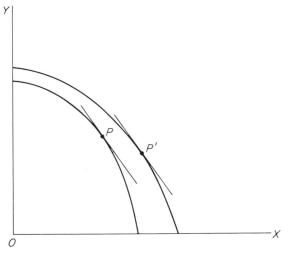

Fig. 3-7(a)

example, Nicaragua, which is too small to affect its terms of trade. Nicaragua is experiencing a population growth more rapid than either its capital accumulation or its technological progress; for simplicity, assume the latter two items do not change at all. Further, assume that the box diagram appropriate to the economy is that of Fig. 3-3, which is reproduced as the solid lines in Fig. 3-7(b) for convenience. We may show population growth by extending the labor axis of the box, as shown by the dashed lines in the diagram. Assume there are no distorting tariffs or frictions that inhibit the movement of factors from one industry to another. Then we may predict two consequences of population growth:

1. The transformation curve will shift outward, as in Fig. 3-7(a).

2. The equilibrium production point will shift from P to P'.

[7] Charles P. Kindleberger, "International Trade and United States Experience: 1870–1955," in *Postwar Economic Trends in the United States*, ed. R. E. Freeman (New York: Harper & Row, Publishers, 1960), pp. 365–66.

P' must involve less production of Y (the capital-intensive good) and more production of X (the labor-intensive good).

Why *must* this particular change in production occur? It is the result of a fairly subtle chain of reasoning that starts from the assumption of constant terms of trade. P_X/P_Y constant implies MC_X/MC_Y constant. There is a proposition in microeconomics that $P_X = MC_X = W/MP_L^X = R/MP_K^X$, and $P_Y = MC_Y = W/MP_L^Y = R/MP_K^Y$, where W and R are the

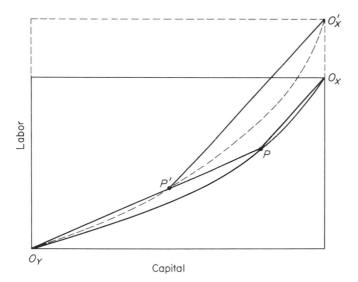

Fig. 3-7(b)

prices of labor and capital, respectively. It follows by division that $P_X/P_Y = MP_L^Y/MP_L^X = MP_K^Y/MP_K^X$, and these ratios will be constant in our example. Rearranging the last equality, we get $MP_K^X/MP_L^X = MP_K^Y/MP_L^Y$. This ratio is the absolute value of the slope of the isoquants, and it will also be constant. In the model we are using, the slope of the isoquants is constant only if the factor proportions are constant. So the conclusion is that the increased labor supply stemming from population growth will not change the factor proportions used by X and Y manufacturers. That means that the new equilibrium, P', must be along the line O_YP, which gave the original factor proportions in industry Y. It also means that the line $O_X'P'$ must have the same slope as line O_XP, since the slopes of these lines are the factor proportions in X. As shown in the diagram, these considerations imply that P' must lie closer to O_Y than did P. But this is simply another way of stating that the production of Y falls and the production of X rises.[8]

---

[8] This conclusion is called the Rybczynski theorem; it is presented in T. N. Rybczynski, "Factor Endowment and Relative Commodity Prices," *Economica*, XXII, No. 4 (November 1955), 336–41.

A less formal but helpful way to establish the conclusion is to argue that the new labor must be supplied with capital in order to be productive. The capital is provided by a reduction in the output of Y, the capital-intensive industry. The precise amount of reduction of Y is determined by the requirement that the original factor proportions must be retained.

The result of the analysis is that Nicaragua, faced with population growth, should reduce the output of its capital-intensive industry. Such a conclusion flies in the face of the development aspirations of most underdeveloped countries. Their great ambition is to increase rather than reduce their industrial output. This is one example of a theme to which we shall return: the opposition to the theory of comparative advantage by the planners in underdeveloped countries.

CHAPTER 4

INDIFFERENCE CURVES AND OFFER CURVES

IN CHAP. 3 THE TRANSFORMATION CURVE was used as a graphic device to summarize the production aspects of an economy. Now the scene shifts to the demand and consumption side. The tools developed to handle demand problems have a prominent place in international trade literature, and we need to have a firm grasp of them before tackling contemporary theories of tariffs, customs unions, and the like. These tools are indifference curves and offer curves.

COMMUNITY INDIFFERENCE MAPS

The use of indifference curves has given international economists some headaches.[1] The curves proved so handy in consumer theory that it seemed natural to apply them to international problems, and many writers

[1] It may be helpful at this point to remind the student of the essential facts about the use of indifference curves in consumer theory. We shall state the facts in a summary manner; if more review is needed, consult any price theory text.

In Fig. 4-1, quantities of the two goods, X and Y, are shown on the axes. It is assumed that the consumer, when confronted with a choice between combinations of the two goods, can tell whether he likes one combination better than another or is indifferent between them. In the diagram he is shown to be indifferent among points A, B, and C, but prefers D to any of the first three. Consequently A, B, and C lie on the same indifference curve and D on a higher one, showing more satisfaction to the consumer. The assumption of a rational consumer leads to the indifference curve properties of (1) a negative slope, (2) convex to the origin, and (3) nonintersection of the curves.

The straight line tangent to the indifference curve at point C is the budget line showing the income of the consumer and the prices the consumer must pay. Its slope is $-P_X/P_Y$. The consumer's equilibrium is the highest indifference curve he can reach, given his income and the prevailing prices. As shown by point C, this requires that the budget line and the indifference curve be tangent (i.e., have equal slopes).

have treated a nation as though it were a single consumer. The great pitfall in such an approach is that a nation is not one consumer; it is a group of individuals with widely different tastes. In general this fact makes it impossible to derive a unique set of indifference curves for the country.

Why is this so? We can show it by an intellectual experiment. Suppose there is a given total of goods in the country; this will establish one point

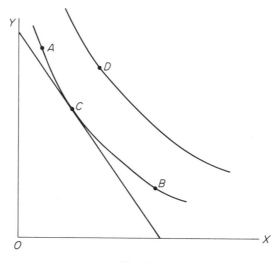

Fig. 4-1

on the indifference map. Suppose these goods are distributed among the citizens in some fashion. If trade is allowed, the market will establish an equilibrium price ratio. By analogy with point C of Fig. 4-1, we may say that the slope of the indifference curve through the given-total-of-goods point has been established. But now suppose the same total is distributed in an entirely different way. We would expect demands and supplies to change so that different prices are established. This implies an indifference curve with an entirely different slope; that is, the indifference map is not unique. But since the basis of standard consumer theory is a unique, nonintersecting indifference map, we see that we cannot take over the approach used in analyzing the individual consumer.[2]

Faced with this problem, economists have the choice of abandoning the use of indifference curves in international trade or of specifying assumptions

[2] Professor Paul Samuelson gives a mathematical proof of the nonexistence of community indifference curves in "Social Indifference Curves," *Quarterly Journal of Economics*, LXX, No. 1 (February 1956), 1–22. He also points out that if every consumer has an income elasticity of unity for every good, the hypothetical redistribution will not affect demand in total, so that a unique indifference map could exist in that case.

under which it would be proper to use them. For example, it may be assumed that everyone in the country has the same tastes and the same income. Then there is no problem in using a community indifference curve (but will the conclusions of the theory be applicable generally?).[3]

A very different approach to a logically rigorous community indifference curve relies on an assumption of optimal redistribution of goods.[4] Because this sort of curve is widely referred to, we shall explain it in some detail.

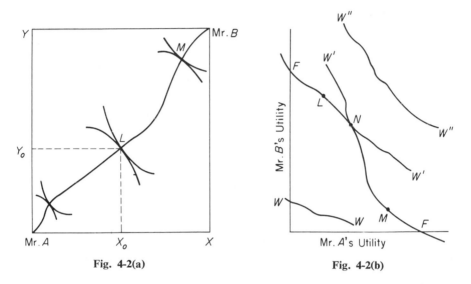

Fig. 4-2(a)   Fig. 4-2(b)

The starting point is a box diagram, similar to the production box diagram of Chap. 3, but applied to two consumers of two products. Fig. 4-2(a) shows this box. The products are X and Y. Mr. A's indifference map has its origin at the lower left-hand corner of the box; Mr. B's indifference map originates at the upper right-hand corner. The total amount of X and Y available for distribution between the two consumers is shown by the dimensions of the box. At point L, for example, Mr. A receives an amount of X equal to the distance between his origin and X_o; Mr. B gets the rest. Similarly, Mr. A has a quantity of Y equal to the distance between his origin and Y_o; Mr. B gets the rest. The points of tangency of the two sets of indifference curves are connected by the contract curve; notice that along the contract curve it is not possible to move A to a higher indifference curve without moving B to a lower one.

[3] This is the assumption of James Meade in his influential book, *A Geometry of International Trade* (London: George Allen & Unwin Ltd., 1952).

[4] This approach, due to Samuelson, is explained in his article cited in footnote 2. It is adapted by permission of the publishers from Paul A. Samuelson, *The Quarterly Journal of Economics* (Cambridge, Mass.: Harvard University Press), copyright 1956 by the President and Fellows of Harvard College.

Suppose we start at A's origin and move uphill along the contract curve. A will steadily feel better off and B worse off. We can show this in Fig. 4-2(b). Here the axes of the diagram show the utilities of the consumers. Since indifference curves show only greater or less, not absolute, quantities of utility, the axes should not be interpreted as measuring quantities but only directions. A redistribution from point L in the box diagram to point M would move the consumers from point L to point M in the utility diagram. [Professor Samuelson calls the line connecting L and M in Fig. 4-2(b) a utility frontier, since it shows for a given utility of Mr. B the most utility Mr. A can achieve with the total amount of products at their disposal. The frontier is labeled FF in the diagram.] Of course, if the dimensions of the box were bigger, the utility frontier would lie farther up and to the right.

The next step is to draw in curves representing the social welfare function in Fig. 4-2(b). (These curves are the ones labeled WW, $W'W'$, and $W''W''$.) These curves make explicit our ethical judgment about the relative importance society should give to the utilities of each of its citizens. They demonstrate in a formal way the necessity of decisions about how incomes should be distributed in making or recommending policies. (Of course, finding the social welfare function for a given society is a difficult problem, perhaps more suited to the skills of the political scientist than the economist.) Once we have the function, it is easy to see how to redistribute the total of commodities among the public: Welfare is obviously maximized at point N, the highest of the social welfare contours available along the utility frontier.

It seems obvious that if every time the economy has the fixed total of X and Y given by the dimensions of the box diagram in Fig. 4-2(a) this total is redistributed to achieve point N, and if for every other possible box size the total is redistributed by the same criterion, then the amounts traded and the prices set must always be the same. Professor Samuelson's article shows that this is indeed the case: This sort of optimal redistribution does generate well-behaved community demands which imply community indifference curves with the desired slope, convexity, and absence of intersection properties. It is therefore possible to define conditions under which it is proper to use the concept of a community indifference curve without assuming that everyone has the same tastes.[5]

Of course, when it is inappropriate to assume the conditions leading to community indifference curves, we get along without them and start directly with demand functions based on empirical generalizations. Because of their common use and the neat exposition they make possible, we shall use them in the rest of this chapter.

[5] The student interested in seeing how these social indifference curves are applied might consult Jaroslav Vanek, *General Equilibrium of International Discrimination* (Cambridge, Mass.: Harvard University Press, 1965); or Harry Johnson's article, "Optimal Trade Intervention in the Presence of Domestic Distortions," in *Trade, Growth, and the Balance of Payments*, eds. Richard E. Caves, Harry G. Johnson, and Peter B. Kenen (Skokie, Ill.: Rand McNally & Company, 1965).

OFFER CURVES

The next order of business is to investigate the particular kind of demand curves used in international economics. They are sometimes called offer curves and sometimes reciprocal demand curves (because they simultaneously show a supply of exports that reciprocates for a demand for imports). The first point to make is that they may be applied either to a pure barter problem, where each country is endowed with a quantity of goods to trade

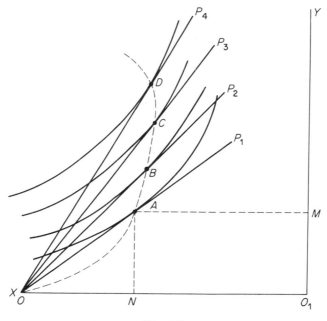

Fig. 4-3

(like manna from heaven), or to a mixed trade and production setting. It is easiest to start with the simple barter model.

To see what is involved, see Fig. 4-3. Because it is common to draw the offer curves with their origin in the southwest corner, it is necessary to place the origin of the indifference map in the southeast corner. Suppose country 1 is endowed with a quantity of product X, OO_1 in amount, and no Y. Then give it a chance to trade at terms of trade given by the line P_1 (as in Chaps. 2 and 3, the slope of the terms-of-trade line is $dy/dx = P_X/P_Y$). The equilibrium point A is on the highest indifference curve that can be reached at that price. To go from point O to point A, ON of X is exported and NA of Y is imported. The other price lines, P_2 and so on, involve higher prices of X relative to Y and lead to different quantities of imports and exports. The curve connecting the equilibrium points A, B, . . . , is the offer curve of country 1. The offer curve may thus be defined: It is the locus of the pairs of export and import quantities desired at each possible price ratio.

The offer curve of country 2 is derived in a similar way, with the origin for its indifference curves in the northwest corner and with an initial endowment of Y but no X. It therefore trades Y for X along an offer curve such as that shown in Fig. 4-4. In this figure the offer curves for both countries are shown. The equilibrium terms of trade, P_1, are found, as you would expect, by the intersection of the two offer curves. There the amount of Y

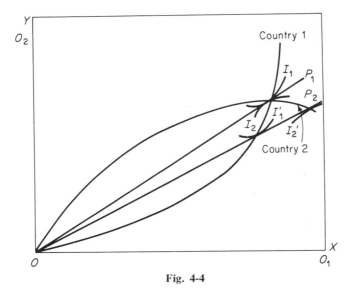

Fig. 4-4

demanded by country 1 is equal to the amount offered by country 2, and the desired supply and demand for X are also equal. At another price, such as P_2, supplies and demands do not mesh. The amount of X supplied by country 1 is less than the amount demanded by country 2, and the amount of Y demanded by country 1 is less than the amount offered by country 2. Therefore one would expect the price of X to rise and the price of Y to fall, with the result that P_X/P_Y rises and the price line becomes steeper.

Notice that the characteristic of the equilibrium is that the indifference curves of each country, being tangent to the same price line, are tangent to one another (with the slope of mutual tangency pointing toward the origin). The trade equilibrium lies on the contract curve (not drawn in, to avoid clutter), which runs between O_2 and O_1. At other prices the indifference curves are tangent to the same price line but not to each other, as curves I_2' and I_1' show.

This pure barter model is perhaps at the opposite extreme from Ricardo's comparative advantage model. Here cost of production is not a consideration at all; the course of trade is governed purely by tastes. In Ricardo, on the other hand, the emphasis is on the influence of costs, with demand getting a minimum of attention. Complete models giving attention to both production and tastes may be constructed algebraically or geometrically, and from these models offer curves that are very similar in appearance to the ones in Fig. 4-4 can be derived. Their interpretation is different, of course. Before we get involved with this, there are some helpful facts about offer curves to learn.

ELASTICITY OF OFFER CURVES

The first fact is how to measure elasticity. Since an offer curve is a type of demand curve, it does have an elasticity; but since it is a different animal than the demand curves met in microeconomics, the elasticity measure has to be modified. There are in fact two measures that are in common use.

1. The elasticity of the offer curve (denoted by E_{oc}). The offer curve of country 1 shows the demand for Y in exchange for X. It can be regarded as a functional relation whose form is $X = f(Y)$. The elasticity of this function is the percentage change in Y divided by the percentage change in X:

$$\frac{\frac{dY}{Y}}{\frac{dX}{X}} = \frac{dY}{dX} \cdot \frac{X}{Y}.$$

In Fig. 4-5, this definition is applied to the offer curve at point A. dY/dX is the slope of the tangent line at A and is equal to AB/BG. X/Y is equal to BO/AB. The product is then $BO/BG = E_{oc}$.

2. The elasticity of the demand for imports (denoted by E_{id}). In this approach, the demand for Y is regarded as a function of its relative price, $Y = f(X/Y)$. The elasticity is, as usual, defined as the percentage change in quantity divided by the percentage change in price, that is, as $dY/Y \div d(X/Y)/(X/Y)$. This formidable definition has a simple geometrical counterpart, which is illustrated by point A in Fig. 4-5. Suppose the terms of trade change from the slope of the line P_1 to the slope of the line P_2. Then the percentage change in the quantity demanded of Y is CA/AB. The percentage change in the price ratio is FA/AB, so E_{id} is CA/FA.[6]

[6] *Exercises:* Define analogous measures of elasticity for the offer curve of country 2. Show that E_{id} for country 1 is equal to 1 when the offer curve is vertical, is less than 1 when the offer curve has a negative slope, and is infinite when the offer curve is a straight line from the origin. For more on the geometry of elasticity measures, see Harry G. Johnson, "Optimum Welfare and Maximum Revenue Tariffs," *Review of Economic Studies*, XIX, No. 48 (1951–1952), 28–35; and R. A. Mundell, "The Pure Theory of International Trade," *American Economic Review*, L, No. 1 (March 1960), 74; the first definition explained in the text was developed by Johnson, and the second by Mundell.

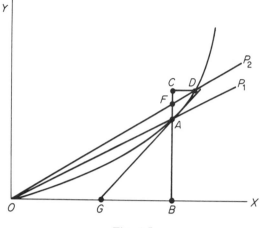

Fig. 4-5

These elasticities have an enormous influence on the outcome of many events in international trade. Prices and the amounts traded change when tariffs are levied, tastes change, technology is improved, and the like, and the extent of the trade changes depend on the elasticities. We shall cover all this in due course. At the moment the problem is the second of the facts about offer curves: When is equilibrium stable? Will a small disturbance away from the equilibrium (caused by some random event such as a dock strike or a poor monsoon) be followed by events leading to a return to equilibrium? One common answer is that it will if the sum of the elasticities of demand for imports is greater than 1.[7] Stability and instability are illustrated in Figs. 4-6(a) and 4-6(b). In part (a), the equilibrium point E is stable. If the terms-of-trade line is displaced to P_2, the demand for Y (point

[7] *Proof:* Write country 1's demand for imports as a function of the relative price of Y: $I_1 = I_1(P)$. Country 2's demand for imports is a function of the relative price of X, which is the reciprocal of the relative price of Y, so we have $I_2 = I_2(1/P)$. Country 1's balance of payments, B, is the value of its exports minus the value of its imports; in terms of good X this is $B = I_2(1/P) - PI_1(P)$. If we choose the commodity units properly, we can make $P = 1$ and hence $I_2 = I_1 = I$ at equilibrium (since the balance of payments must be zero in this model with no capital movements for equilibrium to prevail). To see what happens to B when the price of country 1's imports change, we differentiate the balance-of-payments equation. The result is

$$\frac{dB}{dP} = -\frac{dI_2}{d(1/P)}\frac{1}{P^2} - P\frac{dI_1}{dP} - I_1 = I\left(\frac{dI_2}{d(1/P)}\frac{1/P}{I_2} - \frac{P}{I_1}\frac{dI_1}{dP} - 1\right).$$

The first two terms in the parentheses are the elasticities of import demand, written in terms of prices rather than the alternative and equivalent terms of commodities used in the text. Stability requires that a rise in the price of country 1's imports leads to an improvement in its balance of payments, so that $dB/dP > 0$. Since $I > 0$, stability occurs when the sum of the terms in parentheses is positive, or, finally, when $E_{id1} + E_{id2} > 1$. This particular development of the stability conditions follows Mundell, *American Economic Review*, L, 72. A complete investigation of stability requires investigating the dynamic properties of the trade model; see Kemp, *The Pure Theory of International Trade*, Chap. 5.

A) exceeds the supply (point *B*), and the price of *Y* will rise. Since the slope of the price line is P_X/P_Y, the price line shifts in the direction of P_1 and so returns to equilibrium. But in part (b) the demand is less than the quantity supplied along P_2, so P_Y will continue to fall and the price line will shift farther from equilibrium at *E*. (*Question*: is *E'* a point of stable equilibrium?) Notice that the elasticities of import demand are both less than 1 at *E* in both parts of Fig. 4-6; the difference lies in the sum of the elasticities.[8]

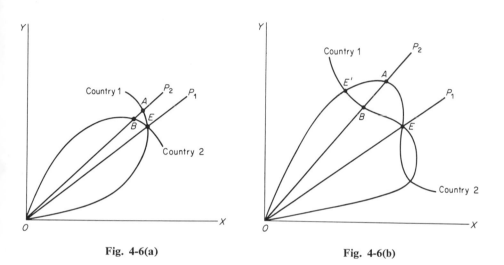

Fig. 4-6(a)   Fig. 4-6(b)

EFFECTS OF SHIFTS IN OFFER CURVES

The offer curves are used to handle a wide variety of trade problems. By way of illustration, here is one of them. A rise in the demand of one country for the products of the other would cause the price of the imported commodity to rise and this would cause a deterioration in the terms of trade for the country whose offer curve had changed. For example, if the offer curve of country 1 in Fig. 4-4 shifts to the right (showing an increase in demand), at the new equilibrium the terms-of-trade line will have a lower slope than *OP*. So far, so good. But by how much will the terms of trade fall? Will they fall more if country 1's offer curve is elastic or if it is inelastic? And what is the role of the elasticity of country 2's offer curve? The answers are not as obvious as they might seem, for two famous economists derived

[8] Two references that illustrate the importance of the stability conditions are Mundell, *American Economic Review*, L, 67–110; and J. Bhagwati and H. G. Johnson, "Notes on Some Controversies in the Theory of International Trade," *Economic Journal*, LXX, No. 277 (March 1960), 74–93.

different solutions. Alfred Marshall claimed that a high elasticity for country 2 meant a small fall in the terms of trade, and a low elasticity meant a larger fall. For country 1 a high elasticity caused a large fall, and a low elasticity a smaller fall. Frank Graham agreed as far as country 2 is concerned, but he thought Marshall had country 1 turned around—a high elasticity should

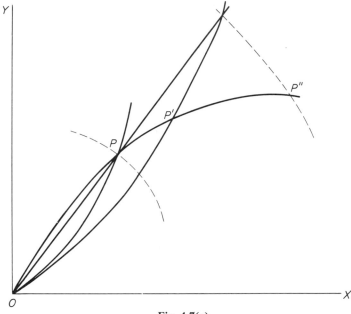

Fig. 4-7(a)

go with a small deterioration, he thought. Others entered the controversy but it was not resolved until recently.[9]

The trouble appears to have been a sort of grand carelessness in the definition of an increase in demand. One plausible definition is that an increase means an increase, in uniform proportion, of the quantity of imports demanded by country 1 at each level of the terms of trade. For example, country 1's offer curve might be twice as far from the origin along each possible price line after the shift than it was before the shift. This sort of demand increase is shown in Fig. 4-7(a) for elastic offer curves (the solid curves) and inelastic curves (the broken lines). It is obvious that in this case Graham's conclusion was correct. The new equilibrium at P' for

[9] Marshall's original proposition appeared in 1923, in *Money Credit and Commerce* (London: Macmillan & Co., Ltd., 1923), p. 177; Graham's solution is in "The Theory of International Values," *Quarterly Journal of Economics*, XLVI, No. 3 (August 1932), 601 2. Kemp resolved the controversy in "The Relation between Changes in International Demand and the Terms of Trade," *Econometrica*, XXVII, No. 1 (January 1956), 41–46; but a simpler solution is in the article by Bhagwati and Johnson cited in footnote 8.

the elastic curve involves less of a deterioration than does P'', the equilibrium for a shift of the inelastic curve in the same proportion.

Marshall, however, apparently had in mind an increase in a uniform proportion of the amount of good X that country 1 would give in return for each quantity of Y imported. For example, for each quantity of Y the new offer curve might lie twice as far to the right as did the old one. This sort of demand shift is shown in Fig. 4-7(b), and now obviously Marshall was correct. The terms of trade do deteriorate more if the elasticity is high than

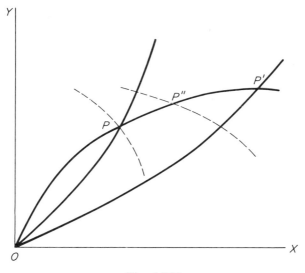

Fig. 4-7(b)

if it is low. The conclusion is that both results are correct by their own proper definitions. Can we say that one definition is correct and the other wrong? No, since both kinds of demand shifts are conceivable (and many other kinds as well); for any case in practice it is a matter of which one fits the facts.

TARIFF PROBLEMS AND OFFER CURVES

Another example of the usefulness of offer curves is in the analysis of tariffs. Toward the end of Chap. 3 we established the Stolper–Samuelson theorem: that a tariff may protect the scarce factor of production in certain circumstances. One of the assumptions used was that the tariff-levying county was too small to affect the international terms of trade. In that case the effect of the tariff was to raise the relative price of the import commodity. But suppose a big country installs a tariff; will the terms of trade then be affected, and, if so, how?

An answer is given in Fig. 4-8. Suppose a free-trade equilibrium has been established between country 1 and country 2 at point *P*, with terms of trade *OP*. Then country 2 levies a tariff on its import good, *X*. The diagram is drawn on the basis of a 50 per cent tariff rate. If we neglect for the moment the effect of the government spending of tariff revenues, the result of the

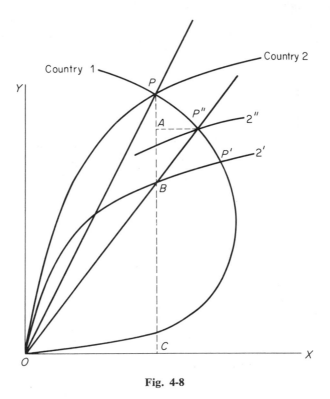

Fig. 4-8

tariff is to shift the offer curve down so that, for example, *BP* is 50 per cent of *CB*, and similarly for other points on the offer curve. This makes the domestic price ratio, *OP*, 50 per cent higher than the international terms of trade, *OB*. Another way to view the tariff is to realize that at point *P* the citizens of country 2 will offer *CP* of *Y* for *OC* of *X*, whether there is a tariff or not. If there is no tariff, the citizens of country 1 would receive *CP* of *Y* for selling *OC* of *X*. If there is a tariff, the government of country 2 may be regarded as intercepting *PB* of *Y*, which is 50 per cent of the net payment of *BC* that is left to go abroad. So offer curve 2' is constructed to be two thirds of the distance from the *X* axis to offer curve 2. If the government spent all the tariff receipts on good *Y*, no further international effects would be observed and the new equilibrium would be found at point P'.[10]

It is customary to regard the government's spending and fiscal policy as fixed independently of the amount of tariff revenue. In that case the tariff simply replaces some other tax, and disposable income is increased by the amount of other taxes that were formerly paid. The extra income will lead to more imports as well as to more consumption of domestic production. We can show the new imports diagrammatically by this technique: Suppose the marginal propensity to import for country 2 is AB/PB (i.e., from an extra income equivalent to PB, AB will be spent on imports). AB of Y will buy AP'' of X at the international price. A new equilibrium would be established at P'', with a total of CA of Y traded for $OC + AP''$ of X. But notice the result of our particular choice of a marginal propensity to import (MPM). The domestic price ratio will not change; it is 50 per cent higher than price line OP'', but OP'' was constructed to be two thirds of OP. With no change in domestic prices, there would be no change in output, factor proportions, or wages. As in the previous case, the Stolper–Samuelson effect is modified by the effect of tariffs on international prices.

Of course, the case of no change in domestic prices is a borderline case. If MPM for country 2 were less, the equilibrium would fall someplace between P' and P'', and domestic prices would fall. If it were higher, domestic prices would rise. Metzler's contribution was to prove that the condition that prevails in the borderline case is that $E_{id1} = 1 - MPM_2$, and that the domestic price will rise if $E_{id1} > 1 - MPM_2$.[11] Similarly, the domestic price

[10] Note that in that case the domestic price ratio of P_X/P_Y would have fallen. If we change the basis of our offer curves from the pure barter model to one that accommodates changes in production, the fall in the relative price of X leads to a fall in the domestic output of X. If we go back to the box diagram, Fig. 3-4, we see that a fall in the output of X leads to a rise in the labor/capital ratio in both industries. This in turn means a fall in the wage rate—the exact opposite of the Stolper–Samuelson effect. This example and the one that follows in the text were developed in a famous paper by Lloyd Metzler, "Tariffs, The Terms of Trade, and the Distribution of National Income," *Journal of Political Economy*, LVII, No. 1 (February 1949), 1–29. Reprinted from *The Journal of Political Economy* by permission of The University of Chicago Press.

[11] *Proof:* Using the notation of footnote 7, it is easiest to prove the inequality under the assumption that country 1 imposes the tariff, but the results are symmetrical. Let t_1 be the ad valorem tariff rate, and let $T_1 = (1 + t_1)$. The domestic price of imports in country 1 is then PT_1. Country 1's imports are a function of the domestic price and the national income: $I_1 = I_1(PT_1, Y_1)$. We may find the effect of a change in t_1 on the international price by first determining the excess demand for imports (at constant terms of trade) caused by the change in t_1, and then see what change in the terms of trade is necessary to eliminate the excess demand. Before allowing for the remission of other taxes, the change in imports is

$$dI_1 = \frac{\partial I_1}{\partial(PT_1)} \frac{d(PT_1)}{dT_1} dT_1 = \frac{\partial I_1}{\partial(PT_1)} \left(P + T_1 \frac{dP}{dT_1}\right) dT_1.$$

of good X falls if the elasticity of import demand of the other country is less than unity minus the home marginal propensity to import. (It is certainly remarkable and not at all obvious that the effect of the tariff depends on the elasticity of import demand of the other country rather than on the elasticity of the tariff-levying country.) When the elasticity of import demand abroad is sufficiently low, the tariff may not protect the domestic industry or raise the income of the factors of production that are intensively employed by it.

This theory is so straightforward that it should be feasible to apply it to actual cases, and an attempt has been made in the case of Australia. In 1929 a committee of Australian economists recommended in an official report that the Australian tariff not be reduced, for tariff reduction would

1. Worsen Australia's terms of trade
2. By forcing labor from manufacturing to agriculture, reduce the relative scarcity of labor and so lower Australian wages.[12]

Since we are temporarily holding P constant, $dP/dT_1 = 0$. Suppose we start with free trade, so that $T_1 = 1$. Then we can write

$$dI_1 = \frac{\partial I_1}{\partial(PT_1)} \frac{PT_1}{I_1} I_1 \, dT_1 = -E_{id1} I_1 \, dT_1.$$

The extra imports resulting from the remission of other taxes is equal to $MPM_1 I_1 \, dT_1$. The sum of the two sources of excess demand is then $(-E_{id1} + MPM_1)I_1 \, dT_1$.

From footnote 7, we know that the excess demand can be eliminated:

$$dB = I_1(E_{id1} + E_{id2} - 1) \, dP.$$

Setting the excess demand equal to dB, we obtain

$$\frac{dP}{dT_1} = \frac{-E_{id1} + MPM_1}{E_{id1} + E_{id2} - 1}.$$

It is now a short step to find the change in domestic price resulting from a tariff change:

$$\frac{d(PT_1)}{dT_1} = P + T_1 \frac{dP}{dT_1}.$$

We know dP/dT_1, so we can substitute for it. Recall from footnote 7 that $P = 1$ initially, by assumption; and $T_1 = 1$ by assumption. Therefore

$$\frac{d(PT_1)}{dT_1} = 1 + \frac{-E_{id1} + MPM_1}{E_{id1} + E_{id2} - 1} = \frac{E_{id2} + MPM_1 - 1}{E_{id1} + E_{id2} - 1}.$$

In stable situations, the domestic price of imports rises if the numerator is positive, i.e., if $E_{id2} > 1 - MPM_1$.

This proof follows Mundell, *American Economic Review*, L, 87–88.

[12] Suppose Australia is country 2 in the model and the rest of the world is country 1. From footnote 11 we know the change in the relative price of Australia's imports is

$$\frac{dP}{dT_2} = \frac{-E_{id2} + MPM_2}{E_{id1} + E_{id2} - 1}.$$

Australia's export products are wheat and wool, products that are generally supposed to have inelastic demands. So on a priori grounds E_{id1} is low, but this term appears in the denominator so that dP/dT_2 would tend to be large and negative (assuming the stability conditions are met). This means that a tariff improves the terms of trade substantially and correspondingly that tariff reduction worsens them, *cet. par.*

Both results were unwelcome. But it can be argued (still on the armchair econometrician's assumption of a low E_{id1}) that this twofold argument is wrong. If E_{id1} is so low that $E_{id1} < 1 - MPM_2$, then the tariff has actually lowered the domestic price of manufactured products. Removing the tariff would raise their relative price, expand their output, pull labor from agriculture, and raise the wage rate. Paradoxically, Australian labor working in import-competing manufacturing industry would be better protected with free trade than with tariffs.[13]

It is not necessary to reply on casual empiricism with the amount of statistical work that has been done over the last several years. I. A. McDougall has recently summarized the evidence.[14] The lowest of several estimates for Australia's *MPM* was .25; using this number, any elasticity of foreign demand less than .75 would suffice for the paradox to exist. The various estimates culled from econometric studies were .48, .66, 1.06, 2.20, and 1.69. These estimates were made for different time periods and using different techniques, but the two lowest ones used a technique that is known to be biased downward. It appears that, after all, labor in Australia's industrial sector would be better protected with a tariff.[15]

APPENDIX

In the course of discussing the Metzler model, we handled the effects of changing prices on production in quite a general fashion to save time. But with the apparatus built up in Chap. 3 it is not hard to be more precise. The neatest (but not the only) technique to show the combined effects of tastes and variable production was developed by James Meade.[16] We make the necessary assumptions so that community indifference curves exist, and we use the transformation curve.

In Fig. 4-9 a set of so-called trade indifference curves are constructed from the underlying taste and production data. The first and third quadrants refer to international trade. The second quadrant shows the domestic consumption and production of country 1, and the fourth is devoted to the domestic economy of country 2. In the second quadrant is, first, the community indifference map, drawn to read increasing amounts of X from right to left beginning with the origin. Let us first determine domestic equilibrium

---

[13] Metzler suggested this as a possibility in his article cited in footnote 10.

[14] "A Note on Tariffs, the Terms of Trade, and the Distribution of National Income," *Journal of Political Economy*, LXX, No. 4 (August 1962), 393–99. Reprinted by permission of The University of Chicago Press, copyright 1962 by the University of Chicago.

[15] The advanced mathematical literature on the subjects of Chaps. 3 and 4 is reviewed by John S. Chipman, "A Survey of the Theory of International Trade: Part 2, The Neo-Classical Theory," *Econometrica*, XXXIII, No. 4 (October 1965), 685–760. The comment of footnote 7, Chap. 2, applies here also.

[16] *A Geometry of International Trade*, Chap. II.

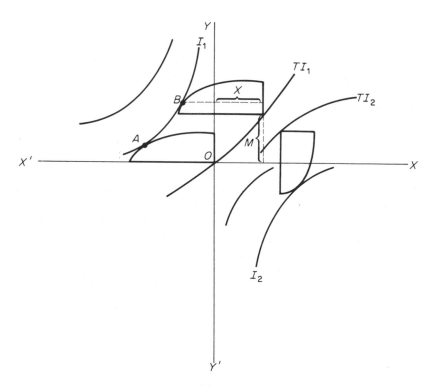

Fig. 4-9

without any trade. This would be shown by the tangency of an indifference curve with the transformation curve (point *A* in the diagram). The domestic price ratio is of course equal to the mutual slopes of these curves.

Now imagine that the transformation curve slides along indifference curve I_1, always with the two tangent. The origin of the transformation curve must then be pushed over into the first quadrant (or the third, if the transformation curve slides down instead of up). As the transformation curve slides up, the indifference curve becomes steeper, so the tangencies occur at steeper points on the transformation curve. That is, the production of *Y* decreases while *X* output increases. But at the same time, as point *B* shows, the consumption of *Y* increases and the consumption of *X* falls. The divergence between consumption and production is taken care of by trade: the surplus *X* production is exported (this is the quantity indicated by braces, marked *X*), and the excess demand for *Y* is met by imports (the braced amount labeled *M*). Thus it is possible to show simultaneously domestic production and consumption as well as exports and imports.

The origin of the transformation curve traces out a curve in the first and third quadrants as it moves up and down a given indifference curve. The curve traced out by the origin shows various import and export combinations which go with a given level of community indifference, so it has been named a *trade indifference curve*. If we go through the sliding routine with each of the community indifference curves, we can trace out a set of trade indifference curves for country 1, each corresponding to a different level of community indifference.

It is then no trouble at all to derive an offer curve for country 1 using the trade indifference curves. All we need is the technique used in Fig. 4-3: For each possible price ratio, what is the highest trade indifference curve that can be reached? The difference now is that for each point on the offer curve we know how much is being produced and consumed as well as how much is traded.

Exactly the same method is used to derive the trade indifference curves of country 2. They are based on the community indifference map drawn in the fourth quadrant (now X is read from left to right, but increasing Y is read from the origin downward). Some of its trade indifference curves, transformation, and community indifference curves are shown. Once again, when the trade indifference curves are known, an offer curve can be drawn. From there the considerations of equilibrium, stability, terms of trade, and so on, follow exactly as in Chap. 4.

CHAPTER 5

THE HECKSCHER–OHLIN MODEL

ONE OF THE MOST INFLUENTIAL APPROACHES to international trade theory in the last generation has been the Heckscher–Ohlin model.[1] This theory presented a new approach to the problem of comparative advantage. In essence it is a general equilibrium model of the type developed in Chap. 4, taking account of both tastes and production conditions, but singling out for particular emphasis the factors of production as controlling variables in trade.

THE ASSUMPTIONS

The Heckscher–Ohlin theory (the H–O theory for brevity) starts with some of the same assumptions we have been using—competition prevails, and transportation cost is ignored for the time being. A new assumption is that production functions are the same everywhere: A given amount of land, labor, and capital inputs will produce the same output in all countries in the world.[2] This seems rather an extreme position; the progress of knowledge and organizational ability differs so much between, for example, Germany and New Guinea that the functional relation between inputs and output should differ considerably. But let us follow up this idea to see where it leads.

[1] The originator was Eli Heckscher, who published in Swedish an article called "The Effect of Foreign Trade on the Distribution of Income" (published in English in A.E.A., *Readings in the Theory of International Trade*). The theory was further developed and elaborated in Bertil Ohlin, *Interregional and International Trade* (Cambridge, Mass.: Harvard University Press, 1933).

[2] Although Ohlin did not restrict himself to linear homogeneous production functions (in fact he spent a lot of time talking about increasing returns to scale), it is convenient to do so at this point. Also, diminishing returns to each input are assumed.

The importance of the factors of production in the H–O model comes from three assumptions. The first is obvious: Different countries are differently endowed with land, labor, and capital (and their various subdivisions). The next is more debatable: Any kind of productive input is similar among various countries (unskilled labor in France is qualitatively similar to unskilled labor in Italy, wheat land in Argentina is identical to wheat land in Australia, and so on). That means that factor endowments may be compared in a precise form. And finally, different commodities have different factor intensities (steel production always uses more capital relative to labor than does market gardening) at all ratios of factor prices—or at least at all the ratios we observe. This assumption, we shall see, is contradicted by much of the empirical evidence put together in recent years.

The assumptions concerning the factors of production and the production functions together suffice to derive the transformation curves for each country. Knowing the production functions and the factor supplies, a box diagram can be drawn for each country, as in Fig. 3-3. Because factor endowments differ, the box will have different dimensions for each country. From the assumption about factor intensities in each country, the contract curve in each box diagram will form an arc on one side of the diagonal, as in Fig. 3-3. The two box diagrams will generate two different transformation curves for each country. If country 2 has a relative abundance of labor, it will be able to produce more labor-intensive good X for a given amount of Y than country 1 can.

Generally it might be expected that wages would be relatively low in the labor-intensive country and high in the capital-intensive country. This would be true only if the demands for the products did not offset the relative factor supplies. If in country 2 the tastes and income patterns led to a high demand for X compared to Y, the derived demand for labor would be high and could lead to high wages even though labor was relatively abundant. The H–O assumption is that such offsetting demand patterns are not important and that we may regard the relatively abundant factor as having a low return relative to the other one.[3]

THE CONCLUSION

In that case the labor-intensive good will be relatively cheap in the labor-intensive country. This follows because a large amount of the cheap factor of production is used in its production. And, of course, in the capital-intensive country the capital-intensive product is relatively cheaper. This

---

[3] Bhagwati points out that the assumption that the consumption pattern is the same in both counties at all income levels is all that is needed for the H–O theorem to hold when factor abundance is defined in terms of the ratios of physical quantities of the resources. But if the abundant factor is defined as the cheap one, more stringent demand assumptions are needed. See Bhagwati, *Economic Journal*, LXXVII.

means that comparative advantage depends on relative factor supplies. The outcome of this reasoning is what has come to be known as the Heckscher–Ohlin theorem: Each country's comparative advantage lies in the production of commodities that use a large amount of factors relatively cheap and plentiful in that country.

Now this is a simple and striking result with many obvious applications. The case of Australian and Argentinian wheat has already been mentioned (Canada could be added). Here the ratio of land to labor and capital is high. The United States, presumably a capital-intensive country, exported $1,430 million of chemical products in 1960–1961 and imported only $372 million.[4] Natural resource examples abound—Arabian oil, Chilean nitrates. Japanese silk in the 1920's rested on a labor-intensive commodity in a labor-intensive country.[5] The wide range of application and the simplicity of the results led many writers to adopt the H–O model as the theory of international trade.

Further research has reduced the emphasis on the H–O model, however. There have been two major lines of development. One of these is theoretical, stemming from work on the effects of trade on factor prices; the other is statistical, involving techniques for testing the H–O model.

AN IMPLICATION: FACTOR-PRICE EQUALIZATION

Turning first to the theory, it was noticed by Ohlin that since a country would import commodities relying heavily on its scarce factor, the demand for that factor would be reduced. At the same time there is an additional demand stemming from exports for the plentiful factor. The price of the scarce factor will fall and that of the abundant one will rise. Abroad, the same things are happening. But since the plentiful factor at home is the scarce one abroad, its price rises at home while falling abroad. The prices of factors tend to become equalized as a result of trade.[6] This line of thought, if applicable, leads on to the conclusion that the fact that the United States had severe immigration quotas makes much less difference in the long run. India can trade labor-intensive products and raise its wages just as though it had been possible for Indians to migrate to the United States.

Why did Ohlin say that factor prices "tend" to become equalized instead of making the unqualified statement that they do become equal?

[4] Hal B. Lary, *Problems of the United States as World Trader and Banker* (New York: National Bureau of Economic Research, Inc., 1963), pp. 92–93.
[5] Many other examples can be gleaned from Ohlin, as well as from Charles P. Kindleberger, *Foreign Trade and the National Economy* (New Haven: Yale University Press, 1962).
[6] Since the same thing would happen if the abundant factor migrated to a region where it is scarce, it is sometimes said that trade substitutes for factor movements. See Ohlin, *Interregional and International Trade*, pp. 35ff.

This innocent-sounding question set off a line of research that culminated in the realization that the H–O model may well be unrealistic enough not to be useful trade theory.[7] Two assumptions are needed, in addition to the ones made earlier in the chapter, to prove that trade does make factor prices equal in both countries. The first is that trade does not result in complete specialization, so that both countries continue to produce something of both goods after trade. The other is of importance for generalizing beyond the

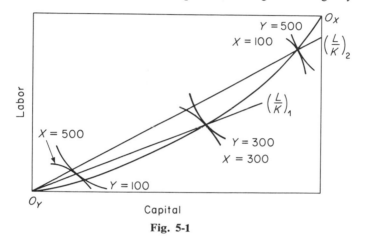

Fig. 5-1

2×2 model we have been using: The number of factors must not be greater than the number of goods.

There are many proofs in existence of the factor-price equalization theorem. The one we shall explore is based on consideration of the box diagram. Figure 5-1 reproduces the box diagram of Chap. 3. The equilibrium of production, remember, lies someplace on the contract curve. As we move along the contract curve from O_Y, observe how the labor/capital ratio increases. $(L/K)_1$ and $(L/K)_2$ are two sample input ratios that illustrate this crucial fact: As the output of Y increases, X output falls and the L/K ratio increases. The ratio increases for X as well as for Y. As the L/K ratio increases, what happens to the factor-price ratio? More labor per unit of capital means that MP_L falls and MP_K rises; but since the slope of the isoquants is MP_K/MP_L, we know that the isoquants are becoming steeper as L/K increases. In other words, the rentals on capital goods increase while wages are falling.

This establishes the first fact: P_K/P_L falls when K/L increases. The right-hand part of Fig. 5-2 illustrates this fact. Notice that for any

[7] See in particular Paul A. Samuelson, "International Trade and the Equalization of Factor Prices," *Economic Journal*, LVIII, No. 230 (June 1948), 163–84, and "International Factor Price Equalization Once Again," *Economic Journal*, LIX, No. 234 (June 1949), 181–97.

factor-price ratio the capital/labor ratio is higher in industry Y than it is in industry X; that is, Y is the capital-intensive industry.

The second fact is that Fig. 5-2 applies to both countries under the H–O assumptions. That is because we assume that the production functions are the same in both countries and the relations between factor prices and factor ratios depend only on the production functions. The only difference between the countries lies in their overall factor endowments. If country 2

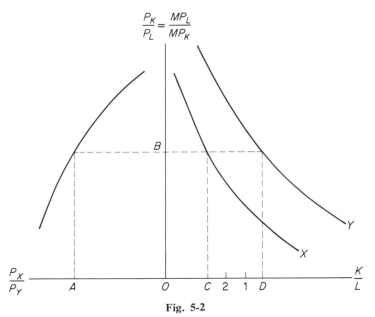

Fig. 5-2

is labor intensive, its K/L ratio might be given by $O2$, while $O1$ would indicate the higher K/L ratio in the capital-intensive country.

Now the relationship between commodity prices and factor prices must be established. In the second quadrant of Fig. 5-2 this relationship is shown as a rise in P_X/P_Y going along with a fall in P_K/P_L. Once again this relationship comes from the box diagram (but may be clearer if the transformation curve in Fig. 5-3 is consulted also). We already know that a fall in the factor-price ratio lowers the L/K ratio. From the box diagram, it also reduces the output of Y and raises the output of X. From the transformation curve, less Y and more X means a shift to a higher P_X/P_Y ratio. In Fig. 5-3, point A and its associated price line go along with a given factor-price ratio. If the factor-price ratio falls, the new transformation curve equilibrium will be at a point like B. Here P_X/P_Y is higher than in the original equilibrium, as we have just seen must be the case. This is the geometry. The economics of the relationship is that a rise in the price of X and the consequent increase in X output and fall in Y output changes the allocation of factors among industries. Because of the different factor intensities, the amount of capital released by cutting the output of Y is greater than can be absorbed at the previous factor price in X. Meanwhile industry X wishes to use more labor than industry Y releases. Therefore P_K must fall while P_L rises.

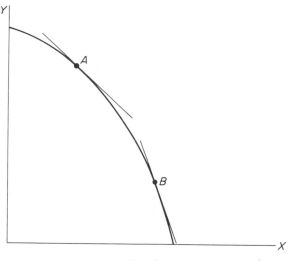

Fig. 5-3

Once more it should be emphasized that this relationship comes from the production functions, which are the same in both countries. Therefore the second quadrant of Fig. 5-2 applies to both countries.

We are almost home. Trade makes the P_X/P_Y ratio the same in both countries, for example, OA. Then in both countries the factor-price ratio must be OB, and in each country the K/L ratio in industry X will be OC and in industry Y will be OD. The theorem is proved.

It often heightens the appreciation of what is involved in factor-price equalization if a diagram such as Fig. 5-4 is carefully studied.[8] The box diagrams of both countries are superimposed, beginning with a common origin for good Y. Of course, the isoquants in each diagram conform with the assumption of identical constant-returns-to-scale production functions in each country. The assumption that country 1 is capital-intensive while country 2 is labor-intensive appears in the dimension of each box. The origins

[8] Diagrams similar to Fig. 5-4 were used in the analysis of trade and factor prices by Romney Robinson, "Factor Proportions and Comparative Advantage: Part I," *Quarterly Journal of Economics*, LXX, No. 2 (May 1956), 169–92. Adapted by permission of the publishers from *The Quarterly Journal of Economics* (Cambridge, Mass.: Harvard University Press), copyright 1956 by the President and Fellows of Harvard College

of the isoquants for good X must therefore be displaced from each other, as shown.

Production and consumption before trade occurred at some point on the contract curve of each country; points C and D might have been such pretrade equilibria. The factor proportions, the factor prices, and the product-price ratios were different in each country. But after trade, as we have seen, the equalization of product-price ratios implies the equalization of factor-price ratios. This requires the labor-capital ratio to be the same in

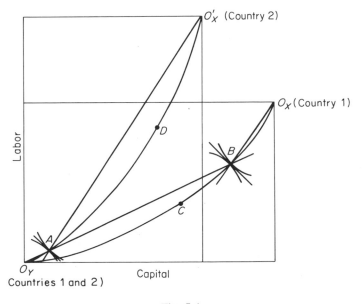

Fig. 5-4

the respective products in both countries. In the diagram the common L/K ratio in good Y is the slope of the line $O_Y B$. Product X's common L/K ratio is the slope of the line $O_X B$ equals the slope of the line $O'_X A$. At A and B the isoquants have the same slopes, because the factor proportions are the same, and hence the factor-price ratio is the same. (This is not a proof of the factor-price equalization theorem; it simply illustrates the way the equilibrium must look.)

There is only one unfinished bit of business. How can each country have the same K/L ratios in their industries when their overall K/L ratio is different? It is possible because the overall ratio is really a weighted average of uses in each industry:

$$\frac{K}{L} = \frac{K_X + K_Y}{L} = \frac{K_X}{L_X} \cdot \frac{L_X}{L} + \frac{K_Y}{L_Y} \cdot \frac{L_Y}{L}.$$

Industry X, with its low K/L ratio, gets a high weight in country 2, the labor-intensive country. And likewise, the capital-intensive industry gets the high weight in the capital-intensive country.[9]

The factor-price equalization theorem states that, given the appropriate assumptions, trade will make wages, rents, and so on equal around the world. This result has stimulated a lot of theoretical and empircal research. It is

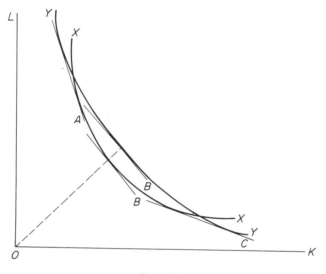

Fig. 5-5

obviously at variance with the way the world works—wages in India and Peru show no sign of becoming equalized with wages in America and Europe. We expect reality to diverge from the model somewhat because of many distortions that the theory ignores (monopoly, tariffs, transportation cost, and the like). Intuitively the divergence seems greater than can be accounted for by these elements. Where has the model gone wrong?

The particular assumption that has been treated most severely is that commodities are uniquely factor-intensive. It is easy to draw isoquants such that the factor-intensity varies with P_K/P_L. For example, in Fig. 5-5 X is capital-intensive at factor-price ratio A. The capital intensities are equal at factor-price ratio B; and at price ratio C, Y has become capital-intensive.

---

[9] For a discussion of what happens when the number of factors is greater than the number of products, or when one country specializes completely, see Samuelson's articles cited in footnote 7. A recent addition to the literature that explores a number of capital models in which trade leads to the equalization of interest rates is Paul A. Samuelson, "Equalization by Trade of the Interest Rate along with the Real Wage," in Caves, Johnson, and Kenen, eds., *Trade, Growth, and the Balance of Payments*, pp. 35–52.

The results for factor-price equalization are shown in Fig. 5-6. In the first quadrant the commodities change factor intensities as the factor-price ratio falls. In the second quadrant the line relating goods prices with factor prices becomes backward-bending. This phenomenon is caused by the change in factor intensities. At factor-price ratios below B, Y is capital-intensive and the goods-factor prices relation is the same as in Fig. 5-2 (higher relative price for X is associated with a lower relative price of capital). At higher factor-price ratios, however, a rise in P_X/P_Y and the associated shift in production in favor of X increases the demand for capital. Why is this true? Because in this range X is the capital-intensive good. As a result, a rise in P_X/P_Y leads to a higher P_K/P_L.

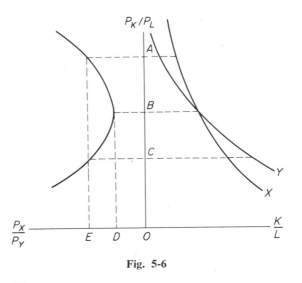

Fig. 5-6

This is fatal for factor-price equalization. Suppose the equilibrium terms of trade are represented by E in Fig. 5-6. The factor-price ratio could then be high (at A) in one country and low (at C) in the other. But note that such isoquants are fatal for the H–O theorem as well. No longer are exports tied in with factor proportions. In the example in Fig. 5-6, Y is capital-intensive at low P_K/P_L ratios. Since country 1 is capital-intensive in its overall factor endownment, there should be a low rental on capital goods. Y would be produced there with more capital-intensive techniques than are used in the manufacture of X. Country 2 is labor-intensive, has a high P_K/P_L ratio, and according to Fig. 5-6 would produce X by capital-intensive techniques. Suppose that the trade pattern involves the export of Y from country 1 and X from country 2; that is, both export their capital-intensive products. The H–O model, in other words, falls down when Fig. 5-5 isoquants are the order of the day.[10]

TESTING FACTOR-PRICE EQUALIZATION

Are such factor-intensity reversals more than curiosa? Do they occur often enough to remove the H–O theory from the center of the stage? Here we are in the middle of the turmoil of current research, with the reports from all the precincts not yet in. The most ambitious piece of research was performed by B. S. Minhas.[11] Minhas employed the H–O assumption that the same production function exists around the world, and computed what are called CES production functions for 24 industries, using data from 19 countries.[12] He computed diagrams similar to Fig. 5-6 for six of these industries and found five intersections or factor-intensity crossovers within the range of observed factor-price ratios. For example, his data show that the dairy products industry is more capital-intensive than the pulp and paper business when the wage-return-on-capital ratio is less than $2,136 (wages in dollars per man-year). Thereafter pulp and paper is more capital-intensive. Another example is textiles versus nonferrous metals: The former is more capital-intensive up to a wage/rate-of-return ratio of $1,350. His conclusion was that there is little practical validity to the H–O assumption of unambiguous factor intensity.

This conclusion is not unanimously accepted. One critic did additional calculations based on Minhas' data for 21 of the industries and found that of a possible 210 crossover points in the factor-intensity diagram, only 17 were found.[13] This suggests that factor reversals are rather infrequent. Perhaps the most questionable part of this empirical research is the attempt to fit the same production function to 19 countries. On a priori grounds, the efficiency of labor, managerial skill, climate, transportation facilities, scale, level of technology, and composition of capital vary so widely that different

[10] This formulation of factor-intensity reversals follows Michael Michaely, "Factor Proportions in International Trade: Current State of the Theory," *Kyklos*, XVII, No. 4 (1964), 529–49.

[11] *An International Comparison of Factor Costs and Factor Use* (Amsterdam: North-Holland Publishing Company, 1963).

[12] A CES production function is one with the property of constant elasticity of substitution. Like the Cobb–Douglas function it has the property of constant returns to scale, but the elasticity of substitution in the Cobb–Douglas function is always 1. The equation for the CES function is $V = (AK^{-\beta} + \alpha L^{-\beta})^{1/\beta}$, where V is the output, A, α, and β are parameters, and K and L are capital and labor. A review of the marginal productivity and isoquant slope formulas of CES functions is given by Minhas.

[13] Wassily Leontief, "International Factor Costs and Factor Use," *American Economic Review*, LIV, No. 4 (June 1964), 335–45.

production functions must be present.[14] Of course, different production functions are just as damaging to the H–O theory as are factor-intensity reversals.

TESTING THE H–O MODEL:
THE LEONTIEF PARADOX

The factor-price equalization theorem is a famous part of the theory of international trade. The H–O theory fostered a test that is just as famous in empirical work: Leontief's study of the factor intensity of U.S. trade.[15] His results became famous because they were unexpected. Although the United States is obviously one of the most capital-intensive countries in the world, his data showed American exports to be labor-intensive, while imports were capital-intensive!

These results came from applying a technique that is more and more being used in international economics. The technique is to use the input-output data gathered in the study of the domestic economy to answer questions dealing with international transactions. In Leontief's case the question was: What are the total requirements of direct plus indirect capital and labor per unit of output? The direct requirements are easy; it is only necessary to discover how much capital and labor are used in the industry under question. Indirect requirements are tougher; the question becomes something like the following: How many workers make the steel used in the automobile industry; how many mine the coal and the ore used in making the steel; how many are needed to make the machines to mine the coal; how many to make the steel to make the machines to mine the coal; ... ? This sort of question is answered by use of input-output data. The solution to the backward projection into time of input requirements comes from the solution of the simultaneous set of input-output equations.

A simple example should help clarify the matter. Suppose the economy consists of three goods, each used as inputs for the other goods as well as for final consumption (domestic or foreign). In addition, there are primary inputs—labor and capital—needed to produce each good. Denote the net output, the amount finally consumed, by X_i, and the gross output (net output plus the amount used in the production of other goods) by x_i. The input-output relations for the economy are

$$
\begin{aligned}
x_1 &= \;.2x_2 + .1x_3 + X_1 \\
x_2 &= .3x_1 + .4x_3 + X_2 \\
x_3 &= \;.4x_2 + X_3.
\end{aligned}
\tag{5-1}
$$

[14] Cf. Joan Robinson, "Factor Price Not Equalized," *Quarterly Journal of Economics*, LXXVIII, No. 2 (May 1964), 202–7.

[15] W. W. Leontief, "Domestic Production and Foreign Trade: The American Capital Position Re-examined," *Proceedings of the American Philosophical Society*, XCVII, No. 4 (September 1953), 331–49.

The equations have this interpretation: Each dollar of the gross output of x_2 requires 20 cents of x_1, and each dollar of x_3 uses 10 cents of x_1. The total output of x_1 is then the sum of the amounts used to produce the other two items, plus the final consumption, X_1. Notice that the production of each good depends on inputs of the others. x_1 requires an input of x_2; it does not directly use x_3; but since x_2 uses x_3, there is an indirect use. These direct and indirect uses mean that the total input of the primary factors of production are different from the direct use of these factors in each industry.

To use the input-output equations, it is easiest to transform them slightly. Change Eq. **(5-1)** into the following form:

$$\begin{aligned} x_1 - .2x_2 - .1x_3 &= X_1 \\ -.3x_1 + x_2 - .4x_3 &= X_2 \\ 0x_1 - .4x_2 + x_3 &= X_3. \end{aligned} \quad (5\text{-}2)$$

In this form, it is not difficult to find the gross outputs necessary to produce any given menu of net outputs. For example, suppose the net outputs are $X_1 = 1$, $X_2 = X_3 = 0$. Using these values in **(5-2)**, a little substitution gives

$$\begin{aligned} x_1 &= 1.1 \\ x_2 &= .39 \\ x_3 &= .16. \end{aligned} \quad (5\text{-}3)$$

If net outputs are changed, a quite different pattern of gross outputs emerges. When $X_3 = 1$, $X_1 = X_2 = 0$, the result is

$$\begin{aligned} x_1 &= .23 \\ x_2 &= .56 \\ x_3 &= 1.2. \end{aligned} \quad (5\text{-}4)$$

We shall use these results in a minute, but first we should handle the primary factors of production.

Assume that input-output research gives the capital and labor requirements for \$1 of gross output as

$$\begin{aligned} K_1 &= 3 & L_1 &= 1 \\ K_2 &= 20 & L_2 &= 1 \\ K_3 &= 2 & L_3 &= 1. \end{aligned} \quad (5\text{-}5)$$

That is, \$3 of capital are needed for \$1 output of x_1, and so on.

For purposes of the example, let us take x_2 as a domestic good such as haircuts that are neither exported nor imported, and the other two as foreign trade goods. As far as direct requirements are concerned, x_1 is more capital-intensive than x_3. If the economy is capital-intensive in overall endowment, the H–O prediction is that x_1 has a comparative advantage and will be exported. But what happens when intermediate goods are accounted for?

If \$1 of X_1 is exported, the capital and labor requirements including intermediate goods are easily calculated by multiplying the factor requirements in (5-5) by the output requirements in (5-3). That is,

$$K = 3(1.1) + 20(.39) + 2(.16) = 11.42$$
$$L = 1(1.1) + 1(.39) + 1(.16) = 1.65. \qquad \text{(5-6)}$$

The capital/labor ratio when intermediate goods are in the picture is somewhat higher than the direct requirements; it is, in fact, $11.42/1.65 = 6.95$.

Table 5-1

	Exports	Imports
Capital (dollars in 1947 prices)	2,550,780	3,091,339
Labor (man-years)	182.313	170.004

SOURCE: W. W. Leontief, "Domestic Production and Foreign Trade: The American Position Re-examined," *Proceedings of the American Philosophical Society*, XCVII, No. 4 (September 1953), pp. 332–49.

We can use the same method to find the capital and labor used in x_3. If X_3 is now being imported, and we reduce imports by \$1, replacing the foreign source by domestic production, the needed capital and labor are found by multiplying the factor requirements in (5-5) by the output requirements in (5-4). The result is

$$K = 3(.23) + 20(.56) + 2(1.2) = 14.29$$
$$L = 1(.23) + 1(.56) + 1(1.2) = 1.99. \qquad \text{(5-7)}$$

Notice that now the K/L ratio is $14.29/1.99 = 8.2$. X_3 is more capital-intensive than X_1 when intermediate goods are in the picture.

Leontief's study was an application of this technique on a grand scale. He computed requirements for \$1 million of exports whose percentage composition was the same as total U.S. exports for 1947, and for U.S. production of \$1 million of import replacements. The results are summarized in Table 5-1. Obviously, U.S. exports were labor-intensive in 1947. Here is a challenge to the H–O theory. Why did not exports prove to be capital-intensive, in line with the factor-proportions theory of trade?

One way to meet the challenge is to repeat the experiment on other countries to see if the results for the United States were a fluke or if generally the H–O prediction is wrong. It has been found that:

1. In Japan, exports are capital-intensive and imports labor-intensive. Since Japan is labor-intensive, this is contrary to the H–O hypothesis.

2. In East Germany, exports are capital-intensive and imports labor-intensive. This result is in accord with H–O reasoning, as East Germany trades with less-industrialized members of the Communist bloc.

3. India's exports are labor-intensive while imports are capital-intensive. Clearly this in accord with the H–O theorem.

4. Canadian exports are capital-intensive and imports labor-intensive. Since Canada trades mostly with the United States, this outcome violates the H–O theorem.[16]

It appears that about half the time a prediction based on factor proportions would be correct—not enough, presumably to give one much confidence in the theory.

Another way in which the challenge of Leontief's perverse results may be met is to point to neglected factors in his study. Currently the concept of human capital is in vogue in many circles, under the energetic promotion of Professor T. W. Schultz of the University of Chicago. It has been suggested that when reliable measures are developed, adding human capital to the capital listed in Table 5-1 will change the results. One clue pointing in this direction is the finding that U.S. exports involve more nonagricultural labor than do U.S. import replacements. Presumably more human capital is tied up in nonagricultural labor than in traditionally low-skilled farm workers.[17] More recently a direct attack on the problem has been mounted by Professor Kenen. A more detailed account of his approach is reserved for Chap. 13, dealing with problems of capital theory in international trade. It is appropriate to note here that his estimates are based on the notion that different amounts of skilled labor in the production pattern result from different amounts of investment in human capital. The value of this capital depends on the amount by which the skilled worker's income exceeds an unskilled worker's wage, capitalized at a suitable interest rate. When the direct and indirect human capital requirements (present discounted value based on a 9 per cent rate of return) are added to the physical capital requirements, American exports become more capital-intensive than do import replacements.[18] This seems one of the most promising solutions of the Leontief paradox yet proposed.

[16] M. Tatemoto and S. Ichimura, "Factor Proportions and Foreign Trade: The Case of Japan," *Review of Economics and Statistics*, XLI, No. 4 (November 1959), 442–46; W. Stolper and K. Roskamp, "Input-Output Table for East Germany with Applications to Foreign Trade," *Bulletin of the Oxford University Institute of Statistics*, XIII, No. 3 (November 1961), 379–92; R. Bharadwaj, *Structural Basis of India's Foreign Trade* (Bombay: University of Bombay, 1962); and D. F. Wahl, "Capital and Labor Requirements for Canada's Foreign Trade," *Canadian Journal of Economics and Political Science*, XXVII, No. 3 (August 1961), 349–58. The methodology of these studies is similar to that of Leontief.

[17] See M. A. Diab, *The United States Capital Position and the Structure of Its Foreign Trade* (Amsterdam: North-Holland Publishing Company, 1956), pp. 52–53.

[18] Peter B. Kenen, "Nature, Capital and Trade," *Journal of Political Economy*, LXXIII, No. 5 (October 1965), 437–60.

Another factor neglected by Leontief from lack of data was natural resources. This lack has been partly repaired by Jaroslav Vanek, who contributed another line to be added to Table 5-1 [Table 5-1 (addendum)]. Natural resource products (i.e., raw materials and crude foodstuffs) are used as a proxy for natural resources themselves. As in Table 5-1, the natural resource products requirements are computed as the total of direct plus indirect requirements. The result is that the United States is a resource-deficient country whose imports are raw-material-intensive. If one argues that capital is complementary with raw-material production, he can claim that the capital intensity of U.S. imports is not basic in the trade pattern but is simply the reflection of raw-material intensity abroad.

Table 5-1 (addendum)

	Exports	*Imports*
Natural resource products	340,000	630,000
(*dollars in 1947 prices*)		

SOURCE: Jaroslav Vanek, *The Natural Resource Content of U.S. Foreign Trade, 1870–1955* (Cambridge, Mass.: The M.I.T. Press, 1963), p. 132.

Leontief's own reaction was to claim that his results were in accord both with the H–O theorem and with reality, because the common view that the United States is capital-intensive is wrong. He suggests that U.S. labor is three times as productive as its foreign counterpart, so that it would be appropriate to multiply the U.S. labor force by three. Then the overall endowment would be labor- rather than capital-intensive. This suggestion has generally been rejected because Leontief could not show any reason why U.S. capital would not also be made more productive by anything that made labor more productive (entrepreneurship, for example).

Recently an intriguing alternative approach has been proposed. One might accept both the H–O theorem and the validity of Leontief's tests, including the hypothesis that the United States is capital-intensive. The paradoxical finding that exports are labor-intensive could be attributed to the effects of tariffs and other protective devices. It is possible that protection in the United States and abroad might bias trade flows in such a way that the observed factor proportions do not correspond with the actual ones. To predict trade flows, one would need to know the commercial policies of nations as well as their factor endowments.[19] This idea seems worth further development.

[19] See W. P. Travis, *The Theory of Trade and Protection* (Cambridge, Mass.: Harvard University Press, 1964).

A rather different approach to investigating the relation of factor proportions to trade was taken by Professor L. Tarshis.[20] He first obtained data establishing price patterns for comparable commodities in several countries (85 items in four countries, 97 items in three countries). Then he used the input-output data to determine the labor/capital ratios for goods that were especially high or low priced in one country compared to their

Table 5-2

AVERAGE VALUE OF RATIO
Labor (man-years)

Capital ($10,000)
FOR HIGH- AND LOW-PRICED GOODS

High in price in United States	1.416
Low in price in United States	.842
High in price in the United Kingdom	1.426
Low in price in the United Kingdom	1.026
High in price in Soviet Union	.889
Low in price in Soviet Union	1.070
High in price in Japan	.884
Low in price in Japan	1.477

SOURCE: Lorie Tarshis, in "Factor Inputs and International Price Comparisons" in *The Allocation of Economic Resources*, eds. Moses Abramoritz and others (Stanford, Calif.: Stanford University Press, 1959), p. 241.

price in the others. Following the H–O assumption of identical production functions and no factor-intensity crossovers, he used the U.S. input-output data to establish the labor/capital ratios in each country. The result are summarized in Table 5-2.

These data are in accord with the H–O theorem, for the presumed overall labor/capital ratio is lowest in the United States, slightly higher in the United Kingdom, still higher in Russia, and highest of all in Japan. The table shows that high-priced U.S. products have a high labor/capital ratio, that low-priced Japanese goods have a high labor/capital ratio, and so on. Relative prices in this test do follow factor endowments.

Tarshis notes, however, that trade flows do not correspond well with the price patterns. The United States exports a number of its high-priced items and imports some items that have a relatively low price at home.

[20] The following material is adapted from Lorie Tarshis, "Factor Inputs and International Price Comparisons," in *The Allocation of Economic Resources*, eds. Moses Abramovitz and others (Stanford, Calif.: Stanford University Press, 1959), pp. 236–44.

These variances might be explained by quality considerations, earlier availability, tied loans, hidden discounts, incorrectly valued exchange rates, a demonstration effect in which foreign items are preferred in spite of their high prices, and perhaps other influences. The divergence between price levels and trade flows might explain some of the Leontief paradox—at the expense of the H–O model.

All the foregoing empirical work has been devoted to international tests of the H–O model. But the first word in the title of Ohlin's book is "interregional" and indeed some of the criticisms of the model lead in the direction of greater relevance for interregional trade. Presumably demands are more alike and production functions not so likely to differ among regions of one country than they are among several countries, and tariff distortions are absent. Factor-intensity reversals cannot be excluded so easily, however. In any event, a test of the H–O proposition is available: Since the southern part of the United States is labor-intensive, there will be a concentration of production of labor-intensive commodities in that region. The test, involving direct labor and capital requirements in 1957, failed: Petroleum, chemicals, and paper are highly capital-intensive and at the same time have a heavy concentration in the South. But it also appears that during the 1949–1957 period the South attracted labor-intensive industries rather than capital-intensive ones. These findings lead the authors of the study on the South, Messrs. Moroney and Walker, to conjecture that while natural resources must be included in a proper testing of the H–O model, this may be appropriate to only the initial pattern of comparative advantage. Subsequent growth and industrial change may depend on the capital/labor ratio.[21] This "growth-pattern" interpretation of the H–O model, based on only one empirical example, needs both more theoretical backbone and more verification in other instances.

The testing of the H–O model has stirred up a hornet's nest of empirical work. None of it perhaps can be called conclusive—Professor Caves calls it "the swamp of uncertainty wherein Leontief and his critics clash by night."[22] We are left, it seems, with the proposition that sometimes the Heckscher–Ohlin theorem fits the facts, but it is an ex post explanation, not to be relied on for predictions in advance. The explanation of trade patterns requires more than knowledge of factor endowments.[23]

[21] John R. Moroney and James M. Walker, "A Regional Test of the Heckscher–Ohlin Hypothesis," *Journal of Political Economy*, LXXIV, No. 6 (December 1966), 573–85.

[22] Caves, *Trade and Economic Structure*, p. 282. Reprinted by permission of the publishers from *Trade and Economic Structure* (Cambridge, Mass.: Harvard University Press), copyright 1960 by the President and Fellows of Harvard College.

[23] The advanced mathematical literature on the H–O model is reviewed by John S. Chipman, "A Survey of the Theory of International Trade: Part 3, The Modern Theory," *Econometrica*, XXIV, No. 1 (January 1966), pp. 18–76. The comment in footnote 7, Chap. 2, applies here also.

CHAPTER 6

TRANSPORTATION COSTS AND INTERNATIONAL TRADE

THE THEORY DEVELOPED in the previous chapters simplified reality in many ways, some of which may be quite important to the course of international trade. The next several chapters take up some of the important omissions one by one, beginning with transport costs in this chapter. Since the purpose of leaving out complications like transportation was to be able to handle problems as simply as possible in the first instance, we expect to find the models increasingly complicated—and such is the case.

Transportation not only requires additional dimensions in the theory, but it also gives headaches to the researcher because it is difficult to find out about empirically. For example, most nations do not report imports in their balance-of-payments data on an f.o.b. basis (free on board; i.e., the cost in the country of export) but on a c.i.f. basis (cost, insurance, and freight, i.e., the total cost of getting the product to the country of import). And the transportation accounts in the balance-of-payments reports involve many errors and inconsistencies.[1]

[1] Thus, to get f.o.b. values, Balassa, in a major study, was forced to use assumptions rather than solid data; he assumed that freight and insurance together amounted to 10 per cent of the c.i.f. value of imports. Bela Balassa, *Trade Prospects for Developing Countries* (Homewood, Ill.: Richard D. Irwin, Inc., 1964), p. 100. The actual percentages run as low as 2 per cent for tin and as high as 40 per cent for bananas and iron ore; *ibid.*, p. 369. An attempt to straighten out the transportation accounts for 1951 was reported by Karreman; after making adjustments for items that should have been reported but were not, he found that total world receipts for transportation services were $7,475 million, while total world payments were $8,641 million. Since total payments must equal total receipts, nearly $1 billion was lost someplace in the reporting. See H. F. Karreman, "World Transportation Account, 1950–1953," *Review of Economics and Statistics*, XL, No. 1, Part 2 (Supplement: February 1958), 36–41. Adapted by permission of the publishers from *The Review of Economics and Statistics* (Cambridge, Mass.: Harvard University Press), copyright 1958 by the President and Fellows of Harvard College. See also his paper, *Methods for Improving World Transportation Accounts*, Technical Paper 15 (New York: National Bureau for Economic Research, 1961).

PARTIAL-EQUILIBRIUM APPROACH

Before looking further at empirical aspects, however, we should see how to handle transportation in theory. The simplest way is to use a partial-equilibrium supply-and-demand model; this is simple but amounts in principle to only a rough first approximation because it neglects feedback effects of changes in trade on the partial-equilibrium demand schedules and, through changes in factor prices, on supply schedules.[2] But it does provide a convenient opening gambit.

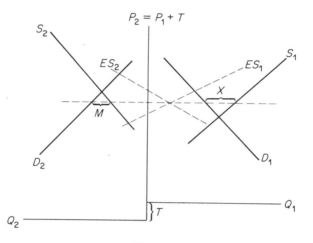

Fig. 6-1

Figure 6-1 shows one of the standard tools of international trade theory, a "back-to-back diagram." The supply-and-demand curves for the same product in each of two countries are shown, with a common price axis. In the right-hand part is the domestic supply and demand in country 1, drawn in the usual way, with domestic price established at the intersection of the two curves. (Alternatively, an excess supply curve, ES_1, can be constructed by subtracting the demand curve horizontally from the supply curve; then domestic equilibrium requires excess supply to be zero.) Country 2's supply-and-demand curves are drawn in the left-hand part, with quantities to be read from right to left. The origin for country 2 is placed downward from country 1's origin by T, the per unit transportation cost from country 1 to country 2. This reflects the fact that with trade the price in country 2 must be higher than in country 1 by the cost of shipment. Why? Because if the

[2] In many cases there may be no harm in neglecting feedback effects because trade is a relatively unimportant fraction of total economic activity. Corden suggests that as this point becomes more obvious there probably will result a "general rehabilitation of partial techniques in trade theory." Corden, *Recent Developments in the Theory of International Trade*, p. 51.

price differential exceeds the freight, it is profitable to ship more, reducing price in country 2 and raising it in country 1; and if the price differential is less, shipments will cease. Because the pretrade intercountry price difference is greater than T, country 1 exports and country 2 imports. The equilibrium, of course, requires that the quantity of exports equals the quantity of imports, which can be seen alternatively as the distances in braces, $X = M$, or the distance from the price axis to the intersection of the excess supply curves.

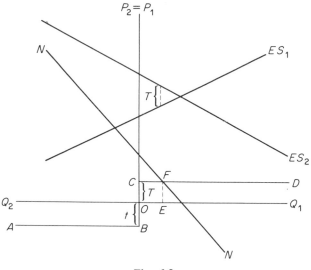

Fig. 6-2

(For country 2, the negative excess supply is the same thing as a positive excess demand.)

What has been the effect of transportation costs? If $T = 0$, the axes of country 2 would be shifted up; ES_2 would intersect ES_1 farther to the right; more would be traded; and the price in country 1 would be higher, while the price in country 2 would be lower (and both prices would be equal.) Much the same would happen if an improvement in transportation occurred that did not reduce T to zero, except that prices would not be equal. Transportation acts as an impediment to trade, from the point of view of the models developed in the earlier chapters.

An extension and modification of Fig. 6-1 brings out some other features of transportation. In Fig. 6-2, the excess supply curves of Fig. 6-1 have been reproduced, but with the axes of the left-hand side aligned with those of the right-hand side. The condition of equilibrium now is that the vertical distance between the excess supply curves be equal to T, reflecting the price divergence caused by freight charges. The equilibrium is the same as in the previous figure, with OE equal to the exports of country 1.

The distinctive features of Fig. 6-2 are, first, that transportation costs in both directions are shown by the line $ABCD$. T represents, as before, the cost of shipment from country 1 to country 2; now shipment charges in the other direction are shown as t. Notice that it is not necessary that $T = t$; with both sailing ships and jet aircraft it is cheaper to cross the Atlantic from west to east than in the opposite direction because of the prevailing west to east wind pattern. Low back-haul rates are another feature of transportation that makes freight rates in opposite directions unequal.

The second novel aspect of Fig. 6-2 is the curve NN, which is a net excess supply curve obtained by subtracting ES_1 from ES_2 vertically. This gives us another way to determine equilibrium, by the intersection of NN with CD at F. This is equilibrium because the vertical distance between excess supply curves is equal to the transport costs; in other words, at F the prices in the two countries differ by T, and the quantity of exports equals the quantity of imports. This construction makes it easy to see the effects on trade of changes in tastes, incomes, factor supplies, or technology in any market—any of these changes will shift the excess supply curve of the country concerned, which in turn changes NN. Suppose, for example, that an improvement in technology in country 2 shifts S_2 to the left. NN must then fall. If it falls so far that it intersects the transportation cost curve in the BC segment, trade is halted, since the difference in domestic prices is less than the transportion costs in either direction. If the S_2 curve fell still further, so that NN intersected the transportation cost curve along its AB segment, the direction of trade would change. Country 2 would become the exporter.[3]

GENERAL-EQUILIBRIUM APPROACH

The partial-equilibrium approach has yielded some ideas about the effect of transportation on trade models. Is it possible to do anything with general-equilibrium models? Yes, again at the expense of complicating life. The simplest general equilibrium to work with is the offer curve model in a barter setting, discussed in Chap. 4. Part of Fig. 4-4 is reproduced here as Fig. 6-3 to give a starting point for the analysis. In this example, country 1 exports X and country 2 exports Y. The equilibrium is established by the intersection of the offer curves, and at equilibrium the terms-of-trade line is tangent to an indifference curve of each country. We already know that $P_X/P_Y = Y/X$. The slope of an indifference curve is called the marginal

---

[3] This development is adapted from Paul A. Samuelson, "Spatial Price Equilibrium and Linear Programming," *American Economic Review*, XLII, No. 3 (June 1952), 283–303. In his article Professor Samuelson shows how this model may be generalized into a many-country, many-commodity model capable of answering complex questions such as the effect of a change in the excess supply curve of country 1 on prices in all counties and exports and imports in all countries. Furthermore, he shows how this model may be related to the transportation problem as defined in linear programming.

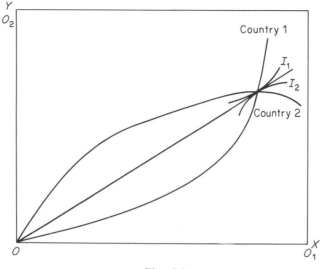

Fig. 6-3

rate of substitution; as a handy abbreviation we may denote the slope by $m_i(i = 1, 2)$.[4] Since the tangency condition means that the slope of the terms-of-trade line is equal to the slope of the two indifference curves, the equilibrium conditions of Fig. 6-3 are

$$m_1 = \frac{P_X}{P_Y} = \frac{Y}{X} = m_2. \tag{6-1}$$

These are the three equations needed to determine the unknowns X and Y traded and the price ratio.

To bring transportation costs into the picture, it is necessary to incorporate the fact that transportation uses up resources. In the partial-equilibrium model, transportation costs were viewed in money terms; but the money payment after all was needed to buy the resources used in moving the products. In this two-commodity barter model, the resources used up have to be the goods available. It is easiest to view it in this way: Suppose X is coal. Then country 1 ships out a cargo of coal, some of which is shoveled into the furnaces of the freighter on the way across the ocean. If quantity X is shipped from country 1, quantity $a_x X$ arrives in country 2, where $0 < a_x < 1$. For example, if one-third of the shipment is consumed as fuel, $a_x = 2/3$. Similarly, the amount of Y received in country 1 is $a_y Y$.

[4] The marginal rate of substitution for country i is a function of the consumption of X and of Y. More specifically, by using the same reasoning as that employed in Chap. 3 to demonstrate that the slope of an isoquant is $-MP_K/MP_L$, it can be shown that the slope of an indifference curve is the ratio of the marginal utilities, MU_X/MU_Y.

Equilibrium requires that in each country the indifference curves are tangent to the domestic price line. The price lines are now different, because the amount of the import good available for consumption is less than the quantity exported by the other country. Specifically,

$$m_1 = \left(\frac{P_x}{P_y}\right)_1 = \frac{a_y Y}{X}, \qquad (6\text{-}2)$$

and

$$m_2 = \left(\frac{P_x}{P_y}\right)_2 = \frac{Y}{a_x X}. \qquad (6\text{-}3)$$

In the partial-equilibrium model, the prices in the two countries were tied together by the transportation cost. Is it possible to tie together the relative prices in this model by the real transportation cost? Yes, but it takes several steps:

$$\left(\frac{P_x}{P_y}\right)_1 = \frac{a_y Y}{X} = a_x \frac{a_y Y}{a_x X} = a_x a_y \left(\frac{P_x}{P_y}\right)_2 < \left(\frac{P_x}{P_y}\right)_2. \qquad (6\text{-}4)$$

X is relatively cheaper in the country that exports it and is cheaper by a factor that is the product of the proportions of the goods that are used up in transportation. (*Problem*: Is Y relatively cheaper in country 2, and, if so, by how much?)

With no transportation cost, three variables had to be determined in this model; now there are four: X, Y, and one price ratio for each country. To set up the necessary four equations, recall that the marginal rates of substitution are functions of the quantities of goods consumed. If we call the initial endowment of country 1 $\bar{X}$, assuming it had no Y to start with, the amount of domestic consumption is the initial endowment less exports: $\bar{X} - X$. Its consumption Y is, as we know, $a_y Y$. Similarly, country 2's consumption pattern is $a_x X$ and $\bar{Y} - Y$. The equilibrium conditions are as follows: The marginal rates of substitution, expressed as functions of these consumption patterns, are equal to the domestic price ratios; and the domestic price ratios are spread apart by the real cost of transportation. A neat way to express the equilibrium conditions, involving a little bit of juggling with the a_x and a_y factors, is

$$\frac{1}{a_y} m_1(\bar{X} - X, a_y Y) = \frac{1}{a_y}\left(\frac{P_x}{P_y}\right)_1 = \frac{Y}{X} = a_x\left(\frac{P_x}{P_y}\right)_2 = a_x m_2(a_x X, \bar{Y} - Y). \quad (6\text{-}5)$$

These are the four equations needed to determine the four unknowns.

The transportation cost considerations can be added to the offer curve diagram by the technique shown in Fig. 6-4. Here the offer curves

increasing the volume of trade and of bringing the two domestic price ratios closer together.[5]

SOME EMPIRICAL ASPECTS

Now that we have learned some of the ways in which international economists incorporate transportation considerations into their theory, it is time to look at some examples of the effects of the costs of moving products. Location studies and regional economics provide a wealth of examples. It is interesting, by the way, to note that while some use of the results of location analysis appears in international economics, the two fields largely pursue their separate ways. Professor Haberler explains the distinction in this way:

> The traditional theory of international trade is at a higher level of abstraction . . . . Location theory, on the other hand, emphasizes the space factor and operates "closer to reality." For the very reason that it is less abstract, however, this theory has as yet been unable to develop a comprehensive general equilibrium system . . . . Only when this theory succeeds in developing a system of general equilibrium will the theory of international trade become merely a special case within such a general framework.[6]

One way of viewing the importance of transportation is provided by Fig. 6-5. The diagram is based on data compiled in the 1920's by the German National Bureau of Statistics. It shows the tonnage of world ocean-going freight related to distance shipped in 1925 and displays a remarkable drop-off of shipments for the more distant ports. Because the data are aggregated by 2,000-mile zones, they conceal some irregularities based on resource distribution, tariff patterns, imperial preference, and the like; but in general the negative relationship prevails.

[5] The algebraic approach described in this section was developed by Paul A. Samuelson in "The Transfer Problem and Transport Costs, II: Analysis of Effects of Trade Impediments," *Economic Journal*, LXIV, No. 254 (June 1954), 264–89. Robert A. Mundell originated the offer curve version of the transportation model in "Transport Costs in International Trade Theory," *Canadian Journal of Economics and Political Science*, XXIII, No. 4 (August 1957), 331–48. He also applies this model to a study of the effects of transportation costs on various problems such as tariffs and the real earnings of factors. A more sophisticated approach that allows for the joint supply features of inward and outward freight haulers is to be found in the programming approach adopted by Louis Lefeber, *Allocation in Space* (Amsterdam: North-Holland Publishing Company, 1958), and in Chap. 10 of Kemp, *The Pure Theory of International Trade*.

[6] Gottfried Haberler, *A Survey of International Trade Theory* (rev. ed.), Special Papers in International Economics No. 1 (Princeton, N.J.: Princeton University, International Finance Section, 1961), p. 4. As a matter of fact, a general theory of location has been developed by A. Losch in *The Economics of Location* (New Haven: Yale University Press, 1953), but regional scientists believe that the more eclectic though less logically elegant theory developed by Walter Isard in *Location and Space-Economy* (New York: John Wiley & Sons, Inc., and the M.I.T. Press, Cambridge, Mass., 1956) has more practical utility. For a discussion of these issues and for other references see John Meyer, "Regional Economics: A Survey," *American Economic Review*, LIII, No. 1, Part 1 (March 1963), 19–54.

This relationship is important in international economics; for example, it is a factor in the problem of the concentration of exports in a few commodities. The spokesmen for underdeveloped countries attribute many of their difficulties, such as exposure to violent fluctuations in the terms of trade and the lack of social progress in one-crop economies, to heavy concentration in a few products. Much development policy is oriented toward diversification of the economies. While concentration depends partly on the

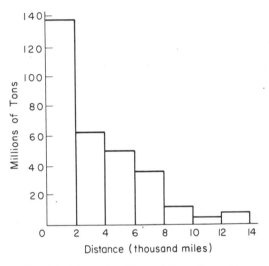

Reprinted from *Location and Space Economy* by Walter Isard, by permission of the M.I.T. Press, Cambridge, Mass., Copyright 1956 by The Massachusetts Institute of Technology.

Fig. 6-5

size of the country and on its resources, it has also been found that distance is important. Professor Michaely points out that the heavier the transportation costs, the larger will be the range of domestic goods and the smaller the range of export and import goods, as we saw in the theoretical section. He cites the example of Australia and Canada, which are similar in terms of size, economic development, and resources, but Australia is far from any major market. Australia's "coefficients of commodity concentration" as computed by Michaely are 50.8 for exports and 27.0 for imports, compared to 24.9 for exports and 18.0 for imports in Canada.[7] Similar results were found in comparing the less-developed countries of Europe (Spain, Portugal, Greece) with some of the better-developed countries of Latin America (Brazil,

[7] Michael Michaely, *Concentration in International Trade* (Amsterdam: North-Holland Publishing Company, 1962), p. 17.

Argentina). This suggests that there may be a natural barrier to the attempts to diversify exports from some of the underdeveloped world.

Innovations in transportation mean that the height of such barriers declines continuously, which has implications for international competition as well as for economic development programs. International oil pipelines, high-voltage electrical distribution systems, and giant tankers are contemporary examples of low-cost transportation. When Japan can import iron ore from Latin America and coal from the United States to make barbed wire that is exported to the United States, transportation cost is not much of a barrier. Over time we may expect the range of international trade to increase from transport cost reductions.[8]

[8] See Kindleberger, *Foreign Trade and the National Economy*, Chap. 2.

CHAPTER 7

INTERMEDIATE
GOODS

A MAJOR DEVELOPMENT in economics generally during the last twenty years has been the growth of theories and methods of research that take account of the fact that much productive activity is not for direct final use by the consumer but is an intermediate step in a productive process. Raw materials, fuel, and semifinished goods of various kinds are used as inputs in other industries and are called intermediate goods in contrast to final goods that are all ready for the consumer.[1] Input-output analysis, growth theory, economic planning, and other branches of economics have incorporated intermediate goods into their analysis.

In international economics, one application of an intermediate-goods model is the testing of the Heckscher–Ohlin model that was described in Chap. 5. In this chapter we explore the two other important developments of international economics that rest on the introduction of intermediate goods. The first is the modification of the structure of a tariff system that results when tariffs on inputs are considered; we shall see that this is of first-rate importance. The other is the question of whether the general conclusions of trade theory that is built on the assumption that only final goods are produced and traded must be modified when intermediates are included. To anticipate the results, in general no great change results.

[1] Professor Leontief's data for 1958 show that, if in that year the gross national product of the United States had been $600 billion, the total transactions including intermediate goods would have been $1,032 billion. Hence about 40 per cent of economic activity was in the intermediate-goods sector. Wassily Leontief, "The Structure of the U.S. Economy," *Scientific American*, CCXII, No. 4 (April 1965), 33.

THE STRUCTURE OF THE TARIFF SYSTEM

The example of the input-output system in Chap. 5 is a convenient place to begin. The following brief review is meant to call to mind the salient points, not to serve as a substitute for re-reading the relevant part of Chap. 5 if needed.

There are three products whose gross outputs are called x_1, x_2, and x_3. Some of the gross output of each is used as an input by other industries; after subtracting the amounts used as intermediate goods, the rest (X_1, X_2, and X_3) is available as the net output for final consumption. Each dollar of the output of x_i ($i = 1, 2, 3$) requires some fixed value of input from industry j. In the example of Chap. 5, we had

$$x_1 - .2x_2 - .1x_3 = X_1$$
$$-.3x_1 + x_2 - .4x_3 = X_2 \qquad (7\text{-}1)$$
$$0x_1 - .4x_2 + x_3 = X_3.$$

Equations (7-1) are simply a reproduction of Eqs. (5-2) and have, it should be recalled, the interpretation that the gross output of industry 1, x_1, minus the amounts used up in industries 2 and 3 equals the net output of industry 1, X_1, and so on.

It is common to call the coefficients .2, .1, and so on "a_{ij}"; they represent the value of the input of the ith good for each dollar of output of the jth good. Thus, in the first equation of (7-1), $a_{12} = .2$. This means that 20 cents of industry 1's output is used as an input in producing \$1.00 of output in industry 2. Similarly, in the next equation $a_{23} = .4$.

The next step is to compute the value added (or, what is the same thing, the incomes earned) in each industry. If industry 1 has a gross output of \$1.00, something less than \$1.00 has been contributed to the value of the output by industry 1. After all, industry 1 took inputs that already had some value and contributed some further processing to them. (It has been said that manufacturing has two branches: making big ones out of little ones or little ones out of big ones.) To find the value added per dollar output in industry j, it is necessary to subtract the value of the inputs per dollar of output. Symbolically,

$$v_j = 1 - \sum_i a_{ij}. \qquad (7\text{-}2)$$

For example, in industry 1 the value added for each dollar of output is \$1.00 minus the 30 cents of industry 2 input used; it happens that $a_{31} = 0$, so no industry 3 input is used directly. Hence $v_1 = .70$.

The recent writing on tariff structure emphasizes that the effects of a tariff on the allocation of resources in an economy depend on the way in which the tariff structure affects the value added in an industry rather than simply depending on the tariff on the value of the output. Steel may have a tariff, but domestic producers may find that they cannot compete with foreign steel because the price of the pig iron input has been raised by a tariff. Or an underdeveloped country may attempt to protect industry in general with tariffs, only to find that the amount of protection to value added in a given industry is very low because the inputs used by the industry have prices that are inflated by tariffs. To work with these problems, the concept of effective or implicit tariff rates has been developed.

To explain the idea of an effective tariff rate, let us start first with the ordinary or nominal rates. Suppose that the tariff laws have given the nominal rates t_i for each industry: $t_1 = 30$ percent, $t_2 = 80$ per cent, and $t_3 = 0$. (x_3 is an export good, requiring no tariff.) Domestic prices will be higher than world prices by the amounts of the tariff. In world prices, assuming that world market prices are fixed, we have Eq. **(7-2)** holding as the definition for value added. But in domestic prices the domestic tariff rate must be added to the world price. If v'_j is the value added in industry j in domestic prices, we have

$$v'_j = 1 + t_j - \sum_i a_{ij}(1 + t_i). \qquad (7\text{-}3)$$

Notice that the price of both the outputs and the inputs must be increased by the rate of the tariff.

The effective tariff in industry j, T_j, is defined as the rate that, when applied to v_j, changes v_j to v'_j. That is, the effective rate changes value added in world prices into value added in domestic prices. Symbolically,

$$v'_j = (1 + T_j)v_j. \qquad (7\text{-}4)$$

With a bit of manipulation, using Eqs. **(7-3)** and **(7-4)**, T_j can be expressed in terms of t_j:

$$T_j = \frac{t_j - \sum_i a_{ij}t_i}{v_j}. \qquad (7\text{-}5)$$

Equation **(7-5)** is the important result that allows us to calculate the effective rate for any industry.[2]

---

[2] This development follows Harry G. Johnson, "The Theory of Tariff Structure, with Special Reference to World Trade and Development," in *Trade and Development*, Études et Travaux de l'Institut Universitaire de Hautes Études Internationales No. 4, eds. Harry G. Johnson and Peter B. Kenen (Geneva: Librairie Droz, 1965), pp. 9–29. Other important articles explaining the new approach of effective tariff rates are W. M. Corden, "The Structure of a Tariff System and the Effective Protective Rate," *Journal of Political Economy*, LXXIV, No. 3 (June 1966), 221–37, covering theoretical points; and, for empirical calculations, Bela Balassa, "Tariff Protection in Industrial Countries, An Evaluation," *Journal of Political Economy*, LXXIII, No. 6 (December 1965), 573–94, and Giorgio Basevi, "The United States Tariff Structure: Estimates of Effective Rates of Protection of United States Industries and Industrial Labor," *Review of Economics and Statistics*, XLVIII, No. 2 (May 1966), 147–60.

The effective rate of protection is not directly set by the Congress or other tariff-making authority. It is the result of the tariffs on the various commodities, in combination with the input-output structure of industry.

To illustrate the effective rate, we may use the numbers in the simple model of Eqs. **(7-1)**, substituting them into **(7-5)**, together with the nominal rates of tariffs $t_1 = .3$, $t_2 = .8$, and $t_3 = 0$. The results are

$$T_1 = \frac{.3 - (.3)(.8) - (0)(0)}{1 - (.3 + 0)} = .086$$

$$T_2 = \frac{.8 - (.2)(.3) - (.4)(0)}{1 - (.2 + .4)} = 1.85 \qquad (7\text{-}6)$$

$$T_3 = \frac{0 - (.1)(.3) - (.4)(.8)}{1 - (.1 + .4)} = -.7.$$

These results demonstrate the way in which the effective rates may diverge from the nominal rates. In industry 1 the effective rate of protection is considerably below the nominal rate, because the rate of the tariff on its input from industry 2 is so high. Rate T_3 carries this effect even further; the negative rate of effective protection means that in fact industry 3 is paying a tax for its uses of protected inputs. And T_2 shows an effective rate much higher than the nominal rate, since industry 2 enjoys much more protection from its nominal tariff than do the industries from which it buys inputs.

This analysis calls attention to deficiencies and difficulties in many attempts to measure tariff levels and to conduct tariff negotiations. Computations of the average level of tariffs may run afoul of many divergences between nominal and effective rates. In most cases in industrially advanced countries the effective rates exceed the nominal ones; for example, in the United States the nominal rate on thread and yarn is 11.7 but the effective rate is 31.8; the nominal rate on ingots and other primary steel forms is 10.6, with an effective rate of 106.7. In a list of 180 effective rates (36 industries in each of five countries) there are only 11 negative rates, including rolling-mill products and agricultural machinery in the United States.[3]

When the rates on individual commodities are averaged into a general tariff level for the country, the effective rates may give some startling information. The average of nominal tariffs in the United States (computed by weighting with the combined imports of the United States, the United Kingdom, the Common Market, Sweden, and Japan) is 11.6, slightly below the Common Market average of 11.9. But when an average is made of effective rates, the U.S. average of 20.0 exceeds that of the Common Market at 18.6.[4]

[3] Balassa, *Journal of Political Economy*, LXXIII, p. 580.
[4] Balassa, *ibid.*, p. 588. Other calculations of effective rates, including the effective rate of protection on the value added by labor in various industries and averages calculated by different weighting schemes are presented in Basevi, *Review of Economics and Statistics*, XLVIII, 147–60.

The conclusions of effective tariff analysis have immediate practical relevance for underdeveloped countries. For one thing, this analysis turns into a precise form one of the contentions of underdeveloped nations: The tariff structure of the industrially advanced world is so designed that it forces underdeveloped lands to continue as specialists in raw-material production, since it offsets whatever comparative advantage they might have in labor-intensive industrial lines. The difficulty lies in what is called the escalated tariff structure of the advanced nations, that is, in a pattern of low tariffs on raw materials and semifinished products with higher tariffs on more nearly completed items.[5] The result of this pattern is similar to that of T_2 in our example—a rate of effective tariff much above the nominal rates. Economic development programs stressing attempts to industrialize run into barriers in their potential export markets.[6] No doubt the years ahead will see pressure from the underdeveloped nations to ease the unfavorable tariff structure that faces them.

It should not be thought, however, that deficiencies in tariff structure exist only in the advanced countries. The underdeveloped world has a great fondness for protecting its own infant industries. The result can be to render the higher stages of production unable to compete with foreign imports (as in the case of T_3 in the example, which came out with a negative rate of protection) and to saddle the country with excess costs.[7] The effective tariff approach should be a remarkably useful tool for economic planners and analysts.

INTERMEDIATE GOODS IN GENERAL INTERNATIONAL TRADE THEORY

Now we turn to the broader aspects of intermediate goods in trade models. This requires a modification of the two-good, two-factor model of Chap. 4. The basic feature of that model was that the two primary factors of production, labor and capital, are substitutes for one another in producing the outputs x_1 and x_2. (The notation is changed from the X and Y of Chap. 4 to the more usual notation for input-output models.) x_1 and x_2 are goods that may be either consumed or traded. The departure from the model in

[5] Travis, *The Theory of Trade and Protection*, pp. 187–226, gives many details supporting this generalization.

[6] Concern about the tariff structure of advanced countries was a main theme of the 1964 United Nations Conference on Trade and Development, but without the tool of effective tariff analysis the discussion tended to be general rather than forcefully precise. See *Towards a New Trade Policy for Development*, Report by the Secretary-General of the United Nations Conference on Trade and Development, E/Conf.46/3 (New York: United Nations, 1964) pp. 23–25 and 59–78; and Sidney Weintraub's analysis of the conference, *The Foreign-Exchange Gap of the Developing Countries*, Essays in International Finance No. 48 (Princeton, N.J.: International Finance Section, Princeton University, 1965), pp. 14–15.

[7] Johnson analyzes the excess costs in the context of the effective tariff model in *Trade and Development*, pp. 23–29.

Chap. 4 comes in the assumption that x_1 and x_2 are also intermediate goods that are used in the production of one another. For example, coal is both an intermediate and a consumer's good: It is fuel in industrial processes but a consumer's good when burned in a fireplace.

As in the effective tariff model, the coefficients a_{ij}, the input of x_i per unit output of x_j, are treated as constants. In the effective tariff model the a_{ij}'s referred to values of inputs; in this context it is better to take them as referring to physical quantities. Again we denote the gross outputs by x_i and

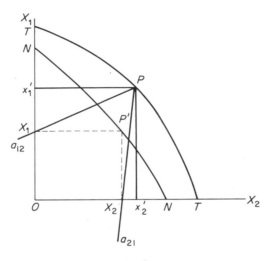

Fig. 7-1

the net outputs by X_i; they also refer to physical quantities rather than to dollar worth. We can now write a two-good version of the input-output model:

$$x_1 - a_{12}x_2 = X_1$$
$$-a_{21}x_1 + \quad x_2 = X_2. \tag{7-7}$$

The gross outputs are functions of the amounts of labor and capital used in each industry. With given supplies of the two primary factors of production, the gross outputs are related by a transformation curve. The first question to ask is whether or not the net outputs are also related by a transformation curve. The answer is: Yes, in the following way.

In Fig. 7-1, draw TT as the transformation curve when there are no intermediate goods required for production. It is hence identical to the transformation curves of our earlier work. From any arbitrary point on TT, such as P, draw a vertical and a horizontal line, x_1' and x_2'. (These are the gross outputs at P.) Beginning at P, move to the left 1 unit along line x_1'; this is equivalent to 1 unit of output of x_2. The production of this unit requires a_{12} units of x_1, so a_{12} units of x_1 must be subtracted from the gross output. If we continue this process, moving farther to the left along x_1', we obtain a line that gives the net outputs of X_1 for the fixed x_1' and for the various gross outputs x_2 beginning at point P. This line has the slope $-a_{12}$ with respect to the x_2' axis by construction. The intersection of the a_{12} line with the x_1 axis at X_1 tells us how much must be subtracted from x_1' for intermediate-goods purposes (i.e., $x_1' - X_1$) and how much is left for final consumption ($X_1 - 0$).

The net output X_2 can be traced out in exactly the same way. Begin again at point P, only this time go down 1 unit along the x_2' axis. This corresponds to 1 unit of output of x_1. a_{21} units of x_2 are to be set aside for intermediate goods. The outcome of continuing this process is a line beginning at P whose slope with respect to the x_1' axis is $-a_{21}$. Extending the a_{21} line to the x_2 axis gives the net output $X_2 - 0$ and the intermediate-goods production $x_2' - X_2$.

Point P' in Fig. 7-1 is determined by drawing perpendiculars from X_1 and X_2. P' gives the maximum amount of X_1 that can be produced for a fixed X_2; it is one point on the transformation curve NN between *net* outputs of the two commodities. To find the other points, it is necessary to repeat this construction for every point on TT.

It can be shown that the slope of the net transformation curve NN, dX_1/dX_2, is equal to the price ratio $-P_{X_2}/P_{X_1}$, just as in the previous work with transformation curves. The rigorous proof is straightforward but too lengthy to bother with here.[8] It seems intuitively reasonable, however, because of the proportionalities involved in the constant a_{ij}'s.

It turns out that many of the propositions already established remain valid when intermediate goods are included. For example, the factor-price equalization theorem of Chap. 5 still holds if we make all the assumptions of Chap. 5 plus intermediate goods as a part of the production process. The reason is that intermediate goods do not change the fact that under those assumptions there is a one-to-one correspondence between product prices and factor prices, no matter what the factor endowment is. For example, suppose the factor supplies of labor and capital for one economy are given as the dimensions of the box diagram in Fig. 7-2. At the factor price ratio P_C/P_L, the point of efficient production is given by the tangency of the isoquants with that slope (of course we know that there is a contract curve giving many points of tangency, but point P is the only one where the tangency involves this particular slope). P in Fig. 7-2 corresponds to P in Fig. 7-1,

[8] See Jaroslav Vanek, "Variable Factor Proportions and Interindustry Flows in the Theory of International Trade," *Quarterly Journal of Economics*, LXXVII, No. 1 (February 1963), 129–42. This article is the source of the diagrammatic analysis used here. Adapted by permission of the publishers from *The Quarterly Journal of Economics* (Cambridge, Mass.: Harvard University Press), copyright 1963 by the President and Fellows of Harvard College.

on the transformation curve *TT*, which includes intermediate-goods production. But to point *P* on *TT* corresponds point *P'* on *NN*. So to any set of factor prices corresponds a point on the net transformation curve, which means a set of product prices, and vice versa. Under trade, when the economies differ only in their factor endowments, the product prices are the same in both countries. Since the factor prices depend only on the proportions used in production and not on total endowments, the factor prices will be the same.

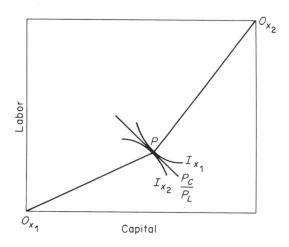

Fig. 7-2

It can be shown that some other results are not changed; for example, the Stolper–Samuelson theorem of Chap. 3 that stated that a rise in the price of the labor-intensive good (caused, for example, by a tariff) will raise real wages remains valid whether intermediate goods are present or not. Also, if the intermediate-goods model is added to the Heckscher–Ohlin assumptions, the conclusion still follows that a country will export products requiring a relatively large proportion of the primary factor with which it happens to be relatively well endowed.[9]

There are, however, points at which the conclusions of theory are changed by including intermediate goods. These involve cases where the number of commodities and of countries is greater than 2. When trade in intermediate goods is allowed, assuming that labor is the only primary factor of production (all other inputs being intermediate goods), the pattern of specialization in a Ricardo-type model is determined by direct labor costs. But if trade in intermediate goods is not allowed (perhaps because of protective tariffs), the trade pattern depends on both direct and indirect labor costs, which may be quite different. The example has been suggested that

[9] For proofs, see Vanek, *Quarterly Journal of Economics*, LXXVII, 129–42.

Lancashire would be unlikely to produce cotton cloth if the cotton had to be grown in England. And if the structures of the economies are different (in our example, if the a_{12} and a_{21} coefficients are different) in the different countries, with free trade in intermediate goods, the trade patterns become very complicated. In that case, differences in technology and in labor costs both affect trade.[10]

We began the chapter with the empirically important example of intermediate goods in the tariff structure; let us close it with another empirically relevant point. The point is exemplified by the problem of Italy in the "dollar shortage" days after World War II. Italy had plenty of labor but lacked other resources so that it needed to import the intermediate goods for its industrial processes. But the lira was not convertible and imports had to be severely restricted. More imports provided by Marshall Plan aid allowed a multiplier-type rise in income, investment, and consumption. Imports are usually regarded as reducing domestic spending and hence reducing the national income, but in the situation of countries like Italy the contrary effect of stimulating the national income was observed. Similar considerations probably hold for imports of intermediate goods in countries attempting economic development.[11]

[10] These propositions are worked out by Ronald Jones in "Comparative Advantage and the Theory of Tariffs: A Multi-Country, Multi-Commodity Model," *Review of Economic Studies*, XXVIII, No. 77 (June 1961), 161–75.

[11] Cf. Wolfgang Stolper, "Notes on the Dollar Shortage," *American Economic Review*, XL, No. 3 (June 1950), 286–300, and "The Multiplier if Imports are for Investments," in Caves, Johnson, and Kenen, eds., *Trade, Growth, and the Balance of Payments*, pp. 126–39.

CHAPTER 8

MONOPOLY

ALTHOUGH THE BASIC THEORY of international trade is developed with the use of competitive models, this does considerable violence to reality. International trade is full of monopoly and imperfect competition problems. The sizable exports of U.S. agricultural products are produced and marketed under various government programs that cannot fit a competitive model. In the industrial sphere, concentration and giant corporations make oligopoly models more appropriate.

Imperfect competition in international trade shows up in various ways. For example, Tinbergen notes that a rise of 1 per cent in the export price level of any given country appears to be followed in the first year or so by a fall in the share of world exports of no more than 2 per cent on the average. If competition were perfect, the share would fall to zero (assuming others' prices remain constant).[1] In the longer run, more competition generally appears and the elasticity becomes higher.

DUMPING

Many texts in international economics pay a great deal of attention to two particular types of monopoly behavior: dumping and cartels. Dumping is the international version of discriminatory monopoly pricing, handled in all microeconomics texts. It involves different prices in the home and the foreign market, transportation costs apart. If the foreign price is lower, it is called dumping; if the home price is lower, reverse dumping is the usual term. The requisites for dumping are monopoly behavior in equating

[1] Jan Tinbergen, *International Economic Integration*, 2nd ed. (Amsterdam: Elsevier Publishing Company, 1965), p. 22.

marginal revenue to marginal cost, rather than price to marginal cost; two markets, kept separate from another since otherwise there could not be two prices; and different elasticities of demand in each market. With marginal revenue in each market set equal to marginal cost, and with price related to marginal revenue by the equation $MR = P(1 - 1/E)$, where E is the elasticity of demand, different prices will be set in each market in order to maximize profits.[2]

Dumping has a long and controversial history. Competing home producers strongly react to any suspicion that their overseas competitors are dumping. For example, the United States first began selling government-held agricultural surpluses for local currency at the world price to underdeveloped countries that were receiving our aid in 1953. Canada, Argentina, Denmark, and the Netherlands all protested that this was dumping because the home U.S. price was held above the world price by the agricultural support program.[3] On the other hand, the dumpee often benefits by being dumped on (one begins to suspect that a better term than dumping could have been chosen). In the 1920's the German steel cartel sold iron and steel to Holland and the United Kingdom at prices as much as 50 per cent below the home price; Dutch and U.K. shipbuilders were thereby turned into low-cost competitors of the German shipping industry. And European sugar producers dumped in the United Kingdom before an agreement made in 1902; in the process a phenomenal development of U.K. jam and candy production was promoted.[4]

As a result of the protests of producers, the United States has had an Anti-Dumping Law since 1921 under which the tariff can be raised to offset dumping when it has been proven to occur. Many cases have been brought under this act.[5]

CARTELS

Cartels are the other monopolistic behavior pattern that has been much discussed. They involve agreements among producers in various countries about market sharing, price-fixing, exchange of patents and technological information, and the like. The interested student may find a good reference for the sort of things that go on in George W. Stocking and Myron W. Watkins, *Cartels in Action* (New York: The Twentieth Century Fund, 1946); the theory is handled in Stigler, *The Theory of Price*, Chap. 13. While

[2] See, for example, George J. Stigler, *The Theory of Price* (3rd ed.) (New York: The Macmillan Company, 1966), pp. 209–14.

[3] L. W. Towle, *International Trade and Commercial Policy* (2nd ed.) (New York: Harper & Row, Publishers, 1956), p. 671.

[4] Gottfried Haberler, *The Theory of International Trade* (Edinburgh: William Hodge and Company Limited, 1936), p. 315.

[5] See Don D. Humphrey, *American Imports* (New York: The Twentieth Century Fund, 1955), pp. 195–96.

interest ran high in cartels and cartel policy in the years after World War II, the discussion has by now abated. The reason may be in the difficulty of controlling them (the Sherman Act controls domestic U.S. cartels, but international cartels are harder to deal with) and in the problems in working out criteria for regulation. The prominent current attempt to do so is in the European Common Market, where Articles 85 and 86 of the Treaty of Rome prohibit cartel activity—unless specific vital economic functions or unusual contributions to technical or economic progress are involved.[6]

Professor Caves holds that the analysis of dumping and other monopolistic phenomena in international trade generally suffers from the partial-equilibrium approach taken, whereas the distinctive characteristic of trade is the general-equilibrium nature of the relationships. When general-equilibrium considerations are introduced into the picture, however, the pattern of trade under monopoly must depend on demand functions as well as on cost conditions. But the simple demand function of partial-equilibrium theory has to be qualified by cross-elasticities, complementarity, and substitutability. Sharp, well-defined conclusions become rare indeed, since general treatment is difficult.[7] (If this line of thought makes you despair look back at p. 68 and decide whether it is really true that the relative unimportance of changes in international trade make partial-equilibrium techniques more applicable.)

Professor Johnson has suggested that another reason for the minor impact of monopoly considerations on international trade theory is that the two major theoretical problems of contemporary interest—working out the implications of the H–O model and applying welfare economics to trade problems—required the assumption of perfect competition.[8]

TEMPORARY MONOPOLY:
THE TECHNOLOGICAL GAP

Recent research has emphasized neither theory nor the well-trodden empirical study of dumping and cartel behavior, but instead has taken up the Schumpeterian notion of temporary monopoly gained by technological progress. Part of the impact of technological change is in improved ways of producing existing products, and some theory has been

[6] See F. B. Jensen and Ingo Walter, *The Common Market* (Philadelphia: J. B. Lippincott Company, 1965), pp. 132–41.

[7] Caves, *Trade and Economic Structure*, pp. 181, 186. Adapted by permission of the publishers *Trade and Economic Structure* (Cambridge, Mass.: Harvard University Press), copyright 1960 by the President and Fellows of Harvard College. An initial step toward general treatment has been made by Daniel M. Schydlowsky and Ammar Siamwalla in their article, "Monopoly under General Equilibrium: A Geometric Exercise," *Quarterly Journal of Economics*, LXXX, No. 1 (February 1966), 147–53.

[8] Harry G. Johnson, "International Trade Theory and Monopolistic Competition Theory," in *Monopolistic Competition Theory: Studies in Impact, Essays in Honor of Edward H. Chamberlin*, ed. Robert E. Kuenne (New York: John Wiley & Sons, Inc., 1967), pp. 203–18.

worked out about the effects on international trade of these improvements in the theory of economic growth. Chap. 13 deals with this material in some detail. But another part of technological change is in the introduction of new products. This gives rise to trade that cannot be explained by factor productivities, demands, factor proportions, economies of scale, or the other causes we have looked at. One influential writer calls this "technological gap trade."[9] A new product is introduced in country 1; after some lag necessary for others to become aware of the existence and merits of the product, exports develop. The future course of trade according to this notion depends on a race between the rise of imitation in country 2 and the economies of large-scale production and the hints for future innovation derived by the manufacturing experience of country 1. Finally, when the product has been around long enough to become a standard item of manufacture, the standard theories of trade become applicable. Eventually a new product may be developed that completely eliminates the demand for the original innovation. But during a large part of its life the basis for trade has been the existence of a monopoly based on being the first to arrive. Dr. Hufbauer has illustrated this sequence with many examples taken from such synthetics as plastics, synthetic rubber and various man-made fibers, and finds that the "technological gap" is a good framework for analysis of this branch of trade.

A related line of research about the monopoly elements springing from innovations involves statistical tests of the trade patterns of U.S. industries in their relationship to the research and development (R&D) efforts of the firms. For example, it has been shown that U.S. industries with high research effort (measured by R&D spending as a percentage of sales or by the employment of R&D personnel as a percentage of total employment) also have a strong export position—either exports as a percentage of total sales or the excess of exports over imports as a percentage of sales.[10] It further turns out that the industries with a large R&D commitment are typically large and concentrated, but not necessarily capital-intensive. This research, based on rank correlation techniques, has been supplemented by multiple correlation work in which U.S. exports as a percentage of the sales of advanced countries are computed as a function of R&D effort, capital requirements, natural resource requirements, labor skills, and scale economies. The results show a high correlation of exports and R&D (e.g., the correlation between export shares and R&D in terms of scientists and engineers as a percentage of total employment is .88 for a recent year).[11]

[9] G. C. Hufbauer, *Synthetic Materials and the Theory of International Trade*, (Cambridge, Mass.: Harvard University Press, 1966), p. 29.

[10] William Gruber, Dileep Mehta, and Raymond Vernon, "The R & D factor in International Trade and International Investment of U.S. Industries," *Journal of Political Economy*, LXXV, No. 1 (February 1967), 20–37.

[11] Donald B. Keesing, "The Impact of Research and Development on United States Trade," *Journal of Political Economy*, LXXV, No. 1 (February 1967), 38–48. Reprinted by permission of the University of Chicago Press, copyright 1967 by the University of Chicago.

While the empirical work needs refining of the data and investigation of the interrelationships among the various suggested causes of trade, as pointed out in the articles cited, it is clear that an important line of inquiry is being opened up. Before the implications of temporary or technological gap monopoly can be incorporated into trade theory in a formal, systematic way, the general problem of monopoly in trade theory will have to be cleared up a bit. If Professor Caves is correct, that may not be easy; if Professor Johnson's suggestion, that monopoly has been to one side of the prevailing interest, is accurate, then it may not be such a problem.

MONOPOLISTIC FACTOR MARKETS

There is a famous article by Haberler that works out the consequences of monopoly in a factor market (caused, e.g., by a strong labor union) in a general-equilibrium setting. This shows monopoly as having adverse effects on trade and is quite a contrast to the trade-creating idea of technological progress.

The idea is shown in Fig. 8-1. Begin with curve NN; this is the familiar old transformation curve, drawn under the assumptions of Chap. 4. Equilibrium before trade is at P; if the international terms of trade are given by the line TT, production changes to P' and consumption to C after trade. But suppose that resources are not perfectly mobile. Then reducing the output of Y releases resources, but they do not all transfer to X. The output of X does not expand as much as along NN. This is shown by the transformation curve nn. Here, after trade, production becomes P'' and consumption C'. However, the tangency of the terms-of-trade line and the transformation curve means that the price ratio is equal to the marginal cost ratio. This implies that resource prices are flexible. Resources that are mobile receive

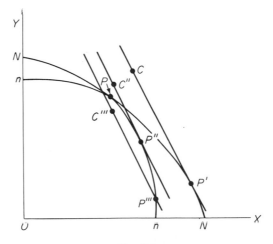

Fig. 8-1

the same pay in industries X and Y; immobile resources become unemployed in industry Y and their rate of pay falls to zero.

But suppose there is a labor union that prevents the real wage rate for the unemployed factors from falling. Production equilibrium must then occur at a point such as P''', where Y output is less than at P''. The reasoning is somewhat subtle. It may be easiest to approach it by remembering that the equilibrium condition for the producers, selling in a competitive market, is price equals marginal cost. Comparing the equilibrium before and after trade, we see that the price of Y has fallen (the terms-of-trade line is steeper than the slope of the transformation curve at the pretrade equilibrium). To restore the $P = MC$ condition, the output of Y must fall—assuming, of course, that MC has a positive slope.

Now marginal cost is equal to the wage divided by the marginal physical product of labor.[12] In the case of immobile resources but flexible wages, marginal cost falls to equality with the new lower price not only because wages fall but also because the marginal product rises. The rise in the marginal product is the result of using a smaller amount of labor in production of Y. In the case of rigid wages only the rising marginal product can change marginal cost; hence the employment of labor and the output of Y must fall further with a monopoly price in the factor market than without it.

We have established an equilibrium for the producers. But although marginal cost equals price in each industry, the price ratio and the private marginal cost ratio is no longer equal to the transformation ratio. The price and private marginal cost ratios imply that a unit reduction in the output of Y will allow the output of X to increase by a larger amount than will in fact be the case. Some of the Y resources will become unemployed rather than be transferred to the X industry.[13]

The diagrammatic example shows a tremendous fall in the output of Y, not much increase in the output of the exportable good X, and a consumption equilibrium inside the transformation curve—surely an extreme example of the effects of monopoly. Even if the results were less dramatic, the fundamental result of monopoly would remain. With monopoly in a factor market the price line is no longer tangent to the transformation curve. The same thing happens if the monopoly element occurs in a product market; the monopolist equates marginal cost with marginal revenue rather than price, so tangency cannot occur. We shall investigate some of the welfare effects of monopoly in Chap. 11.

[12] $MC_Y \doteq d(\text{total cost})/dY = [d(\text{labor}) \cdot \text{wage}]/dY$. Since $d(\text{labor})/dY = 1/[dY/d(\text{labor})] = 1/\text{marginal physical product of labor}$, the conclusion follows that $MC_Y = \text{wage}/\text{marginal physical product}$.

[13] See Gottfried Haberler, "Some Problems in the Pure Theory of International Trade," *Economic Journal*, LV, No. 238 (June 1950), 223–40. A more thorough analysis of this case is provided by Harry G. Johnson, "Optimal Trade Intervention in the Presence of Domestic Distortions," in Caves, Johnson, and Kenen, eds., *Trade, Growth, and the Balance of Payments*, pp. 3–34.

CHAPTER 9

INCREASING
RETURNS

THE STANDARD ASSUMPTION of the models we have studied so far is that production functions have the feature of constant returns to scale. But there is much of importance and interest in increasing returns-to-scale production functions. In particular, it is necessary to know about increasing returns to follow much of the literature on tariffs; and the economics of underdeveloped countries puts heavy stress on the possibility of increasing returns.[1]

The basic idea of increasing returns is that if all inputs are increased by the same proportion, output will increase by some greater proportion. The result is that long-run average and marginal costs fall, by contrast with the constant-returns-to-scale case where costs are constant at constant factor prices. For the individual firm, increasing returns can arise because of the possibilities of specialization of labor and of capital equipment as output increases, or because inventories do not have to increase proportionately with sales, or because of the indivisible nature of some investment goods, or from the economies of large-scale purchases of inputs. If these economies of scale persist to a large volume of output, and are not offset by difficulties of managing and coordinating a giant enterprise, some variety of monopoly or oligopoly would typically emerge. One firm by expanding and achieving lower marginal costs can produce and sell more cheaply than its competitors, eventually driving them out of the industry. Or only a few giants may remain, with product differentiation allowing them to survive simultaneously.

[1] There is a long literature stemming from Frank Graham, "Some Aspects of Protection Further Considered," *Quarterly Journal of Economics*, XXXVII (February 1923), 199–227. For the relevance of increasing returns to underdeveloped countries see Charles P. Kindleberger, *Economic Development* (2nd ed.) (New York: McGraw-Hill, Inc., 1965), Chap. 9.

The literature on the economies of scale classifies such happenings as internal technological economies of scale, since they occur within the firm and are aspects of the relations between physical inputs and outputs. External economies, by contrast, involve impacts on outsiders from an expansion in the output of a firm or the industry. Alfred Marshall analyzed these effects in detail, pointing out that unlike internal economies they are compatible with competition. Improved marketing arrangements and transportation facilities are examples of external economies.[2]

INCREASING RETURNS AND THE TRANSFORMATION CURVE

We do not need to linger on internal economies, since they are related to monopoly and Chap. 8 covered the monopoly problem. Most of the discussion in international economics is devoted to the case of technological economies, assuming that the output of an entire industry increases more than in proportion to its inputs and not bothering about what effects this might have on the division of outputs among firms. In particular, in the economics of the firm the effects on costs are derived on the assumption of constant factor prices. But in international trade's general equilibrium it is not permissable to hold factor prices constant. As one industry expands and the other contracts, the price of the factor used intensively in the expanding industry rises relative to the price of the other. Therefore the factor proportions change in each industry. So the transformation curve must reflect the combination of scale changes and of factor-proportions changes. With constant returns to scale, the factor-proportions changes lead to a concave production function, as we saw in Chap. 4. A mildly increasing-returns production function might still be concave when transformed into a transformation curve; convex transformation curves would require still stronger increasing returns.[3]

---

[2] There can also be external diseconomies, as, for example, the overcrowding of highways. In addition to the internal-external classification, one sometimes sees a technological-pecuniary distinction, where the long-run marginal cost of a firm falls in the first case because of physical considerations as developed in the text, and in the second case because the expansion of output allows it to purchase some inputs more cheaply. This is typically the result of internal technological economies in some supplying firm. There are also external pecuniary diseconomies, as, for example, an expansion in the output of all wheat farms increasing land rents. Jacob Viner, "Cost Curves and Supply Curves," *Zeitschrift für Nationalökonomie*, III (September 1931), 23–46, has much to say on all these classifications. A rather different approach to the same phenomena is in Francis M. Bator, "The Anatomy of Market Failure," *Quarterly Journal of Economics*, LXXII, No. 3 (August 1958), 351–79.

[3] This point is developed and illustrated in K. M. Savosnick, "The Box Diagram and the Production Possibility Curve," *Ekonomisk Tidsskrift*, LX (September 1958), 183–97.

One of the important aspects of increasing returns is shown in Fig. 9-1. It is assumed that industry Y has constant returns to scale, but industry X eventually shows such strongly increasing returns that the transformation curve becomes convex when the output of X has increased enough. The more X that is produced, the bigger the increment in X that will be produced by the resources released from a small decrease in Y.

In Fig. 9-1, point P is the production and consumption point before trade, with equilibrium in the convex part of the transformation curve. Then

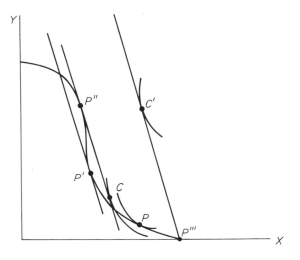

Fig. 9-1

trade is opened up, with international terms of trade given by the slope of the line $P''C$. There are three possible new equilibrium points: P', P'', and P'''. P' is an unstable equilibrium. If production is displaced a bit from P', for example, in the direction of more X and less Y, the slope of the transformation curve is less than the slope of the terms-of-trade line. Therefore $MC_X/MC_Y < P_X/P_Y$, which will induce yet more production of X. A displacement in the other direction leads to more Y output.

The other two possibilities are both stable. Suppose the economy has settled down to producing at P'' and consuming at C; it exports Y and imports X. If we interpret the indifference curves as social welfare contours, the country is worse off with trade. The trouble is that it is specializing in the wrong good. A prohibitive tariff that would halt the imports of X would allow the equilibrium to return to P, which would be a wise move. A still wiser move would be to maintain trade but to induce Y producers to shift over completely to the X industry, perhaps by a subsidy. The country would then specialize in the increasing-returns product, produce at P''', and consume at C'.[4] Increasing returns may thus provide a basis for tariffs; this is, indeed, an argument used by underdeveloped countries in formulating their commercial policies.

This line of thought, however, contains an assumption that is not explicit but that is important. As Fig. 9-1 is drawn, it assumes that the ratio of private marginal costs is equal to the ratio of social marginal costs. The ratio of social marginal costs is always shown by the slope of the transformation curve; it shows that the cost to society of producing more of one good, at the margin, is the amount of the other good that must be sacrificed. With a convex transformation curve, this ratio falls as more of the increasing-returns good is produced. Private marginal cost for one firm may be rising, however. Then the marginal private cost ratio would not equal the social marginal cost ratio, necessarily. It is possible that the two ratios would be equal when external economies are present, but it takes some specialized assumptions such as constant returns to the firm, even though returns to the industry are increasing, and a number of propositions about the exact nature of the external economies.[5] These include the requirement that the economies be internal to the industry, that the output of one firm depends on the outputs of other firms, that the factor/input ratio depends on factor prices but not on the industry output, and that both industries have the same ratio of marginal private costs to marginal social costs. Obviously, these are severe requirements and usually we would expect them not to be met.

Cases that seem to be most often cited of the phenomenon of the expansion of the output of one good involving a lower cost to society than to the entrepreneur are the examples of the training of a labor force, the stimulus to the development of financial institutions, and the creation of an obvious need for better transportation. The pioneering entrepreneur without these services has high costs, but his output leads to their development, and subsequent entrants to the industry will find their costs considerably lower. The cost to society will be less than the cost to the original producer.

One of the consequences of the divergence between marginal social and marginal private costs is shown in Fig. 9-2. The assumption is that the economies of large-scale output are not enough to make the transformation curve convex but that they do make the ratio of marginal social costs (shown by the slope of the transformation curve) less than the ratio of marginal private costs. The price ratio and the marginal cost ratio are initially equal to the slope of the line through P; P is the production and consumption point before trade. If the international terms of trade are given as $P'C$, the production of X should be expanded according to the transformation curve. But since the new price ratio, P_X/P_Y, is less than the original marginal cost

[4] See Tinbergen, *International Economic Integration* (2nd rev. ed.), pp. 132–34; and Caves, *Trade and Economic Structure*, pp. 171–72.

[5] Kemp, *The Pure Theory of International Trade*, p. 111.

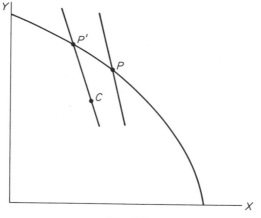

Fig. 9-2

ratio, MC_X/MC_Y, producers will shift out of X. They will find a new equilibrium at some point such as P', expand the output of Y, and trade it for X. They specialize in the wrong commodity. A tariff on X would expand its production, and the country would find that it could produce X more cheaply than it can acquire it through trade.[6]

INCREASING RETURNS AND THE OFFER CURVE

While many things can be done with the analysis of increasing returns in connection with such questions as stability, factor-price equalization, and changes in the terms of trade, we shall consider only the effects on the offer curve. This is most easily done for the case where the effect of increasing returns is strong enough to make the transformation curve convex and where social costs are equal to private costs.

Increasing returns change the nice smooth offer curves we have been using into something much more complex. In Fig. 9-3(a), NN' is the transformation curve. It is possible to derive the offer curve $AP'R'OA$ in Fig. 9-3(b) from the transformation curve. In the first quadrant of 9-3(b), Y is the export good and X is the import good; the export and import roles are reversed in the third quadrant.

N and N' are the points of complete specialization on the transformation curve. The slope of the terms-of-trade line NO is equal to the marginal cost ratio at N, so production equilibrium could occur at N. Then Y would be the export good, X would be imported, and consumption equilibrium would be a point such as O. The same terms-of-trade line is shown as OO' in

[6] Haberler, *Economic Journal*, LV, 223–40. Haberler puts this case forward as an interpretation of Graham's increasing returns case for a tariff (see footnote 1), whereas Tinbergen interprets Graham as thinking of a case such as Fig. 9-1. Graham's own work was in terms of numerical examples of a rather ambigous sort.

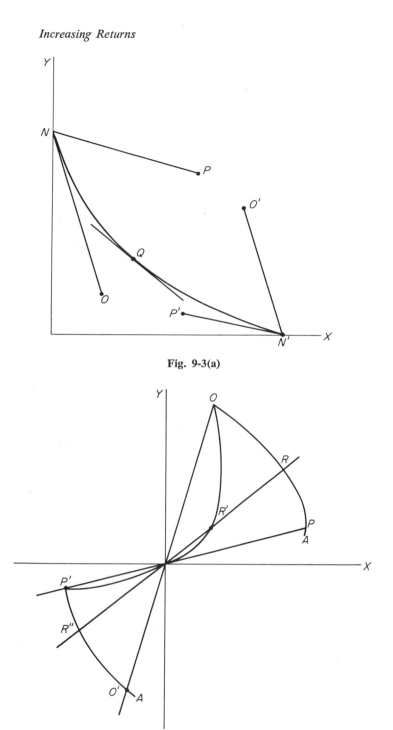

Fig. 9-3(a)

Fig. 9-3(b)

Fig. 9-3(b), with O giving the supply of exports and the demand for imports. But notice that with the same terms of trade, production could take place at N' and consumption at O'. N' is a point of stable equilibrium; with $MC_X/MC_Y < P_X/P_Y$, producers would expand the output of X if they could; they certainly will not wish to reduce it. The export and import roles of X and Y are changed around from the original equilibrium, and O' appears on the offer curve in the third quadrant of Fig. 9-3(b).

In much the same way, $N'P'$ is the terms-of-trade line that is equal to the marginal cost ratio at N', with the associated consumption point of P'. P' appears in the same quadrant as O', but involves more exports of X for fewer imports of Y. However, production could also take place at N, where the relative marginal cost of Y is lower than its relative price. In this case P is the equilibrium consumption point. P is in the same quadrant of the offer curve diagram as O, but requires less exports for more imports.

It appears that there are two possible international trade equilibria for each of the two terms of trade so far considered. For some terms of trade there are actually three possible equilibria. For example, the terms of trade implied by the line tangent to the transformation curve at Q would lead to an equilibrium at Q itself, but also at N and at N'. The trade corresponding with these is shown as R, R', and R'' on the offer curve. Any terms of trade between NO and $N'P'$ will have three possible points of equilibrium. On the other hand, terms of trade outside these limits will involve only one equilibrium point. If P_X/P_Y falls below $N'P'$, the price ratio would be less than the marginal cost ratio and production would never take place at N'. Only N would be an equilibrium. Similarly, for a price line steeper than NO, production would occur only at N'.

In summary, the offer curve under increasing returns has three segments: incomplete specialization, between P' and O; complete specialization in X, the $O'P'$ segment; and complete specialization in Y, to the right of O in the first quadrant.

Trade problems involving the general equilibrium of two countries are now easy to analyze when one or both of them have increasing returns. If only one has increasing returns, its offer curve will be like the ones in Fig. 9-3(b), while the other country's curve will be like the curve in Chap. 4. If both have increasing returns, one curve looks like Fig. 9-3(b), while the other has the same general appearance but the incomplete specialization segment bows the other way while the complete specialization segments point the other way. Figure 9-4 contains an example. The offer curve for country 1 is a duplication of the offer curve developed in Fig. 9-3(b). Country 2's offer curve shows the opposite orientation. It must be drawn that way because the first quadrant shows country 1's offers of Y and demands for X. It must therefore show country 2's demands for Y and offers of X—hence the opposite curvature.

The interesting aspect of these offer curves is the possibility of multiple equilibria. Any of the three points of intersection is a candidate for international trade equilibrium. At E' both countries specialize completely, country 1 in good Y and country 2 in good X. E'' is located in the incomplete specialization segment of both countries' offer curves, while E''' makes country 2 specialize completely in Y and country 1 a producer of both goods.

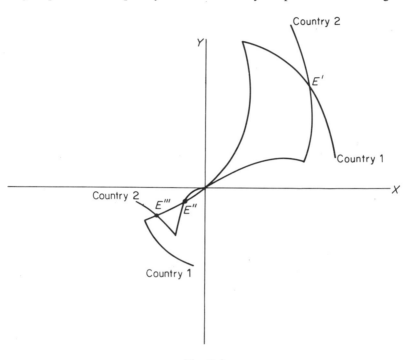

Fig. 9-4

By giving a little different twist to the curves, it is possible to have two, or even just one, points of equilibrium.[7] Increasing returns obviously makes the world of international trade complicated, both in theory and in applied work.

EMPIRICAL EXAMPLES

In fact, increasing returns are important and widely encountered. We have already noticed their relevance to problems of underdeveloped countries. Some additional bits of evidence may be offered. Professor

[7] The pioneer contribution on this subject is R. C. O. Matthews, "Reciprocal Demand and Increasing Returns," *Review of Economic Studies*, XVII (February 1950), 149–58. This discussion follows Kemp, *The Pure Theory of International Trade*, Chap. 8, copyright 1964, by permission of Prentice-Hall, Inc., Englewood Cliffs, N.J.

Johnston summarized some 16 statistical studies of long-run cost functions and found a preponderence of L-shaped long-run average cost patterns; that is, at small outputs, average costs fall sharply, but then they become constant and do not rise as outputs become very large. This argues for internal economies of scale.[8] In an earlier study Caleb A. Smith had found much the same thing, but he noted that the conclusions were complicated because factor prices seemed to rise with the size of the plant so that the factor of scale by itself was hard to sort out.[9] Neither had anything to say about external economies.

In international economics, Taussig's studies of the effects of tariffs put heavy emphasis on scale as a factor in the success of infant industries that have grown up (although in his narrative history approach it is difficult to sort out innovations and Yankee ingenuity as other contributing factors). He claims that large-scale operations allowed a comparative advantage in the late-nineteenth- and early-twentieth-century heavy iron and steel industry, including crude iron, beams, rails, and the like. Similarly, large-scale production gave the United States a comparative advantage in standard sewing machines, but in specialized embroidery and knitting machines the volume was too low to allow interchangeable-parts manufacturing. Imported handmade machines were used.[10]

[8] J. Johnston, *Statistical Cost Analysis* (New York: McGraw-Hill, Inc., 1960), p. 168.

[9] "Survey of the Empirical Evidence on Economies of Scale," a chapter in National Bureau of Economic Research, *Business Concentration and Price Policy* (Princeton, N.J.: Princeton University Press, 1955), pp. 213–30.

[10] Taussig, *International Trade*, pp. 189–91. Taussig's emphasis was on scale; he was writing before Ohlin popularized the factor-proportions analysis, so he did not consider that the high capital/labor ratio in the United States compared to Europe might have been invoked to explain the trade pattern. Which do you think was more important?

CHAPTER 10

OTHER
INFLUENCES ON TRADE

TASTES
AND THE DISTRIBUTION
OF INCOME

THE ASSUMPTION UP TO THIS POINT has been that demands for importables and exportables depend only on prices and incomes. In studying demands, however, researchers have found that relative prices and real incomes do not completely explain demand patterns. They have found it necessary to add time trends and variables representing "social factors," taste changes, and income distribution effects. The reason is that the data for the statistical demand studies are collected from transactions for several years. Over the years factors that for theoretical purposes are "impounded in *ceteris paribus*" (i.e., held constant) do in fact change.[1] For example, in a study of tobacco consumption in the United Kingdom between 1870 and 1938, a regression equation with independent variables of time and a dummy variable to represent a demand shift (with the value of zero before 1914 and the value of 1 after 1920) had a correlation coefficient of .987. When price and income data were added, the correlation coefficient became .991, which is not much higher (indeed, it could not be much higher than .987). In tea, a 1 per cent per year cumulative trend in consumption, quite apart from price and income changes, was found to be important. In beer, spirits, coffee, imported wine, and coal, the other factors seemed to be as evident as the price and income effects.[2]

---

[1] A very clear discussion of this point and the ways in which statisticians handle it is found in Lawrence R. Klein, *An Introduction to Econometrics* (Englewood Cliffs, N.J.: Prentice-Hall, Inc., 1962), Chap. 2.

[2] A. R. Prest, "Some Experiments in Demand Analysis," *Review of Economics and Statistics*, XXXI, No. 1 (February 1949), 33–49. Adapted by permission of the publishers from *The Review of Ecomomics and Statistics* (Cambridge, Mass.: Harvard University Press), copyright 1949 by the President and Fellows of Harvard College.

THE DEMONSTRATION EFFECT

The importance of these other factors, which are called nuisance variables by Klein, has led to some attempts to develop theories that show their effects on the course of international trade. In the field of tastes perhaps the most famous of these theories is the demonstration effect, emphasized by Ragnar Nurkse.[3] The idea of the demonstration effect is that at one time in the past, for example, a century ago, the underdeveloped countries had a well-established, traditional standard of living that did not change much over the years. In particular, it did not change as the result of trade, partly because contacts between cultures were fairly limited, and partly because the difference between the living standards of the advanced and the under-developed countries was not so large as today.

By contrast, today the developing countries are well aware of the living standards of advanced countries, thanks to movies, television, and cheaper travel costs. The result is that the offer curves shift in the direction of a higher demand for importables. At the same time the propensity to save falls, as the developing country's citizens try to emulate the standard of living of more wealthy countries. Development efforts are made more difficult by a lower propensity to save, and the achievement of equilibrium in trade is hampered by continued shifts in the offer curve.[4]

THE LINDER HYPOTHESIS

A relatively new idea on the influence of tastes on trade has been advanced by Stefan B. Linder.[5] He was intrigued by the phenomenon of the large volume of trade in manufactured products among the advanced countries. The questions are: Why do these countries import manufactured products instead of producing their own, and why is the volume of trade in manufactured items greater among advanced countries than between advanced and underdeveloped countries? Linder's suggestion is that trade in manufactures will be greatest, potentially, when demand structures are similar. Furthermore, the important thing in determining demand structure is the level of per capita income, because tastes do not differ much among countries with the same average incomes. (This approach ignores the effects of the distribution of incomes.) In effect, the thesis is that tastes are not an

---

[3] *Problems of Capital Formation in Underdeveloped Countries* (New York; Oxford University Press, 1953), Chap. III.

[4] See Kindleberger, *Economic Development*, pp. 141–48, for a review of the evidence for and against the existence of the demonstration effect. He also notices that a demonstration effect in technology may be favorable for growth if the technology of advanced countries is not only imitated but is also adapted to local conditions, whereas a transplantation of technology into inappropriate conditions such as different factor proportions may be less than optimal.

[5] *An Essay on Trade and Transformation* (New York: John Wiley & Sons, Inc,. 1961).

independent variable affecting trade, since tastes are a function of per capita income.

It is worthwhile to go into this suggestion a little more. Why exactly, is the volume of trade higher when demand structures are similar? The argument, as summarized and interpreted by Bhagwati,[6] is that a manufactured item will not be a candidate for an export position unless there is a domestic demand. Primary commodities may be produced for a fundamentally export clientele, but manufacturing concerns treat exports as only a branch of their domestic operation. Therefore the internal demand pattern gives the domain of possible exports. When two countries have similar demand patterns, their domains of possible exports overlap, which leads to a large volume of trade (subject to the qualifications of the effects of transportation costs, monopoly, increasing returns, and tariffs). But if one country has a high per capita income while the other has a low one, the existence of possible exports from the high-income country will not be followed by a large volume of actual exports. The low-income country simply does not have the tastes that lead to a demand for those exportables.[7]

Of course, Linder was not the first to notice the large volume of trade among the industrial countries.[8] The usual explanations have not appealed to the demand side but rather to comparative advantage. For one thing, it is suggested that increasing returns leads one country to specialize in manufactured product X and another in manufactured product Y, with a trade equilibrium such as E' in Figure 9-4. Alternatively, or also, the hypothesis is offered that an innovating country gains at least a temporary advantage in the industry in which the new products or processes are introduced.[9] Linder's suggestion adds a new possibility for research in this field.

INCOME REDISTRIBUTION AND THE OFFER CURVE

Both the demonstration effect and the Linder thesis derive from empirical observation. By contrast, theorizing about the other "nuisance variable," income distribution, has tended to involve modification of already-received theoretical models. The most fully-developed work has been devoted

---

[6] *Economic Journal*, LXXIV, 28–29.

[7] It is obvious that this view is contrary to the demonstration effect thesis. The statistical tests Linder uses are unsophisticated but do seem to support his thesis as far as they go; see *An Essay on Trade and Transformation*, pp. 110–23.

[8] For example, in 1957 a report by the General Agreement on Tariffs and Trade's panel of experts showed that of about $66.5 billion of exports from the total industrial area, about $40.5 billion went to the industrial areas and only $26 billion to the total nonindustrial areas. *Trends in World Trade* (Geneva: The Contracting Parties to the General Agreement on Tariffs and Trade, 1958), p. 130.

[9] Charles P. Kindleberger, *International Economics* (3rd ed.) (Homewood, Ill.: Richard D. Irwin, Inc., 1963), p. 103 and Chap. 7; also Erik Hoffmeyer, *Dollar Shortage and the Structure of U.S. Foreign Trade* (Copenhagen: Ejnar Munksgaard, 1958), Chap. 7; as well as our discussion in Chap. 8 of R&D for the argument that the comparative advantage of the United States lies in "research-intensive" commodities.

to incorporating income-distribution considerations into the Heckscher-Ohlin model. To take a specific case, let us retain all the assumptions of the H–O model of Chap. 5 except those pertaining to demand. We assume, that is, that the same constant-returns-to-scale production functions exist in both countries 1 and 2, and that labor and capital are the same in both countries. Perfect competition is the order of the day, there are no tariffs, and transportation costs are ignored. If Country 1 is the labor-intensive country and X the labor-intensive good, under the H–O model Country 1 exports X while Country 2 exports Y. The change to be made on the demand side is this: in the H–O model the demands are assumed to be so nearly the same that the factor-proportions considerations dominate. Now for the purposes of this chapter it is assumed that in Country 1 incomes are always redistributed optimally, as in the development of the Samuelson type of community indifference curves, but that in Country 2 no income redistribution occurs. Each factor keeps what it earns (which will be its marginal product times the quantity of the factor, under the H–O assumptions). This will permit us to examine the impact of trade on income distribution and vice versa. As to the precise nature of the demand functions of each factor of production, it is supposed that each factor has a high marginal propensity to consume the product in which it has the higher production intensity—labor has a high marginal propensity to consume X and a low marginal propensity to consume Y, while the owners of capital have the opposite consumption pattern.

One way to show the effects on international trade of these assumptions is to try to trace out the offer curve of Country 2. This is shown in Figure 10-1. Suppose we are at point B on Country 2's offer curve, and that then P_X rises; that is, the slope of the terms of trade line increases. Now, as experts on the Stolper-Samuelson theorem (Chap. 3) and the factor-price equalization theorem (Chap. 5), we know that a rise in the price of the labor-intensive good goes along with a rise in the wage rate; and, with a fixed amount of labor, it must also go along with a redistribution of income from capital to labor. (See, in particular, Fig. 5-2.) The reasoning of Chap. 5 applies perfectly here, and should not need to be repeated.

What is new is the effect on the demand for imports. With labor earning more income, and with a high MPC for X, the result is an increase in the demand for X. Simultaneously, capital loses income and because of its high MPC for Y, the demand for Y falls. This result is like Giffen's paradox—a rise in the price of X leads to an increase in the amount of X demanded—but is a different mechanism.

At the same time, there are other effects of the rise in P_X. One of these is that a rise in the relative price has income and substitution effects. The substitution effect means that the quantity demanded of X falls; so does the income effect of the price rise (note: this is not the income effect from the for the two countries without transport costs are the solid lines. The use of X and Y in transporting themselves is represented by the dashed offer curves $1'$ and $2'$. These show the original offers reduced to the quantities that finally make it to the other shore. For example, if country 2 ships out AE_2 of Y, $AB = a_y(AE_2)$ is received by country 1.

Through the intersection of these displaced offer curves draw a line perpendicular to the X axis and extend it to country 2's offer curve and a line perpendicular to the Y axis extended to country 1's original offer curve. The

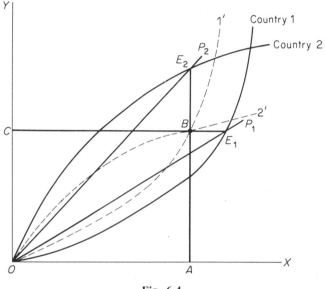

Fig. 6-4

equilibrium for country 1 will be at E_1, with a quantity of X exports equal to CE_1 and a quantity of Y imports equal to AB. The domestic price ratio in country 1 is then the slope of the line P_1. This is tangent to one of country 1's indifference curves, as we know by the way an offer curve is constructed.

In country 2, equilibrium is at point E_2. An amount of Y equal to AE_2 is exported, and imports of X are CB. The domestic price ratio is the slope of the line P_2; this is greater than P_1, as the analysis in Eqs. **(6-4)** showed must be the case. The amounts of resources used in transportation are E_2B of Y and E_1B of X. However, the volume of trade is reduced by more than the amount of resources used up, because of the increase in the relative price of imports in each country.

As in the partial-equilibrium model, the effects of an improvement in the technology of transportation (a reduction in the real cost) can be traced. If a more efficient means to carry Y is developed, the displaced offer curve $2'$ will be moved closer to the original offer curve, with the obvious effects of redistribution of incomes) when X is not an inferior good. There is also an output effect; the rise in P_X gives a new equilibrium on the transformation curve, with a higher X output and a lower Y output. For a given total demand of X, fewer imports will be needed. The output effect shows up very clearly in Meade-type diagrams such as our Fig. 4-9. There three effects work in

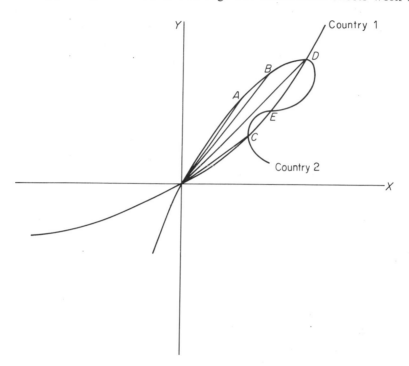

Fig. 10-1

the opposite direction to the income redistribution effect, and the total impact on the demand for imports of X depends on whether the demand-increasing factor offsets the demand-reducing factors. In Fig. 10-1 when the price line is originally OB, a rise in P_X leads to a reduction in the quantity of imports of X demanded; but if the price line is originally at OC, the rise in P_X leads to an increase in the quantity of imports demanded because the income redistribution effect is assumed to outweigh the substitution, income, and production effects.[10]

[10] This presentation follows Harry G. Johnson, "International Trade, Income Distribution, and the Offer Curve," *Manchester School*, XXVII, No. 3 (September 1959), 241–60. Professor Johnson shows that the income redistribution effect cannot outweigh the others over the entire offer curve; and he shows how different assumptions about their relative importance can lead to a complicated case where the offer curve loops back on itself, looking like the string bow ties favored by frontier marshals in Dodge City.

INCOME REDISTRIBUTION AND THE TARIFF

In some ways, the income-redistribution model is reminiscent of the increasing returns model of Chap. 9. For one thing, there are the same multiple equilibrium possibilities. In Fig. 10-1, points C, D, and E are all possible points of equilibrium. (E happens to be unstable.) Also, in the increasing returns model (Fig. 9-4) equilibrium could occur in either the first or the third quadrants—that is, a given country could end up exporting X, or it could find itself importing it. The same thing can happen in the income-redistribution model (although not with the offer curve of Fig. 10-1). But the possibility is there, for consider: Country 2 is importing X. P_X falls, therefore the income of labor falls. With its high MPC for X, the quantity of X imports falls. What is there to prevent the quantity of X imports falling so much that they become negative? That is just another way of saying that the import commodity becomes the export good, and paradoxically, because the price of the import good has fallen. This has the interesting corollary that a prohibitive tariff on X, rather than halting trade, will convert Country 2 into an exporter of X and an importer of Y—a result contrary to the expected outcome from our H–O-like assumptions. The reason is this: we start from a given P_X/P_Y at an equilibrium in the first quadrant where country 2 is exporting Y. Impose a high tariff on X. This raises the domestic P_X/P_Y ratio and raises labor income at the expense of the owners of capital. The latter have a high MPC for Y. If the resulting fall in the quantity demanded of Y is outweighed by the income, substitution, and production effects of the fall in the relative price of Y, then Y may be turned into an import good. This, of course, will not happen unless the world price ratio (that is to say, P_X/P_Y in country 1) falls, because country 1 will not export Y unless its relative price is quite high. The tariff in this case has turned the terms of trade against country 2.[11]

In general, conclusions from the theory that treats the demand of a country as though it behaved like the demand of a single person may need to be modified when the effects of a changing distribution of income are important. Recent empirical evidence from the field of international finance reinforces this conclusion. When money wages are relatively constant compared to the rise in the domestic price level induced by a devaluation of the foreign exchange rate, there is a shift of real income from workers to the owners of land and of manufacturing corporations. With different marginal propensities to save as well as different marginal propensities to spend income on foreign-trade goods in the various social classes, this redistribution of real income has a noticeable impact on the balance of payments. The

[11] See Harry G. Johnson, "Income Distribution, the Offer Curve, and the Effects of Tariffs," *Manchester School*, XXVIII, No. 3 (September 1960), 215–42, for a diagrammatic analysis of this case.

higher marginal propensity to save of the nonwage income-earners might be expected to reduce the demand for imports at constant terms of trade, but a higher marginal propensity to import might increase it. For a more complete description of the process we need some of the tools of international finance; for the moment all we need is the point that income redistribution does indeed influence international demands.[12]

[12] Carlos F. Diaz Alejandro, *Exchange-Rate Devaluation in a Semi-Industrialized Economy: The Experience of Argentina 1955–1961* (Cambridge, Mass.: The M.I.T. Press, 1965), presents both a model of the effects of income redistribution and an empirical study that leads him to the conclusion that the impact of the changing income distribution was as important in Argentina in his period as changes in monetary and fiscal policy in influencing the balance of payments.

CHAPTER 11

TARIFFS

THEORY AND POLICY

TARIFFS HAVE BEEN DISCUSSED REPEATEDLY at many points in the preceding chapters. This is not surprising; tariffs are one of the major concerns of international economics. A minor reason is that the tariff is such a convenient point to show the workings of some theory, but the major reason is that trade controls have been an issue of economic policy since the days of the mercantilists.

Much of the basic theory in the real model has already been developed in the discussion of the Stolper–Samuelson and Metzler contributions in Chaps. 3 and 4. The tariff shifts the offer curve and changes the international terms of trade by an amount that depends on the elasticities of both countries. Normally, the terms of trade are expected to improve, and the improved terms of trade are a source of gain to the tariff-levying country within limits. Often, however, this is less important in the eyes of the tariff-maker than the domestic price effects. As we saw in Chap. 4, the domestic price effects depend on what the government does with its tariff revenue. On the assumption that it reduces other taxes correspondingly, the domestic price change in country 2 has the same sign as $E_1 + MPM_2 - 1$. If the foreign demand for imports is inelastic, it is possible that the home price (including the tariff) will fall. Knowing the direction of the change of the relative price of importable goods, we can predict the effects on local production, as well as on the demand for and the prices of factors of production if the Heckscher–Ohlin model is applicable. If not—if there are factor-intensity reversals and the like—general predictions would not be possible, and each case would have to be handled individually.[1]

[1] Many of the effects of the tariff cannot be examined in terms of the models so far developed; tariffs have balance-of-payments effects and employment effects, which will be discussed in the second half of the book.

THE TERMS OF TRADE

Normally the terms of trade would be expected to improve, according to the previous paragraph; why? To see this, let us regard country 2 as the tariff-imposing country, importing X and exporting Y, as in the discussion of the Metzler model in Chap. 4. The relative price of its imports is $P_X/P_Y = Y/X$. It is convenient to define the commodity units so that the relative price equals 1 to begin with, and to write P instead of always repeating the ratio. Define T as one plus the ad valorem tariff rate. If the international terms of trade are held fixed provisionally, the home price becomes PT when a tariff is imposed. We can tell what the effect on imports will be from the elasticity of demand for imports, E_2. (Remember that the elasticity is the percentage change in imports divided by the percentage change in price, multiplied by -1 to make it a positive number; that is,

$$E_2 = -\frac{dX}{X}\frac{PT}{d(PT)}, \qquad (11\text{-}1)$$

since the relevant price includes the tariff.) To find the change in imports, dX, then,

$$dX = \frac{dX}{X}\frac{PT}{d(PT)} X\, d(PT) = -E_2 X\, d(PT), \qquad (11\text{-}2)$$

assuming that we start from free trade so that $P = T = 1$. Since P is the international price and is being held fixed for the time being, the last term on the right of Eq. **(11-2)** can be rewritten:

$$d(PT) = P(dT) + T(dP) = dT. \qquad (11\text{-}3)$$

(That is, $P = 1$ and $dP = 0$.) Substituting **(11-3)** in **(11-2)** gives the result

$$dX = -E_2 X\, dT. \qquad (11\text{-}4)$$

We have not yet accounted for any effects that might arise from the use of the tariff proceeds. Following Metzler's advice, these will be redistributed to the public. The amount of tariff revenue is $X\, dT$. From this the public spends something on imports, depending on the marginal propensity to import. The extra demand for imports from the remission of taxes is

$$dX = MPM_2 X\, dT. \qquad (11\text{-}5)$$

To find the total change in imports at constant terms of trade, add Eqs. **(11-4)** and **(11-5)**[2]:

$$dX = (-E_2 + MPM_2) X\, dT. \qquad (11\text{-}6)$$

[2] The student with a good microeconomics background can recognize that the expression in parentheses, $-E_2 + MPM_2$, is equal to -1 times the "compensated" or pure substitution elasticity of demand for imports, which we shall call E_2'. This concept is based
(*Continued on p. 110.*)

We now know by how much the demand for imports will fall at constant terms of trade; this represents an improvement in the balance of payments of country 2. For equilibrium, the terms of trade must change so that this surplus is eliminated. But we have already developed an expression for the change in the balance of payments when the terms of trade changed in connection with the stability discussion of Chap. 4 (see footnote 7, Chap. 4):

$$\frac{dB}{dP} = X(E_1 + E_2 - 1), \tag{11-7}$$

in the notation appropriate for this chapter. We can rewrite this to show the desired change in trade balance:

$$dB = X(E_1 + E_2 - 1)\, dP. \tag{11-8}$$

Equilibrium will be restored when dB in Eq. **(11-8)** is equal to dX in Eq. **(11-6)**. We may therefore equate the right-hand side of the two equations:

$$(-E_2 + MPM_2)X\, dT = X(E_1 + E_2 - 1)\, dP. \tag{11-9}$$

Now it is easy to derive an expression showing the change in the international price ratio that results from a small tariff change; simply rearrange Eq. **(11-9)** to read

$$\frac{dP}{dT} = \frac{-E_2 + MPM_2}{E_1 + E_2 - 1}. \tag{11-10}$$

In footnote 2 of this chapter it was established that $-E_2 + MPM_2 = -E_2'$; Eq. **(11-10)** can therefore be changed into

$$\frac{dP}{dT} = \frac{-E_2'}{E_1 + E_2 - 1}. \tag{11-11}$$

We know from Chap. 4 that the denominator is always positive in a stable equilibrium, and since E_2' is always positive, we may conclude that $dP/dT < 0$ whenever the international trade equilibrium is stable. But if the relative price of the import good falls when a tariff is imposed, the terms of trade improve. Therefore, normally the terms of trade are expected to improve when a tariff is levied. (In other words, a stable equilibrium is normal; but the results

---

(Footnote 2 continued.)
on the familiar division of the effects of a price change into income effects and substitution effects, restated in the form of elasticities. For a good exposition, see Milton Friedman, *Price Theory: A Provisional Text* (Chicago: Aldine Publishing Company, 1962), pp. 52–55. E_2' is the elasticity of demand if income effects are eliminated by compensating for the change in real income generated by the price change. The only effect left will be the substitution effect. Since with convex indifference curves the substitution effect always leads to an increase in the quantity demanded when the price falls, and since by convention the expression "percentage change in quantity divided by the percentage change in price" is multiplied by -1 in forming elasticities, E_2' is positive, always.

of the work on increasing returns and income distribution gives warning that it is not universal.)

It is easy to derive Metzler's criterion for the change in the domestic price level from this formulation; the question is, what happens to PT when T changes? To find this, all that is necessary is the product rule for differentiation, $d(PT)/dT = P + T\,dP/dT$. Since $P = 1$ by choice of commodity units, while $T = 1$ when trade is free initially, and since we have just obtained dP/dT in Eq. **(11-10)**, it follows that

$$\frac{d(PT)}{dT} = 1 + \frac{-E_2 + MPM_2}{E_1 + E_2 - 1} = \frac{E_1 + MPM_2 - 1}{E_1 + E_2 - 1}. \tag{11-12}$$

The conclusion: The domestic relative price of imports rises if the sum of the foreigners' elasticity of demand for imports plus the domestic marginal propensity to import is greater than 1, in stable situations.[3]

Equation **(11-10)** or **(11-11)** gives the answer to such questions as these: What happens to the terms of trade as the result of a tariff if the foreign offer curve is perfectly elastic? (In that case, the offer curve of country 1 is a straight line from the origin.) The answer is that as E_1 becomes larger, dP/dT becomes smaller until in the limit it approaches zero. If E_1 is perfectly elastic, then, there will be no change in the terms of trade. But on the other hand if E_2 is perfectly elastic, notice that dP/dT approaches a limit of -1 as E_2 approaches infinity. Hence the terms of trade improve in proportion to the tariff. Finally, suppose that the foreign country has an inelastic demand for imports; since E_1 appears in the denominator, there is a larger fall in import prices as E_1 becomes smaller, and indeed relative prices may fall by more than the tariff rate.[4]

The change in domestic price is given by Eq. **(11-12)**. It is easy to see from this what happens to domestic production—if the price of importables rises, more will be produced. The effect of scarce factors follows; in the H–O model the demand for factors used intensively in the production of importables will rise, and hence their price will rise. There is also a consumption effect: Normally, less is consumed at higher domestic prices. Finally, the tariff has an impact on government revenue, unless the tariff rate is so high that imports cease altogether.

It may sometimes be convenient to use a partial-equilibrium model to analyze the tariff, if the import industry is small and has little repercussion on and feedback from the rest of the economy. In that case the partial-equilibrium transportation model of Chap. 6 is ready-made for the purpose. Simply replace the transportation cost by the amount of the tariff and observe how prices are spread out in the two countries. The price falls in the export

[3] This development follows Mundell, *American Economic Review*, L, 86–88.
[4] It would be a good idea for the student to draw illustrations of each of these three cases.

country and rises in the importer, representing the improved terms of trade, while the quantity of imports is reduced.[5]

Knowledge of the price and output effects of a tariff is not enough by itself to tell anyone whether or not a given tariff is desirable, and tariffs may be imposed for a number of reasons or excuses that we shall look at later. Both tariffs and free trade help some people and injure others, and in working on tariff policy, it is necessary to derive what help is possible from the branch of economics that deals with these matters, welfare economics. The trouble is that welfare economics is not in a state of development suitable to lend very much help,[6] but let us see what can be done with it.

There are three topics in welfare economics of special relevance to the problems of international economics: the gains from trade, the theory of second-best, and the question of welfare weights. The gains from trade may be shown in the transformation curve model developed in Chap. 3. Figure 11-1 reproduces the situation of one of the countries in Fig. 3-5. It is assumed

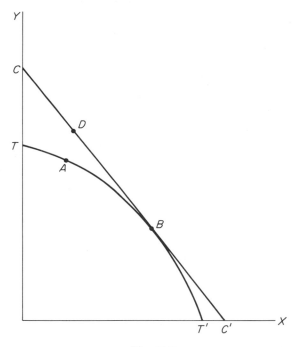

Fig. 11-1

[5] More complicated models, of course, yield more complicated formulas for terms of trade and domestic price changes; see Jagdish Bhagwati and Harry G. Johnson, "A Generalized Theory of the Effects of Tariffs on the Terms of Trade," *Oxford Economic Papers*, XIII, No. 3 (October 1961), 1–29.

[6] "Many of the modern writers on welfare economics take a poor view of its prospects." E. J. Mishan, "A Survey of Welfare Economics, 1939–1959," *Economic Journal*, LXX, No. 278 (June 1960), 251.

that the terms of trade are given by CC' and that the trade equilibrium results in producing at B, exporting X and importing Y, with consumption at D. If the pretrade equilibrium would have been at A, it is obvious that the economy has more consumer goods to dispose of with trade, so that everybody *can* be better off as the result of trade. The question is, will they, and under what circumstances?[7]

TARIFFS AND WELFARE: UTILITY POSSIBILITIES APPROACH

An answer to this question can be obtained by using the welfare-economics tool of the utility possibilities curve. The utility possibilities for our country of Fig. 11-1 are shown in Fig. 11-2. The axes of Fig. 11-2 measure the utilities of two representative citizens of our country. The

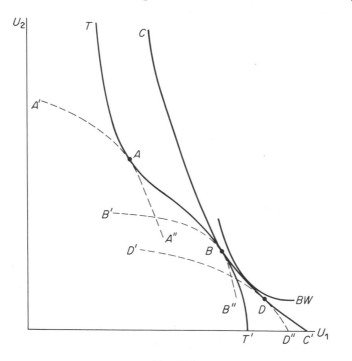

Fig. 11-2

<hr />

[7] As a matter of fact, what is called an optimum tariff policy can push the consumption point to the northeast of D, so that the country can gain still more with tariffs (there is the matter of retaliation to be considered, however). A nonoptimum tariff policy may make things worse. This is considered later in this chapter. For an exposition of the gains from trade on which the following material is based, see Paul A. Samuelson, "The Gains from International Trade Once Again," *Economic Journal*, LXXII, No. 286 (December 1962), 820–29. A more advanced treatment is in Murray C. Kemp, "The Gain from International Trade and Investment: A Neo-Heckscher-Ohlin Approach," *American Economic Review*, LVI, No. 4, Part 1 (September 1966), 788–809.

utilities are in turn derived from the consumers' position in a box diagram of the sort studied in Chap. 4 (see especially Fig. 4-2(a)); the dimensions of the box will depend on the amount of X and Y available at equilibrium. Since we are using ordinal utility, all that can be said is that a higher point on the U_2 axis means that man 2 is on a higher indifference curve, and similarly for the U_1 axis. It cannot be said that a point 2 inches from the origin means twice as much utility as a point 1 inch from the origin. Directions matter, but not distances.

The meaning of Fig. 11-2 can best be explained by beginning with a point such as A. This represents the indifference levels reached by each man from his consumption in the pretrade equilibrium, A in Fig. 11-1. Now, A in Fig. 11-1 is a fixed total of goods that may be made into a consumers' box diagram with Mr. 1's indifference curves having an origin at one corner and Mr. 2's at the opposite corner. The initial equilibrium is along the contract curve, someplace within the box. If the fixed total of goods is reallocated between the consumers in such a way that they are always on the contract curve, a curve such as $A'AA''$ is traced out in Fig. 11-2. When Mr. 1 gains, Mr. 2 loses along the contract curve, so $A'AA''$ must have the general feature of a negative slope.

The next step is to repeat this construction for every point along the transformation curve. B in Fig. 11-1 will give rise to a different box diagram, for example, one that has a longer X axis but a shorter Y axis than the box associated with A. Reallocation of the new X and Y totals might give a path in the utility space that looks like $B'BB''$. This utility possibilities curve for point B has the feature that, in the neighborhood of B, the first man can be made better off (i.e., he is on a higher indifference curve) for a given utility of the second man than is possible with the quantities of products available at point A, Fig. 11-1. They cannot both be better off because B does not involve more of both goods than point A.

After a utility possibilities curve has been drawn up for every point on the transformation curve, the envelope curve TBT' is drawn. As in the process of constructing a long-run average cost curve by drawing an envelope of all the short-run average cost curves, what is involved is picking out an extreme value along one axis for a given point on the other one. In this case, for each utility level of man 2, find the highest possible utility for the first man on any of the available point utility possibilities curves. This will give a point on the envelope. When it is completed, we have the situation utilities possibility curve for autarky (i.e., national economic self-sufficiency). This is a frontier for consumer satisfaction in the absence of trade.

Now, any point along the terms of trade line CC' of Fig. 11-1 is a candidate for the equilibrium of consumption under free trade. Each point may be turned into a box diagram and a utility possibilities curve drawn for it; an envelope may then be constructed for this new set of utilities possibilities curves. This envelope is shown as CBC' in Fig. 11-2. Because more goods are available with trade than under autarky except at point B, the utility possibilities frontier for the free-trade situation is further to the northeast than was the first envelope corresponding to autarky. The reason is obvious: with more goods, both can be better off, or one can be better off and the other no worse off. This approach then shows the gains from trade as existing in a potential sense: Both men *can* be made better off.

In the actual situation of Fig. 11-2, the posttrade point, D, has resulted in a gain for man 1 and loss for man 2 compared to the pretrade point, A. Curve $D'DD''$ shows that it is not possible to reallocate the total X and Y available at D in Fig. 11-1 to compensate man 2 for his loss. But suppose that a lump-sum transfer is made from man 1 to man 2. Then the after-trade equilibrium will change—the consumers have different incomes and different tastes, so the demand for imports will change. As trade changes, the equilibrium point moves along $CBDC'$ until it arrives at a point northeast of A. Then both men in fact are better off with trade, and the potential welfare gain has been converted into an actual gain.[8]

Welfare economics goes on to consider other aspects of the problem. For example, we may imagine that the country has some sort of social policy about the ideal distribution of income. This idea is often formalized as a Bergson social welfare function and is depicted as a set of "welfare contours." Along one of these contours (usually drawn to look like indifference curves) can be shown the gain in the first man's utility that would compensate for a given loss in the second man's utility, in the judgment of the community.[9] If the highest welfare contour touched by CBC' in Fig. 11-2 is BW, then social welfare is maximized by a small redistribution from man 1 to man 2, but man 2 will remain in a worse condition after trade than he was before.

Speaking realistically, governments do not use lump-sum taxes and subsidies, so any move from D will be to the southeast of CBC'. (Income taxes distort leisure-labor decisions, sales taxes distort purchasing decisions, and so on.) Converting the potential gain from trade into an actual gain then becomes hazardous. Nevertheless, the potential gain is there.

This treatment is quite general, and much recent work has been devoted to making the theory more susceptible to application. In particular, James Meade has been promoting a cardinalist measure of welfare in his work on

[8] The transfer must be lump sum so that none of the marginal conditions are changed; both before and after the transfer we want ratios of marginal utility equal to price ratios, ratios of marginal productivity equal to factor/price ratios, marginal cost equal to marginal revenue, and so on, in order that the Pareto conditions for economic welfare are conformed to.

[9] This idea derives from the suggestion of A. Bergson in "A Reformulation of Certain Aspects of Welfare Economics," *Quarterly Journal of Economics*, XLIX, No. 1 (February 1938), 310–34, that decisions require an explicit ranking of the utility combinations of the citizens. Presumably these rankings are the consensus of the community about how it wishes to see goods distributed among the citizens.

trade theory. He assumes that policy-makers can specify the weights to be given to marginal changes in income for the various people; thus, an extra dollar of income might have a weight of 1 for man 1 and of 2 for man 2. If economic analysis shows that man 1's income falls and man 2's rises as the result of eliminating trade barriers, then the system of weights indicates that the change should be made. This technique can handle all sorts of secondary changes in spending brought about by substitution and complementarity effects stemming from the original change.[10]

TARIFFS AND WELFARE: THEORY OF SECOND-BEST

The final welfare tool that we need is the theory of second-best. This is obviously a modification of the rules for the best allocation of resources (what is called the Pareto optimum). These rules are that all the relevant ratios of marginal whatnots should be equal throughout the economy (ratios of marginal utility should be equal for all consumers; ratios of marginal productivity of two factors should be the same in all outputs; ratios of marginal social utility should equal ratios of marginal social cost; and the like).[11] If these ratios are all equal, it is not possible to change any output or consumption without making somebody worse off; this is the sense in which these rules define an optimum (although the situation that satisfies all these rules may not be at an optimum as defined by, e.g., a Bergson social welfare function). Tariffs and monopolies and excise taxes disrupt the optimum conditions, making some of the marginal ratios not equal to others. Eliminating these interferences then would be an optimum or best policy.

But suppose that in the nature of things some of the interferences cannot be removed; for example, if there is a natural monopoly, should every other industry be required to behave as a competitor? Or if some tariffs must be maintained (perhaps to satisfy a powerful pressure group), should every other tariff be reduced to zero? The answer is that if it is impossible to satisfy all the optimum conditions, then a change that brings about the satisfaction of some of them may make things better or worse.[12] All that one can do in this case is try to achieve the best suboptimal situation; but sometimes there is no second-best solution. The general theoretical reason

[10] See Chap. 5 of Meade's book, *Trade and Welfare* (London: Oxford University Press, 1955). W. M. Corden in his survey, *Recent Developments in the Theory of International Trade*, p. 46, remarks that this approach has the virtue of neither ignoring distributional considerations nor assuming (unrealistically) that compensation for injury takes place; and it brings out the dependence of an optimum position on the assignment of the importance of various members of the community in making welfare decisions.

[11] A concise development and explanation of these rules is found in W. J. Baumol, *Economic Theory and Operations Analysis* (2nd ed.) (Englewood Cliffs, N.J.: Prentice-Hall, Inc., 1965), Chap. 16.

[12] Meade, *Trade and Welfare*, Chap. VII. A more analytical presentation is R. G. Lipsey and K. J. Lancaster, "The General Theory of Second Best," *Review of Economic Studies*, XXIVI (1956), 11–32.

for this result is something like this: The rules for a Pareto optimum come from maximizing a function of several variables subject to a constraint, such as the production function in deriving production conditions or a fixed total of goods in deriving exchange conditions. Now if an additional constraint is imposed in the form of requiring an inequality in one of the marginal conditions, the conditions for a maximum must obviously change. One of the standard examples is the relation of price to marginal cost in determining the best output of an industry. The best output is that for which price equals marginal cost—provided that this condition holds for all other industries. If it does not, the second-best rule is to violate the price-marginal cost equality in the industry at hand as well. The reason is that if price equals marginal cost in one industry but is higher than marginal cost in another, the price line will cut the transformation curve. However, if price exceeds marginal cost by the same proportion in both industries, the price line will be tangent to the transformation curve. In the first case it would be possible to reach a higher indifference curve; in the second case it would not.[13]

DISTORTIONS IN THE DOMESTIC ECONOMY

The preceding ideas of welfare economics are rather general. An important, rather more specific application of welfare ideas to international trade problems comes in the case where there is some distortion in the domestic economy. "Distortion" means that the domestic price ratio does not equal the slope of the transformation curve. A monopoly in one industry while competition prevails in the other brings this situation, since the monopolist's price exceeds his marginal cost while price equals marginal cost in the competitive industry. External economies make the slope of the transformation curve unequal to the ratio of private marginal cost and so distort prices away from tangency with the transformation curve. As we shall see later, a variety of impediments in the factor markets also bring distortions

The conclusion of welfare economics in cases like this is that taxes on foreign trade to correct such distortions are inferior to taxes or subsidies on domestic production. To see this point, let us start from a situation where there are no distortions of any kind, such as is depicted in Fig. 11-3. Welfare is maximized, since it is impossible to reach a higher indifference curve than I_1 at the given terms of trade. The important thing about this trade equilibrium is that there is equality between three ratios: the slope of the transformation curve, the slope of the indifference curve, and the slope of the price line. [Bhagwati and Ramaswami call these, respectively, the domestic rate of transformation in production (*DRT*), the domestic rate of substitution in

---

[13] A discussion of this proposition with all of the qualifications necessary for a rigorous treatment is given in Mishan, *Economic Journal*, LXX, 208, 212, and 248.

consumption (*DRS*), and the foreign rate of transformation of *Y* into *X* (*FRT*). The equilibrium is therefore characterized by $DRT = DRS = FRT$].[14]

Now suppose the economy is beset with a domestic distortion of some sort that has the result of making the ratio of private marginal costs in *X* and *Y* diverge from *DRT*. (More detailed analysis of the situations bringing this result appears in the latter part of this chapter.) Producers in Fig. 11-4, guided by the world prices given by *FRT* and by their private marginal costs,

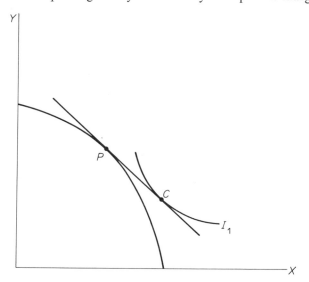

Fig. 11-3

find an equilibrium at *P*, while the consumers' equilibrium is at *C*. But in this situation welfare is not maximized, since $FRT = DRS \neq DRT$. One possible policy is to correct this distortion by subsidizing the production of *X* and taxing the output of *Y*. This policy makes $MC_X/MC_Y < P_X/P_Y$ at point *P* and hence induces a reduction in the output of *Y* and an increase in *X*. If the policy is carried on until production moves to point *P''*, the equality among our three ratios is restored and welfare is maximized.

The alternative policy is to try to correct for the fact that the production of *X* is too low at point *P* by imposing a tariff on *X*. The higher domestic price of *X* encourages an expansion of *X* output, moves the production equilibrium to point *P''*, and, in the diagram, moves the consumers to a higher indifference curve. Notice that domestic production and consumption decisions are guided by the steep P_X/P_Y line, which includes the tariff, while trade takes place at the world terms of trade given by the dashed line with

[14] Jagdish Bhagwati and V. K. Ramaswami, "Domestic Distortions, Tariffs and the Theory of Optimum Subsidy," *Journal of Political Economy*, LXXI, No. 1 (February 1963), 44–50.

the same slope as line *PC*. (That this is not necessarily the case is shown in the article cited in footnote 14; the tariff may leave consumers on a lower indifference curve.) However, this policy is not optimum, for none of the three ratios is equal to any of the others. The moral of the story, as drawn by Bhagwati and Ramiswami, is that use of taxes (or subsidies) on foreign trade to correct *domestic* distortions is inferior to tackling the domestic problems by domestic measures.

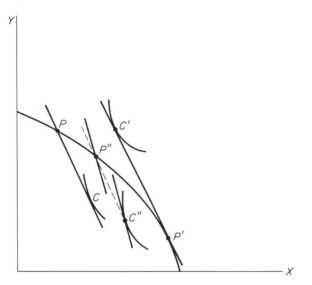

Fig. 11-4

These notions of welfare economics—particularly the gains from trade and the idea of second-best—are important in the evaluation of tariffs and also of common markets, as will soon be apparent.

Before turning to a detailed analysis of the standard pro and con arguments about the tariffs, it might be well to remind ourselves that the fairly abstract analytical theory of the early part of this chapter and the equally abstract welfare theory are not spun in a vacuum. In Chap. 7 it was pointed out that nominal tariffs for the United States are a little more than 10 per cent, while the important effective tariff rate average is 20 per cent. For some other countries the nominal tariffs are even higher.

STANDARD TARIFF ARGUMENTS

It is time-honored practice to list and examine critically the set of arguments for the tariff, although it often appears that the arguments are really rationalizations designed to give window-dressing to deep-seated nationalistic motives for discrimination. A fairly complete list includes the following:

1. *The optimum tariff.* This is the case beloved by trade theorists because it is the only one that is not a second-best argument.[15] In the other cases there are other policy tools available that could accomplish the same goals and do it better. The idea of the optimum tariff is that since the tariff normally improves the terms of trade, the country can behave like a monopolist and

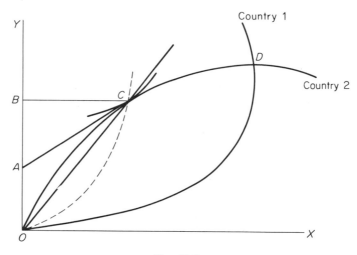

Fig. 11-5

restrict trade in order to get more gain from trade than would be possible with free trade. If we consider only stable situations, the only time this is not possible (barring retaliation) is a condition of perfect elasticity of demand for imports on the part of the foreign country. In that case, its offer curve is a straight line, so that the terms of trade will always be the same.

In the more general case, shown in Fig. 11-5, country 1's optimum tariff is the one that will bring its offer curve (allowing for the redistribution of tariff revenue) to an intersection with country 2's offer curve at point *C*. Here country 2's offer curve is tangent to one of country 1's indifference curves, so this is the highest indifference curve that country 1 can reach—in particular, it is higher than the indifference curve through *D*, the free-trade equilibrium.[16] Thus country 1's welfare is increased with the optimum tariff.

---

[15] Harry G. Johnson, "Optimal Trade Intervention in the Presence of Domestic Distortions," in *Trade, Growth, and the Balance of Payments*, eds. Baldwin et al., pp. 3–34, develops this point at length.

[16] If this indifference curve is of the Scitovsky type, it will depend on the position achieved on the foreign offer curve. It will be a unique curve, however if it is interpreted as a Samuelson social welfare curve, as described in Chap. 4.

In terms of Fig. 11-2, the utility possibility frontier lies to the northeast of CBC' when it is possible to influence the terms of trade.[17]

But if country 1 can gain by an optimum tariff, so can country 2. For example, after point C has been reached in Fig. 11-5, country 2 may levy a tariff that brings the trade equilibrium to a point on country 1's tariff-distorted offer curve someplace to the southwest of C. (By the way, if you do not recall how a tariff shifts the offer curve, refer to the discussion of the Metzler model in Chap. 4.) Then country 1 may retaliate, and so on. It is impossible to say what the outcome will be unless it is known what the responses of the various countries are; this problem is similar to the oligopoly problem of price theory in that respect.[18] Neither is it possible to say that

[17] John Stuart Mill, C. F. Bickerdike, and F. Y. Edgeworth were early pioneers of the idea of improving the terms of trade by a tariff. Many of the writers deal with a formula for the optimum tariff; if E_2 is the elasticity of demand for imports in country 2, the tariff rate t should be $1/(E_2 - 1)$. *Proof:* The home price (P_h) in country 1 is equal to the slope of the indifference curve at C. We are interested in the relative price of the import good, Y, which is $P_X/P_Y = X/Y = CB/BA$. The international price (P_f) of Y is the reciprocal of the slope of the terms-of-trade line; this international price ratio is CB/BO. We also know that P_h exceeds P_f by the tariff rate:

$$P_h = (1 + t)P_f. \tag{11-13}$$

Solving for t,

$$t = \frac{P_h}{P_f} - 1 = \frac{CB}{BA}\frac{OB}{CB} - 1 = \frac{OB}{BA} - 1 = \frac{AO}{BA}. \tag{11-14}$$

To relate t to the elasticity of demand of country 2, write country 2's demand for imports as $X = f(P_X/P_Y) = f(Y/X)$. The elasticity is the percentage change in X divided by the percentage change in the relative price, multiplied by -1 to make the elasticity positive:

$$E_2 = -\frac{dX/X}{[d(Y/X)]/Y/X} = -\frac{Y/X^2}{[d(Y/X)]/dX} = -\frac{Y/X^2}{\dfrac{X(dY/dX) - Y}{X^2}} = -\frac{1}{(X/Y)(dY/dX) - 1}.$$

In terms of Fig. 11-5, this is $\tag{11-15}$

$$E_2 = -\frac{1}{(CB/OB)\cdot(AB/CB) - 1} = \frac{1}{1 - (AB/OB)} = \frac{1}{AO/OB}. \tag{11-16}$$

According to the optimum tariff formula, we want $t = 1/(E_2 - 1)$; that is,

$$t = \frac{1}{E_2 - 1} = \frac{1}{[1/(AO/OB)] - 1} = \frac{1}{(OB/AO) - 1} = \frac{1}{BA/AO} = \frac{AO}{BA}. \tag{11-17}$$

Since **(11-17)** equals **(11-14)**, the formula obviously holds. (For the derivation of this and other related formulas using the elasticity of the offer curve and the partial money elasticities of supply and demand, see Harry G. Johnson, "Optimum Welfare and Maximum Revenue Tariffs," *Review of Economic Studies*, XIX, no. 48 (1951–52), 28–35, reprinted in *International Trade and Economic Growth*, (London: George Allen & Unwin Ltd., 1958), pp. 56ff.)

Notice that knowledge of the elasticity of the foreign demand is not enough; since the elasticity varies with the position on country 2's offer curve, in order to use the formula you must first decide where you want to be on its offer curve.

[18] It sometimes happens that trade policy may have the objective of harming the other country rather than of directly improving your own, as in the refusal of the United States to buy from or to sell to Cuba. Kemp, *The Pure Theory of International Trade*, Chap. 15, discusses this case.

such tariff warfare will cause all countries to wind up worse off than they would have been under free trade, because when an equilibrium has been reached such that neither country gains by imposing further tariffs, it is possible to show that one country may in fact be better off.[19]

How important is the optimum tariff in commercial policies? As a motive influencing public pressure for tariffs in the United States, it seems unimportant, by and large.[20] Interpreted as an influence on the terms of trade, rather than in the sophisticated sense of attempting to maximize welfare, tariffs have on occasion had a noticeable influence. Taussig, for example, wrote that one would have expected the U.S. terms of trade to fall after 1900 in order to achieve a sufficient export surplus with which to pay for immigrants' remittances and interest charges on foreign borrowing. But they did not fall; one interpretation is that the protective tariff installed in the nineteenth century helped maintain the terms of trade in the early twentieth century.[21] However, Professor Kindleberger, after a valiant statistical attempt to determine the influence of commercial policy on Europe's terms of trade, decided that it was impossible to derive significant conclusions about how widely and over how long a period government action had an influence in improving the terms of trade.[22]

The formation of the European Common Market has revived interest in the possibility that a common market can make gains for itself at the expense of the rest of the world by tailoring its common tariff to influence the terms of trade favorably. Historical precedent can be found; for example, during the days before the signing of the American Constitution, the founding fathers argued that the several states were at a disadvantage in dealing with the United Kingdom. This feeling helped to create the state of mind that accepted a closer union with a central tariff policy. Also, much talk was expended in Europe after 1880 about forming a European union to deal with the menacing U.S. commercial policy.[23] Most recently, the threat of adverse Common Market policies has led to the possibility of the sort of retaliation discussed in optimum tariff theory. Section 252 of the Trade Expansion Act of 1962 gave the U.S. president power to retaliate and to discriminate against countries "whenever unjustifiable foreign import restrictions oppress the commerce of the United States."

[19] H. G. Johnson, *International Trade and Economic Growth*, Chap. II.

[20] In his major review of U.S. tariff policies, Professor Don D. Humphrey came to the conclusion that today's desire for tariff protection could largely be regarded as a hangover from the long-drawn nineteenth-century infant-industry tariff debates. See *American Imports*, p. 174.

[21] Taussig, *International Trade*, pp. 303ff.

[22] C. P. Kindleberger, *The Terms of Trade: A European Case Study* (Cambridge, Mass., and New York: The Technology Press of Massachusetts Institute of Technology and John Wiley & Sons, Inc., 1956), p. 90.

[23] For these and other examples see Jacob Viner, *The Customs Union Issue* (New York: Carnegie Endowment for International Peace, 1950), pp. 56–58.

2. *The balance of payments.* The use of tariffs to help eliminate deficits in the balance of payments is one of the prominent current justifications for tariffs. France (1956), Canada (1961), and the United Kingdom (1964) all promptly increased their tariffs when their balance of payments worsened. Indeed, in 1968 France announced a set of export subsidies and import tariffs on the mere prospect of a deficit following the large wage increases won by labor unions during the student-worker rebellion. Professor Galbraith thinks this is the simplest and most straightforward of measures for dealing with disequilibrium; Professor Johnson argues that it is a second-best approach (it assumes that some part of the economy is not in equilibrium), with devaluation or reduction of domestic expenditure the best.[24] We cannot do much with this debate until we take up the balance of payments in the next part of the book.

3. *Promote domestic employment.* This argument for the tariff is seldom heard in recent years. There is, however, a related argument that recent high levels of European growth were promoted by balance-of-payments surpluses generated by undervalued exchange rates.[25] The arguments are related because an undervalued exchange rate is equivalent to a uniform duty on imports and a subsidy on exports. Using the tariff to expand domestic employment involves the sacrifice of the gains from trade to achieve something that can be obtained without sacrifice via monetary and fiscal policy.

4. *Revenue.* The tariff as a device to raise funds for the government has a long history; for example, in 1870 in the United States customs duties yielded $19,450,000, while the internal revenue was $18,490,000.[26] Both import and export taxes are currently used by underdeveloped countries as a revenue device, from the greater ease of enforcing a tax collected at a few ports compared to attempting to collect income taxes or domestic sales taxes. If the purpose of the tariff is really only to collect revenue, a domestic tax of the same height should be imposed on domestic production; otherwise the revenue and protective or other aspects of the tariff get confused and contradictory.

5. *Income redistribution.* This is taken to mean internal redistribution; external redistribution between countries is handled by the optimum tariff analysis. The Stolper–Samuelson theorem of Chap. 3 is the basic tool of analysis for this argument (with Metzler's work, reviewed in Chap. 4,

---

[24] John K. Galbraith, "The Balance of Payments: A Political and Administrative View," *The Review of Economics and Statistics*, XLVI, No. 2 (May 1964), 120; Harry G. Johnson, *Money, Trade and Economic Growth*, (London: George Allen & Unwin, Ltd., 1962), p. 26.

[25] Richard N. Cooper, "Dollar Deficits and Postwar Economic Growth," *Review of Economics and Statistics*, XLVI, No. 2 (May 1964), 155–59.

[26] Frank Taussig, *The Tariff History of the United States* (6th rev. ed.) (New York: G. P. Putnam's Sons, 1914), p. 455. Today, of course, tariff revenue is a tiny fraction of the federal budget.

necessary as a supplement if the terms of trade are changed by the tariff). The idea is, it should be recalled, that a tariff in the H–O model increases the derived demand for the scarce factor of production and so changes the distribution of income. Since other approaches, such as progressive income taxes, social insurance, regional development programs, and the like can redistribute income without distorting international prices and reducing the gains from trade, the use of tariffs for this purpose is a second-best approach.

6. *Strategy*. Adam Smith claimed that defense had a priority over opulence, and ever since then the exigencies of preparedness have been used as a plea for tariff protection. The degree of attention such pleas deserve depends on the sort of conflicts being prepared for, the capabilities of allies, how much time the creation of capacity would require, whether stock-piling is feasible, and (probably most important) whether a strong, progressive economy is not better than a few inefficient strategic industries.[27] The anomalies that appear do nothing to strengthen the argument. For example, it is simultaneously contended that the U.S. heavy electrical equipment industry should be protected for defense reasons and that such equipment should not be exported to Communist China because it would help build up their economy. From the defense argument, however, it should be good strategy to make the Chinese dependent on our supplies; in the event of conflict, they would not be able to service or replace their equipment. Sir Dennis Robertson once had a lot of fun with the exclusion of foreign cheese on defense grounds, suggesting that the cannon-ball-like shape of Gouda cheese was what gave it its deadly quality.[28]

Currently, the restriction of petroleum imports in order to encourage domestic discovery and exploitation is the major use of the strategic argument. Will it have the effect of hastening the exhaustion of local supplies and of more complete dependence on foreign supply? Indeed, was defense any more than a convenient excuse?[29]

7. *Antidumping*. This use of the tariff was discussed in Chap. 8 in connection with the monopolistic practice of discriminatory pricing. In the long run, if dumping by the foreign producer is expected to continue, there is no point in rejecting the gift of the overseas monopolist (see the discussion in Chap. 8 of the U.K. sugar-using industry's development). If the dumping is what is called predatory, where the fear is that the monopolist will raise prices after local competition has been eliminated, the question to ask is why cannot the domestic producers reenter the industry? It may be that they

[27] There is a good discussion in J. Black, "Arguments for Tariffs," *Oxford Economic Papers*, XI, No. 2 (June 1959), 191–208.

[28] *Britain in the World Economy* (London: George Allen & Unwin, Ltd., 1954), p. 66.

[29] "The import restrictions were chiefly designed to protect our independent producers against competition from the big firms with wells abroad, not to foster the national defense." Peter B. Kenen, *Giant Among Nations* (Skokie, Ill.: Rand McNally & Company, 1963), p. 77.

could not because of economies of scale or would not because of the risk of a resumption of dumping. But dumping is not a prima facie case for a tariff.

8. *Increasing returns.* The conditions under which a tariff can improve welfare when increasing returns are present were discussed in Chap. 9. The tariff in Fig. 9-1, for example, moved production from one equilibrium to another one that allowed higher consumption of both goods. At this point it is relevant to add that when increasing returns are present, subsidies are a preferable device for stimulating the industry. Prices are not distorted, consumption is not restricted, there is less likelihood of continuing the special treatment to the industry unjustifiably, and the costs would be paid from the general revenues that presumably are distributed more equitably than would be a tax on the consumers of the industry in question. The subsidy allows the $DRS = DRT = FRT$ relations to exist, whereas the tariff does not.[30]

9. *The infant-industry argument.* The infant-industry argument is very old; Jacob Viner traces it back to 1645.[31] It is a dynamic argument, in contrast to the static nature of the increasing-returns argument. The dynamic sequence is illustrated in Fig. 11-6. In equilibrium 1, the country is assumed to have no tariffs, to specialize in producing Y, and to be an importer of X. It then imposes a tariff on X, which raises the domestic price ratio without changing the world terms of trade. At equilibrium 2, production decisions are guided by the domestic price line DD, while the world prices are given by the slope of TT.

The infant-industry argument then says that as a result in the expansion of the output of X, the transformation curve shifts; furthermore, it shifts in an irreversible fashion, so that the tariff may be removed and the output of X (now an adult industry) will remain large at equilibrium 3, where the original free-trade terms of trade prevail.

There are two points to be examined:

1. Why does the transformation curve shift? The modern versions of the theory explain it in terms of a learning process: Either the firms learn by doing, or they pick up pointers from the experience of other firms, or their labor force acquires new skills.[32]

2. Why, if the transformation curve is going to shift, do not entrepreneurs move in to industry X without the encouragement of tariffs?

The answer might be found in imperfections of the capital market or in fear of trying the unknown; or it might be found in the fact that the transformation curve shows the production alternatives available to society, but

---

[30] A theoretical demonstration of the superiority of subsidies is provided in J. Bhagwati and V. K. Ramaswami, *Journal of Political Economy*, LXXI.

[31] *Studies in the Theory of International Trade*, p. 71.

[32] See Murray C. Kemp, "The Mill-Bastable Infant Industry Dogma," *Journal of Political Economy*, LXVIII, No. 1 (February 1960), 65–67; and Johnson, *Trade, Growth, and the Balance of Payments*, 26–30.

the costs and returns to a given individual business may be something different. For example, it might bear all the cost of an investment in industry X and get some returns but society would get still higher returns from the learning process—other firms can use the knowledge without paying the price.

Subsidies are preferable to tariffs in this case for exactly the same reasons that apply in the increasing-returns case.

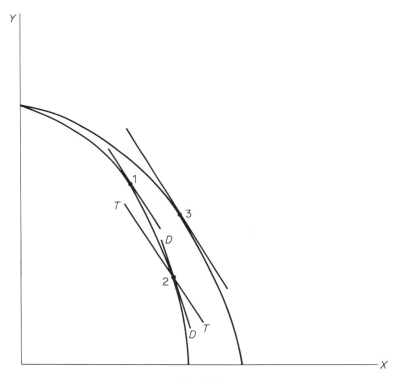

Fig. 11-6

10. *Stimulus to economic development.* A number of arguments for the use of tariffs stem from the special characteristics of underdeveloped countries. The increasing-returns and the infant-industry arguments are prominent; so are propositions based on differences in the wage behavior of advanced and backward sectors of the same economy. Much is made of the alleged monopolistic exploitation of underdeveloped countries by the advanced industrial nations. These ideas are worth a chapter in themselves and are discussed on pp. 159–71.

11. *A "collective preference for industrial production."* The optimum tariff argument was the only one that emerged unscathed from our examination and even that may be faulted as being second-best from a world point

of view. Lump-sum income transfers would avoid the distortions to the world economy brought about by the tariff that benefits the home country.[33] In that case, why have tariffs been such a prominent issue throughout history? Why did President Kennedy have to devote so much presidential power to the passage of the Trade Expansion Act of 1962? Are policy-makers uninformed, or irrational? According to Professor Johnson, an alternative interpretation should be explored. Maybe there is utility attached to industrial production, or to domestic self-sufficiency, apart from the utility of the goods themselves. In that case the public is willing to forego a certain amount of real income in order to have industry, however inefficient it may be.[34] The idea is intriguing and does seem to have explanatory value. But, of course, so does the proposition that the producer interests are narrow and cohesive, while the consumer interest is scattered. It may not be worth any one consumer's time to bring pressure in his own interest. This pattern, sometimes formulated in the phrase "the tariff is a local issue,"[35] seems to fit the development of U.S. commercial policy: Congressmen, sensitive to local interests, put loopholes in the law in the form of escape clauses, peril points, and the like. The constituents try to use the loopholes, and then the president, with an eye toward foreign policy repercussions, more often than not rejects industry's attempts for higher protection.

Of course, the relevant tariff for many of the preceding 11 points is the effective tariff rate of Chap. 7. A tariff justified by the infant-industry argument, for example, is an absurdity if the effective rate of protection is negative. (Which of the 11 arguments require the effective rate, and which may be approached via the nominal rate?)

THE EMPLOYMENT EFFECTS OF TARIFFS

A large part of the research of international economists on the tariff has consisted of attempts to measure the effects of trade restriction. One of these was a major study of the effects on employment of a reduction in the

[33] Corden, *Recent Developments in the Theory of International Trade*, p. 48.

[34] Harry G. Johnson, "An Economic Theory of Protectionism, Tariff Bargaining, and the Formation of Customs Unions," *Journal of Political Economy*, LXXIII, No. 3 (June 1965), 256–83. This article is indeed a development from his idea for computing the ratios of marginal costs to marginal benefits for the economy for tariffs aimed at various goals (strategic and so on); see his article, "The Cost of Protection and the Scientific Tariff," *Journal of Political Economy*, LXVIII, No. 4 (August 1960), 327–45. The idea that there is a collective preference for industry is used as the basis for an analysis of customs unions by C. A. Cooper and B. F. Massell, "Toward a General Theory of Customs Unions for Developing Countries," *Journal of Political Economy*, LXXIII, No. 5 (October 1965), 461–76.

[35] See Percy W. Bidwell, *What the Tariff Means to American Industries* (New York: Harper & Row, Publishers, 1956) for a series of case studies on the tariff as a local issue.

tariff.[36] Salant and Vaccara used the 1953 input-output tables to estimate the total decrease in output that would occur if $1 million of domestic production in a protected industry were to be replaced by imports. The output effects were then translated into employment effects, which were modified by the effects on employment in import-connected industries (ocean freight and shipping) and by the effects of higher income and foreign exchange earnings abroad on U.S. employment in export industries. The results ranged from a net decrease in employment of 175 workers in the apparel industry to a net gain of 5 workers in grain mill products; the median decrease in employment was 86 employees. An increase in imports of $1 billion, they computed, would release 86,000 workers, which was one eighth of 1 per cent of 1959 civilian employment. Since $1 billion was one eleventh of 1959 dutiable imports, the employment cost of liberalization would not be high on a national basis. The conclusion that the employment cost of liberalization is not high can equally be interpreted as meaning that the employment effect of the tariff is not large.

THE HEIGHT OF THE TARIFF

A second long-standing research field, with direct importance for tariff policy and tariff negotiations, is the problem of the concept and technique of measuring the height of various national tariff structures. Chap. 7 developed the important notion of the effective rate of protection of value added, but this is a very recent addition to tariff measures. The typical problem before the introduction of this concept was the measurement of the average level of nominal tariff rates. Scientific curiosity, tariff negotiations under GATT, and the introduction of common markets all made some measure necessary. It has long been recognized as an index number problem without a definitive solution. The two standard methods employed are the weighted average and the unweighted (more properly, the equally weighted) average tariff rate. In the weighted average calculation, each nominal rate is weighted by the fraction of total imports accounted for by the item to which it applies. (It is a simple arithmetical proposition that this is the same thing as dividing the total duty collected by the value of total imports.) The deficiency of this calculation is that low duties are typically given high weights, high duties lower weights insofar as imports are held down, and prohibitive duties, of course, receive a zero weight. And, of course quotas and subsidies are altogether excluded so that in any event the calculation of the tariff height is only a partial picture of commercial policy. The unweighted average consists of the total of tariff rates, divided by the

---

[36] Walter S. Salant and Beatrice N. Vaccara, *Import Liberalization and Employment* (Washington, D.C.: The Brookings Institution, 1961).

number of tariff classifications. Its problem is that it gives undue importance to products with little importance in the picture of world trade, such as the famous example of pregnant mares' urine. Faced with two unsatisfactory measures, it has been suggested that the comparison of the two would be informative. If the unweighted average is much above the weighted average, one can conclude that the high rates in the tariff schedule provide a high degree of protection.[37]

WELFARE COSTS OF TARIFFS

The other line of research that has attracted considerable effort has been the attempt to measure the welfare cost of the tariff. The technique of these studies basically involves the following procedure, tailored to suit the problem at hand; the analysis is based on Fig. 11-7. This is a partial-equilibrium diagram showing the domestic supply and demand for a commodity involving both local production and imports. The world price is assumed fixed at the level P. P'' is the initial home price including a high rate of tariff. After tariff reduction the home price becomes P'. Imports are originally BC; after the tariff cut they expand to AD.

The gains and losses to the economy then break down into these items: Area 1 is a loss to producers, which may be called the loss from reduction of producers' surplus.[38] Area 2 is the loss in tariff revenue from the reduction in tariffs. These losses are offset by, first, a gain in tariff revenue (area 3 + area 4), and, second, the gain to consumers from an increase in consumers' surplus (areas 1 + 5 + 2 + 6). The net gain, in this approach, is then the sum of areas 3, 4, 5, and 6. The research problem is to estimate the supply-and-demand elasticities for the commodities involved in order that the areas may be calculated for assumed tariff cuts and summed over all commodities in order to get the total gain for the economy.

In the case of Germany, tariffs on finished industrial goods were cut by more than 50 per cent in a two-year period, 1956 and 1957, with the result that imports of these products in 1957 and 1958 were about twice as big as their estimated amounts had tariffs not been cut. The welfare gain to the

[37] This suggestion is made by Randall Hinshaw, *The European Community and American Trade: A Study in Atlantic Economics and Policy* (New York: Frederick A. Praeger, Inc., 1964), pp. 78–79. For a good bibliography of the problem of tariff measurement, see Balassa, *Journal of Political Economy*, LXXIII.

[38] The area above the supply curve and below the price line was called producers' surplus by Marshall. It is supposed to measure payments to producers that exceed the amounts needed to call forth the production of the intramarginal units of output. At output OA, for example, the marginal firm has marginal and average costs equal to P'. When the price rises to P'' and industry output expands to OB, the firm that was marginal at price P' is now receiving an excess payment of $P'' - P'$. The total of these excess payments to all the firms whose costs are lower than the marginal firm is producers' surplus.

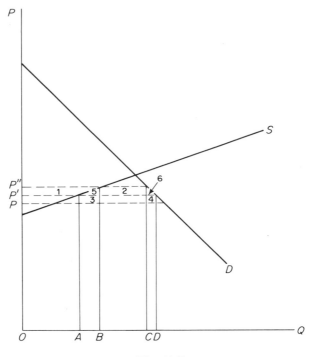

Fig. 11-7

economy, however, was quite small; computed in the fashion outlined above, it amounted to 18/100 of 1 per cent of the 1958 German national income.[39]

Similar small numbers for gains are noted by other studies. In the case of Chile, the welfare gain from trade restriction elimination is estimated as not more than $2\frac{1}{2}$ per cent of the national income; for the United States, complete removal of tariffs and quotas would raise welfare by an estimated 11/100 of 1 per cent of the national income; and the gain to the United Kingdom from the partial tariff reduction involved in participation in a European Free Trade Area is computed to have the order of 1 per cent of the national income.[40]

If these estimates were correct, the tariff would seem hardly worth bothering about. But as the authors point out, the studies are pioneering rather

[39] J. Wemelsfelder, "The Short-Term Effect of the Lowering of Import Duties in Germany," *Economic Journal*, LXX, No. 277 (March 1960), 94–104.

[40] These figures are derived in, respectively, Arnold C. Harberger, "Using the Resources at Hand More Effectively," *American Economic Review, Papers and Proceedings*," XLIX, No. 2 (May 1959), 134–46; Robert M. Stern, "The U.S. Tariff and the Efficiency of the U.S. Economy," *American Economic Review, Papers and Proceedings*, XLIV, No. 2 (May 1964), 459 70; and Harry G. Johnson, "The Gains from Freer Trade with Europe: An Estimate," *The Manchester School*, XXVI, No. 3 (September 1958), 247–55. In the last article, gains from increased exports as well as increased imports are included in the 1 per cent figure.

than definitive. There are the statistical problems of estimating the elasticities, for one thing. Perhaps more serious is the nature of the model used. The notion of consumers' and producers' surplus is beset with difficulties. In particular, if consumers' surplus is to be measured by the area under the demand curve and above the price line, the marginal utility of income must be constant with respect to changes in the prices of the commodities. (This has the interesting result that all income elasticities equal zero.) Clearly, the use of areas 1 + 5 + 2 + 6 in Fig. 11-7 is only a crude approximation. Furthermore, the static partial-equilibrium model does not handle such considerations as the effects of competition from abroad on efficiency and innovation. Then there is the problem of how to handle intermediate goods as distinct from the consumer goods that the demand curve presumably refers to.[41] As an additional complication, the writers on welfare economics point out that lack of perfect competition in the rest of the economy must be taken into account, realistically; there is movement of resources in and out of industries with varying ratios of price to marginal cost as output changes in the import industries. Each such change must change the social benefits and social cost in a most complicated fashion. The general feeling is that consumers' and producers' surplus are far from ideal tools, but, "After all, what other practical procedures are open to us in a comparison of two situations?"[42] In the particular application to the tariff problems, it seems likely that the biases and inadequacies of the model would have to be pretty sizable to change the conclusion that the losses to the economy are modest in the short run.[43] This leaves the important tariff issues to the long run and to the broader international policy aspects of tariffs—for example, how to weigh the claims of western copper producers against our relations with copper exporters such as Chile.

APPENDIX: Quotas

Although tariffs are the most analyzed and empirically documented trade restriction, they are not the only one. Quotas or quantitative restrictions are much used: by the United States and other nations in protecting domestic agriculture, on a "voluntary" basis under the threat of some more drastic action in the case of textile exports from underdeveloped

[41] This is a major problem; in 1960, nonfood consumer goods were only $2.5 billion of the total $14.7 billion of U.S. imports.

[42] Mishan, *Economic Journal*, LXX, 245.

[43] It should be noticed, however, that Jagdish Bhagwati believes that trade restrictions cause considerable waste even from a static, short-run point of view; his contention is that the model's implementation rests on faulty data, and is also based on his experience with less-developed countries. See Jagdish Bhagwati, *The Theory and Practice of Commercial Policy: Departures from Unified Exchange Rates*, Special Papers in International Economics No. 8 (Princeton, N.J.: International Finance Section, Princeton University, January 1968), pp. 50–52.

countries, in cases of balance-of-payments crises, historically in the general disruption of world trade in the 1930's. But studies of the effects of quotas have not yet appeared.[44]

The theory of quotas has usually been subsumed under the theory of tariffs with the proposition that tariffs and quotas are equivalent. In the partial equilibrium analysis, the tariff rate t in Fig. 11-8 results in domestic price P_d, foreign price P_f, imports of AB, and tariff revenue equal to the area

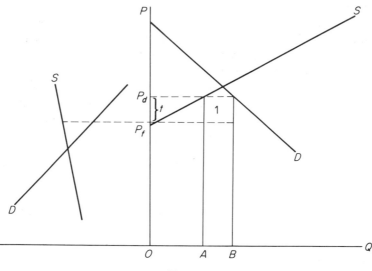

Fig. 11-8

of the rectangle labeled 1. If a quota of AB is set instead, the same foreign and domestic prices result. Foreign price P_f is needed to yield the export supply of AB, and domestic price P_d is needed to hold domestic consumption down to the total of domestic supply plus imports of AB. The difference is that the tariff revenue goes as a monopoly return to the importers, or is captured by the government through the auctioning of import licenses, in the standard treatment. But recently Bhagwati has shown that this equivalence between the tariff and the quota holds only under the assumptions of competition among foreign suppliers, among domestic producers, and among those who receive the import quotas. When monopoly appears in any of the three categories of economic actors, it no longer holds that tariffs and quotas are equivalent: If the tariff rate implied by the quota were to be imposed, the level of imports would differ from the quota amount. Some of the implications of this analysis, noted by Bhagwati, are that it is not reasonable to prefer

[44] Professor Harry G. Johnson lists this as one of the areas needing further research in *Economic Policies Toward Less Developed Countries* (Washington, D.C.: The Brookings Institution, 1967), p. 246.

quotas to tariffs on the ground that quotas have a certain effect on imports, whereas the effect of a tariff is difficult to judge in advance because of uncertainties about supply-and-demand elasticities. The fact is that monopoly actions render the outcome of quotas uncertain too. Also, the auction of quotas does not necessarily simply transfer the area 1 in Fig. 11-6 to the government; it may give monopoly elements among quota-holders that will change the domestic price and the volume of imports. It thus appears that both the theory of quotas and their empirical study are important underdeveloped areas in international trade.[45]

[45] See Bhagwati, "On the Equivalence of Tariffs and Quotas," in *Trade, Growth, and the Balance of Payments*, eds. Baldwin et al., pp. 53–67.

CHAPTER 12

CUSTOMS
UNIONS

THE ECONOMIC THEORY of customs unions is a product of the last decade or two. It has grown rapidly in recent years but is still regarded as incomplete. The motivation for its development was the movement toward the economic integration of Europe that culminated in the Treaty of Rome. The European Economic Community that was formed by the signing of this treaty has been imitated by several groupings of underdeveloped countries.

Economic integration comes in many flavors. Free-trade areas are formed when several countries abolish tariffs and trade controls among themselves but do not attempt to apply a common tariff on imports from the rest of the world. A customs union does have a common, uniform tariff on outsiders. A common market goes a step further by attempting to eliminate restrictions on the movements of the factors of production among its members. A more modest approach is sectoral integration, in which free trade is developed only in one or two industries, such as in the European Coal and Steel Community. The theory is usually stated in terms of customs unions, but clearly many of the conclusions apply to the other forms of integration as well.

In general, the theory of customs unions is treated as a branch of tariff theory and as one of the major applications of the theory of second-best. The result is that the theory tends to be welfare-oriented, so much so that one critic has complained that it fails to contribute much to positive economics.[1] This orientation leads to the following question: Does the formation of a customs union lead to a welfare gain or a loss for the union members and for the rest of the world?

[1] Bhagwati, *Economic Journal*, LXXIV, 47. See also a similar comment by R. G. Lipsey in "The Theory of Customs Unions: A General Survey," *Economic Journal*, LXX, No. 279 (September 1960), 496.

TRADE CREATION AND TRADE DIVERSION

The famous and basic answer to this question in terms of "trade creation" and "trade diversion" was provided by Jacob Viner at the very outset of modern customs union theorizing.[2] The distinction between these two effects is most easily seen in a simple model that concentrates on the production side of the economy by assuming that the demand for a given

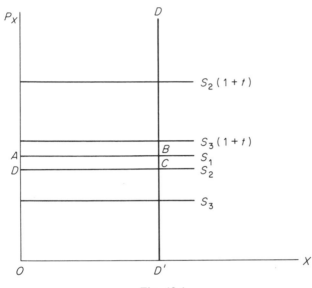

Fig. 12-1

commodity (e.g., X) is perfectly inelastic. The costs of production in countries 1, 2, and 3 are constant but of different levels. In Fig. 12-1 the costs are shown converted into country 1's currency as the solid-line supply curves. In the initial situation country 1 imposes a tariff on imports of such a height that the import price from both countries 2 and 3 exceed its home production costs, and hence it produces X at home. Now suppose that countries 1 and 2 form a customs union; the tariff on imports from country 2 is eliminated and it becomes cheaper to import X from country 2. There is an improved allocation of resources because the same amount of X can be acquired at a saving of resources worth the area of the rectangle $ABCD$. (That is, purchasing OD' of X from country 2 requires exports whose cost is $OD'CD$ compared to the $OD'BA$ that it costs to produce the same quantity at home.) This is trade creation, which occurs whenever production shifts from high-cost home production to lower-cost production in the partner country.

[2] *The Customs Union Issue*, pp. 43–44.

On the other hand, it is possible that the preunion tariff was sufficiently low that the price of imports from country 3, including the tariff, was less than the cost of production in country 1. Figure 12-2 illustrates this case. After the formation of the customs union, imports from country 2 become lower priced than imports from country 3 plus the tariff, so the trade shifts directions from importing from country 3 to importing from country 2. The consumer saves $CEFG$, but this is not a saving to the economy. Previously the resource cost of procuring imports was $OABD'$; when the imports

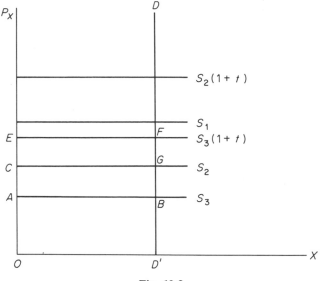

Fig. 12-2

are bought from country 2, the resource cost rises to $OCGD'$. The phenomenon of changing from a low-cost external source to a high-cost intraunion source is called trade diversion. Diversion is well illustrated by the predicted change of $350 million per year in agricultural products from its present U.S. source to undoubtedly higher-cost domestic production in the European Economic Community.[3]

If $S_3(1 + t)$ is less than S_2, and $S_2(1 + t)$ is less than S_1, the customs union will not affect trade in X, so neither trade creation nor trade diversion will occur. The three cases together tell us that anything can happen when a customs union is formed, which is exactly what is claimed in the theory of second-best (see Chap. 11). Ignoring the optimum tariff, the best solution is free trade, as was argued in Chap. 11. The important characteristic of free trade for the problem at hand is that the marginal conditions necessary

[3] Walter S. Salant and associates, *The United States Balance of Payments in 1968* (Washington, D.C.: The Brookings Institution, 1963), pp. 106–111.

for an optimum are met: The marginal rate of transformation in production is equal to the marginal rate of substitution in consumption, not only in domestic production but also in foreign transactions. This is shown in Fig. 12-3, with the free-trade equilibrium involving production at *P* and consumption at *C*. The marginal rate of transformation in production is the slope of the transformation curve; the marginal rate of substitution in consumption is the slope of the indifference curve; and since both are tangent

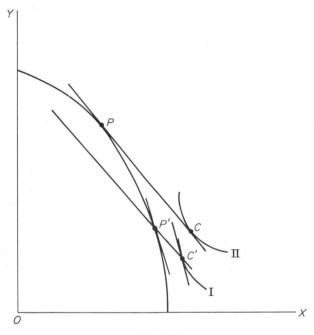

Fig. 12-3

to the terms-of-trade line, the marginal rates are equal in domestic trade as well as in international trade.

The effect of a tariff on the import good, *X*, is, we assume, to raise the domestic price without affecting the terms of trade. The equilibrium after the tariff is imposed is given by *P'* in production and *C'* in consumption. Domestic production and consumption decisions are now governed by the steeper price line involving the tariff, but international trade is carried on along line *P'C'*, which has the same slope as line *PC*. Now the marginal conditions are violated; *MRT* equals *MRS* (i.e., the slope of the indifference curve equals the slope of the transformation curve), but these marginal rates do not equal the marginal rate of transformation of *Y* into *X* through foreign trade. This is demonstrated by the fact that the terms-of-trade line intersects the transformation curve and indifference curve at *P'* and *C'*, respectively, rather than being tangent to them. The result is that welfare is impaired: Indifference curve I in the tariff equilibrium is below indifference curve II in the free-trade equilibrium. Unlike the case in Chap. 11, where the marginal conditions were not met because of domestic distortions, here the trouble is misguided policy.

The best solution is to eliminate the tariff. If that is not possible, the theory of second-best tells that it may or may not be desirable to make a partial change in the tariff. If a trade-creating customs union is formed, the second-best policy is to enter the union. But if the customs union is trade diverting, the second-best policy is to stay out of the union. In any case, no a priori answer can be given. Each customs union must be subjected to individual analysis.

CONSUMPTION EFFECTS

The examples of the effects of customs unions contained in Figs. 12-1 and 12-2 concentrated on production effects, and more particularly on changes in the location of production. Consumption effects were ruled out by the assumptions of inelastic demand and a partial-equilibrium model that ignores repercussions on the consumption of other goods from changes in spending in the market for good X. Actually, of course, customs unions have effects on the consumer because the reduction of tariffs between countries 1 and 2 results in lower prices in the consumers' market.[4]

Consumption effects may be considered independently of production effects by means of a model that fixes output but allows consumption to vary.[5] The model is presented in Fig. 12-4, which represents the situation of country 1. The assumption is that country 1 produces only commodity Y, with a maximum production equal to OA. It can trade Y for X with country 3 at terms of trade equal to the slope of line AB, or with country 2 at the less favorable terms of trade equal to the slope of line AC. In neither case, however, can it affect the terms of trade.

If country 1 initially has a uniform tariff on both countries sufficient to make the domestic price on imports from country 3 equal to the slope of line DE, it will find equilibrium at a point such as F. The equilibrium conditions are fulfilled here, since the indifference curve i_1 is tangent to the domestic price line at F and since F is on the terms-of-trade line. Then a customs union is formed with country 2. The equilibrium changes from F

---

[4] J. E. Meade, *The Theory of Customs Unions* (Amsterdam: North-Holland Publishing Company, 1955), has analyzed a wide variety of possible consumption effects.

[5] The following discussion is based on Lipsey, *Economic Journal*, LXX, 501–3, and F. Gehrels, "Customs Unions from a Single Country Viewpoint," *Review of Economic Studies*, XXIV, No. 1 (1956), 61–64.

to G, at the point of tangency of an indifference curve with country 2's terms-of-trade line. In Fig. 12-4, country 1 has gained from the customs union—i_2 is higher than i_1. In this situation there is a loss and a more-than-offsetting gain from the customs union. The loss is that for the same exports of Y, more X could be obtained by importing from country 3. The gain is in removing the distorting effect of the tariff; a switch in consumption from Y to X has improved welfare.

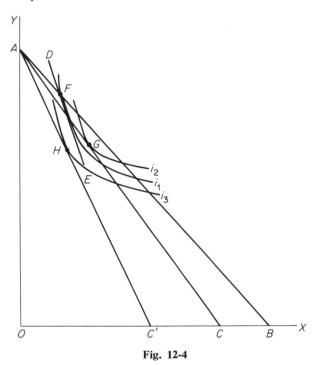

Fig. 12-4

But remember that this is the world of the second-best argument. It is possible that removing the tariff on Y imports from country 2 can reduce welfare instead of increasing it. All we need to do to show that case is to make country 2's terms-of-trade line so steep that it does not touch i_1. Equilibrium in the customs union would then be at a point such as H on i_3, which clearly lowers the welfare of country 1.

PARTIAL-EQUILIBRIUM ANALYSIS

The next step is to move away from these restrictive cases where either production or consumption is frozen into the more general case where both can change. Both partial- and general-equilibrium analyses are available;

since the partial-equilibrium model is less formidable, it is presented here.[6] Figure 12-5 shows the economic conditions affecting a commodity imported by country 1, the home country. The demand curve in the home market is $D_1 D_1'$ and the home supply curve is ES_1. When a customs union is formed, the supply curve of imports from the partner, country 2, will be added to

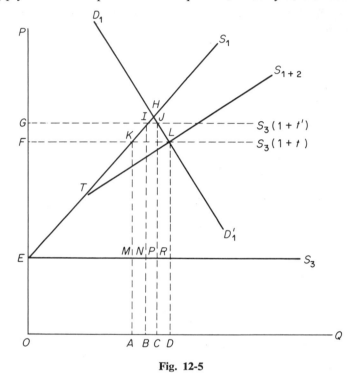

Fig. 12-5

domestic supply to give ETS_{1+2} as the total "domestic" supply. The supply curve of imports from the rest of the world, or country 3, is S_3; as drawn, it reflects the assumption that the customs union, or country 1 by itself, is too small to affect the terms of trade. When the tariff is added to the price in country 3, the supply curve as seen by purchasers in country 1 shifts up. Two examples of the higher import price after the tariff are shown as $S_3(1 + t)$ and $S_3(1 + t')$.

The analysis of the effects of a customs union must proceed by cases, since the outcome in this model depends on how high the tariff is against

[6] This model stems from Johnson, *Money, Trade, and Economic Growth*, pp. 46–74. The general-equilibrium model is carried to a high level of development in Vanek, *General Equilibrium of International Discrimination*. A somewhat amended version of Johnson's model was used by C. A. Cooper and B. F. Massell, "A New Look at Customs Union Theory," *Economic Journal*, LXXV, No. 300 (December 1965), 742–47, from which Fig. 12-5 was taken.

the outside world. Suppose, for our first case, that initially the tariff against both countries 2 and 3 is given by EF. Then the domestic price of the commodity will be OF, domestic consumption OD, domestic production FK, imports from country 3 KL, and imports from country 2 zero. After the customs union is formed, everything remains just as it was except that imports from country 2 replace imports from country 3. Here is an example of trade diversion in a model involving both variable consumption and variable production. It is, however, a borderline case, since the initial tariff level was chosen so that the price before the union is equal to that given by the intersection of D_1 and S_{1+2}. But it is really the trade diversion of Viner's model, with high-cost imports from the partner displacing low-cost imports from the outside. The extra exports that must be shipped out of country 1 when the source of supply shifts are equal in value to the rectangle $MRLK$, which is equal to the foregone tariff revenue. In this case the customs union has imposed a loss on country 1.

A more favorable case emerges if the initial tariff rate is higher, such as a tariff of EG per unit. Then the original domestic price is OG, domestic consumption is $GJ = OC$, domestic production is $GI = OB$, and imports from country 3 are $IJ = BC$. After the customs union is formed, the equilibrium changes to the intersection of D_1 and S_{1+2}. The domestic price falls to OF, domestic consumption expands by CD to OD, domestic production falls by AB to OA, and imports from country 3 vanish while imports from country 2 become AD. This is a mixture of both trade creation and trade diversion: trade creation because some high-cost domestic production is replaced by lower-cost production abroad and because consumption expands, but diversion because the low-cost imports from country 3 are displaced in favor of the higher-cost country 2. Deciding whether the customs union has favorable results then becomes a matter of calculating and weighing the gains against the losses.

Other possible cases, whose analysis is similar to the cases illustrated, are that the initial tariff may be lower than EF or sufficiently high that $S_3(1 + t)$ exceeds the price given by the intersection of D_1 and S_1.

The impact of the customs union on one commodity is thus plain enough. The impact on the entire economy, unfortunately, is not simply a matter of adding up the effects on each product. Relations of substitutability and complementarity become important, as James Meade has emphasized. For example, trade may be diverted in commodity X, but the increased consumption of X may bring along with it more consumption of commodity Z on which sufficient consumers' surplus exists to offset the loss from diversion. In this field the number of combinations is so vast that few generalizations are possible.

It is possible to be a little more precise about the terms of trade, however. In the models covered so far, the terms of trade have been held fixed. This might be appropriate for a small group such as the Central American Common Market, but a union as large as the European Economic Community is bound to change trade relations sufficiently to affect the terms of trade. This in turn has welfare results similar to those of the optimum tariff theory. In general, the model of Fig. 12-5 showed that trade diverson can be expected, whether or not accompanied by trade creation. Furthermore, this diversion would take place in both country 1 and country 2. The effect on country 3 is obvious: It will have a deficit in its balance of trade. In the full-employment real models we are using, country 3 can improve its balance by lowering the price of its imports, which is to say that the terms of the customs union improve while they turn against the outside world. The exception, of course, is the case when the offer curve of country 3 is a straight line through the origin. But the terms of trade of each member do not have to improve; they might improve for country 1 and worsen for country 2, for example.[7]

The customs union theory so far developed has ignored the considerations of the effective rate of the tariff on the value added of domestic production. Not much has been done yet about incorporating effective tariff notions into the analysis, but some more or less preliminary work shows that trade creation might reduce efficiency rather than increase it, and trade diversion might actually bring gains when the effective tariff is considered. If country 1 removes its tariff on the import of product X from country 2, maintaining the tariff on imports from country 3 and also maintaining the tariffs on the inputs into industry X, the domestic production of X will have a negative rate of protection vis-a-vis imports from country 2. (To check this, refer back to the effective tariff discussion in Chap. 7). On the assumption that imports from country 2 displace domestic production rather than imports from the rest of the world, it is possible that the real cost of the imports exceeds the real cost of domestic production. But the conversion of protection into a negative tariff rate would nevertheless allow the imports to enter. Although the general pattern of events corresponds to trade creation, the outcome is a worsening of the pattern of world resource use.[8]

One of the most famous and useful conclusions of customs union theory is that the union is most likely to raise welfare if the partners produce about the same things before union (their actual production is highly competitive) but their opportunity costs are very different so that potentially they are highly complementary in production. This circumstance is just made for trade creation on the production side. It has been argued, for example, that

---

[7] The various possibilities for changes in the terms of trade of member countries, the union itself, and the rest of the world are worked out in Robert A. Mundell, "Tariff Preferences and the Terms of Trade," *Manchester School*, XXXII, No. 1 (January 1964), 1–13.

[8] Harry G. Johnson analyzes a number of cases involving the combination of effective tariff considerations with tariff preferences in *Economic Policies Toward Less Developed Countries*, pp. 185–95.

the Central American Common Market shows promise on this ground since currently all members produce the same agricultural products and have little industry, but potentially three of the members (El Salvador, Guatemala, and Costa Rica) have capabilities for industrial production.[9]

Another famous conclusion, not nearly as useful, is that tariff reduction rather than complete removal among the partners is more likely to raise welfare. This is an example of the theory of second-best proposition that if some distortions cannot be removed it is generally better not to remove the rest of them (but it may be a help to reduce them). The reason the proposition is not useful is that the framers of world trade policy are prepared to allow complete discrimination against outsiders but not partial discrimination, apparently from a prejudice that complete discrimination is trade creating while partial discrimination is trade diverting.[10] Other rather self-evident propositions are that the union is more likely to raise welfare, the higher the initial tariffs; the greater the share of world trade, consumption, and production covered by the union; and the greater the economies of scale.

OTHER FACTORS: SCALE, GROWTH, EFFICIENCY

The basic theory of customs unions is about covered when production, consumption, and terms-of-trade effects have been discussed. There remains a number of effects that are discussed in the voluminous literature on European integration, but that have not been worked into the formal theory. Prominent among these items are questions of scale, growth, and efficiency. A nice quotation that expresses the scale argument is the following: "In many fields there is an urgent need to transcend the many small national markets which are no longer adequate to cope with modern technological developments. On the other hand, many considerations, primarily political, render it impossible to lead this argument to its logical conclusion, i.e., world-wide integration . . . economic integration can only become a reality between such like-minded nations as are already closely linked together . . . ."[11] This quotation expresses the key ideas involved:

1. In a small, isolated market the demand may not be sufficient to allow the most efficient scale of production.
2. With free trade, a country could either use its exports to buy more cheaply the imports from a country that has achieved an economic size of operation, or could itself specialize to achieve the needed volume of sales through exports.

[9] Charles E. Staley, "Central American Economic Integration," *Southern Economic Journal*, XXIX, No. 2 (October 1962), 88–95.

[10] See Clair Wilcox, *A Charter for World Trade* (New York: The Macmillan Company, 1949), pp. 70–71.

[11] Quoted from a publication of the Research Directorate of the Secretariat-General of the Council of Europe by Sidney Dell, "Economic Integration and the American Example," *Economic Journal*, LXIX, No. 273 (March 1959), 39.

3. Because trade is not free, and the efforts of GATT do not seem to be eliminating tariffs nor do the efforts of the IMF eliminate trade restrictions caused by balance-of-payments troubles, a second-best solution is to be found in customs union.

The research that has been done on this proposition suggests that the idea is pertinent for customs unions of quite small countries rather than those of the size of European countries. Dell presented most of the available data in *Economic Journal*, LXIX; his conclusion is that the essential differences between U.S. and the European economies do not include scale. A conference of the International Economic Association concluded that, "It is not going too far, perhaps, to say that it seemed to be our general impression that most of the major industrial economies of scale could be achieved by a relatively high-income nation of 50 million; that nations of 10–15 million were probably too small to get all the technical economies available. . . ." [12] The scale argument has more relevance to unions of underdeveloped countries, consequently.

A second factor of potential importance is the prospect of raising efficiency by forcing business men to meet expanded foreign competition. Again, doing this via a customs union is a second-best policy, since non-discriminatory reduction of tariffs would also expand competition. Within the context of customs unions, this argument was freely used in the debate preceding the first decision of the United Kingdom to seek membership in the European Economic Community. The basis of the argument is that in small protected markets entrepreneurs may prefer to maintain a stable oligopoly situation rather than introduce new techniques or products. Further, business ethics in situations where relations with competitors are friendly and personal may inhibit investments that could change market shares.[13] The evidence is mostly impressionistic, since the proposition has not been systematically tested. One of the bits of evidence is that the U.K. industries that are more heavily concentrated than their U.S. counterparts do not have relatively low productivity.[14] Public policy measures may be needed to promote the competitive effects; hence common market agreements typically include antitrust provisions. In the Treaty of Rome, Article 85 prohibits "any agreement between enterprises, any decisions by associations of enterprises, and any concerted practices which are likely to affect trade

[12] E. A. G. Robinson, ed., *Economic Consequences of the Size of Nations* (London: Macmillan & Co., Ltd., 1960), p. xviii.

[13] The argument is well presented in Tibor Scitovsky, *Economic Theory and Western European Integration* (London: George Allen & Unwin Ltd., 1958), pp. 125 ff.

[14] Dell, *Economic Journal*, LXIX, p. 43. Dell has carried his examination further in *Trade Blocs and Common Markets* (New York: Alfred A. Knopf, 1963), where he suggests that the outcome in Europe may be intensified concentration rather than intensified competition.

between Member States and which have as their object or result the prevention, restriction or distortion of competition within the Common
Market.''

The third effect is the possible stimulus to economic growth within the
customs union. This is the rationale, for example, of the Latin American
Common Market; its proponents begin with the idea that industrialization
and relief from a reliance on unstable external markets are essential for
Latin American growth, and go on to argue that only in a customs union
can these be achieved.[15] The argument for growth partly relies on the scale
and competitive effects, but also includes the extra investment generated by
the expansion of the market. The peculiarly Latin American argument that
the external market is a detriment to economic growth is rather shaky;
Chap. 14 contains an analysis of that thesis. A possible growth stimulus is
an inflow of foreign capital seeking to get behind the external tariff wall of
the customs union. From the point of view of the countries in the customs
union, enhanced growth is a distinct possibility. The enthusiasts who
attribute Europe's rapid growth in the late 1950's and early 1960's to the
EEC ignore too many developments in economic policy, factor supply, and
the foreign exchanges to be entirely convincing. From the point of view of
the world, enhanced growth within the union is matched by reduced growth
outside in the presence of trade diversion, since the diversion reduces markets,
scale, induced investment, and so on. Professor Johnson reminds us that
growth will not result from a customs union if the effects of tariff reduction
are made nugatory by other factors that separate markets, such as high transportation costs or cultural barriers.[16] This is likely to be a problem in the
Latin American Common Market, whose members are as far apart as
Mexico and Argentina.

From a broader perspective, the formation of a customs union is a
political act, and political motivations are mixed in with the evaluation of
the propects of economic gain or loss. In the case of the European Economic
Community, for example, it is said that the motives were to end the historic
Franco-German enmity; to secure the scale, competition, and growth
advantage; and to enable Europe to act as an equal toward the United States
and the Soviet Union.[17] The political element lay behind the United Kingdom's reluctance to join the EEC, and her rejection by the Six when she did
make the attempt, as well as being important in France's decision in 1965
to boycott meetings of various committees of the Six. Of course, the fact
that politics are a major part of the formation and operations of customs

[15] United Nations, *The Latin American Common Market* (New York: United
Nations, 1959), pp. 5–13, 53–93.
[16] *Money, Trade and Economic Growth*, p. 61.
[17] Robert R. Bowie and Theodore Geiger, *The European Economic Community and
the United States*, (Washington, D.C.: Joint Economic Committee, 1961), pp. 1–6.

unions does not preclude an economic analysis of them any more than does the prominent role of politics in fiscal policy preclude economic theorizing about that.

EMPIRICAL STUDIES

The number of factors involved in the analysis of customs unions is so vast and the interest in them is so great that there is an embarrassing surplus of empirical work from which to choose a closing example for this chapter. We may perhaps use the Brookings Institution's study of the effects of the EEC on U.S. exports. For agricultural products, the study must begin with an examination of the EEC's agricultural policy. This involves a transition to a uniform regulated internal price for all six members, a system of variable levies that is designed to ensure that demand for farm products is met first by internal supply with foreigners as residual suppliers, and export subsidies to allow any surpluses to be sold in the world market. The situation is altered compared to previous agricultural policies by the uniform price, which is higher than the average of the previous prices. The agreement also means that the first countries to achieve self-sufficiency will not be under pressures to limit production as before, since their surplus may be exported without difficulty to the other members. Both these changes are designed to increase domestic agricultural output. On the basis of the probable effects of higher prices, the Brookings Institution estimated that by 1968 the U.S. loss in agricultural exports to the EEC would be $350 million compared to 1961.

In estimating the effects on exports of U.S.-manufactured items, the Brookings Institution used a "dominant suppliers'" model. The idea is that in each industrial classification one of the countries is the low-cost producer; this one is defined to be the country that was the largest exporter to other member countries before the EEC was established. The common EEC tariff is then compared to the previous tariff in the low-cost country; the result of this comparison was that the tariff on 75 per cent of all manufactured products would be raised by 25 per cent or more. This calculation, by the way, used the nominal tariff, since it was performed before the more relevant notion of the effective tariff rate had been formulated.

It is assumed by the Brookings researchers that average and marginal costs of the dominant supplier will not be increased as it expands its exports to the other members, and that the difference between the common tariff and the previous tariff of the low-cost country will be reflected in an increase in the price of U.S. products in Europe. These assumptions make it possible to estimate the loss to the United States. This is done by applying the price elasticity of demand for imports from the United States, estimated as -2; since the elasticity is the percentage change in quantity divided by the per-centage change in price, and since the percentage change in price is given by the tariff calculation, it is easy to find the percentage change in quantity. This percentage change applied to 1960 exports gives a loss of $200 million.[18]

The dominant suppliers' model stands or falls depending on whether the assumption of constant cost is a good one. Presumably in well-established industries the increasing returns elements would not be important, but the extent to which costs would rise is debated. The next few years' experience with the EEC will provide a good test.[19]

Some estimates of trade creation and trade diversion eschew the use of models in favor of a more common-sense approach. Professor Balassa, for example, suggests that a comparison of the income elasticity of the demand for imports before and after integration can give a clue. If one assumes that the percentage change of imports compared to the percentage change of GNP would have been constant in the absence of the formation of a common market, then an increase in the income elasticity for trade within the common market indicates trade creation, and a fall in the elasticity for imports from outside the market is a suggestion that trade diversion has occurred. Applying this concept to the European Economic Community, a comparison of income elasticities for the 1953–1959 period with the 1959–1965 period shows that the income elasticity for trade within the market rose from 2.4 to 2.8, for total imports rose from 1.8 to 2.1, and for imports from outside the market rose from 1.6 to 1.7. This indicates trade creation without trade diversion, although the complete story requires examination of separate commodity groups and the different policies followed toward agricultural imports, oil, and manufactured items, as well as analysis of the impact on different suppliers.[20] These common-sense findings are indeed suggestive and can be used as a check on the results derived from research based on more imposing statistical or economic models.

[18] Salant et al., *The United States Balance of Payments in 1968*, Chap. IV. This chapter also contains estimates of the effects on nonagricultural raw materials and on U.S. exports to third countries and comments on the impact of European economic growth and possible retardation of EEC exports as a consequence. The estimate of the total trade diversion from the United States is $750 million per year as of 1968.

[19] For criticism of the dominant suppliers' model along these lines see Peter B. Kenen's statement in *The United States Balance of Payments* (Washington, D.C.: Joint Economic Committee, 1963), pp. 242–43.

[20] See Bela Balassa, "Trade Creation and Trade Diversion in the European Common Market," *Economic Journal*, LXXVII, No. 305 (March 1967), 1–21.

CHAPTER 13

GROWTH,
CAPITAL, AND TRADE

THE THEORY OF THE RELATIONSHIPS among growth, capital, and trade has been developing rapidly in recent years. One obvious reason is the interest in the problems of underdeveloped countries. Another reason has been the rather long periods of disequilibrium in various countries' balances of payments, particularly the dollar shortage that attracted attention until about 1958 and then gave way to concern about the dollar glut. In the discussion of the real aspects of these disequilibria, the theory of trade and growth was advanced.

HICKS' PRODUCTIVITY INCREASE MODEL

A highly important stage in the unfolding of the theory was Sir John Hicks' suggestion that productivity increases may be import- or export-biased (or neutral, for that matter).[1] The picture to have in mind is that of two countries, one of which is growing via improvements in labor productivity (for some reason that will concern us in a moment) while the other is stagnant. If equilibrium prevailed before growth started, what is the effect of the productivity growth? There may be various monetary disturbances; for example, the money supply may not grow enough to prevent a fall in the price level of country 1 (the growth country). This would lead to a balance-of-payments deficit for country 2 as it imported more and exported less to country 1. Country 2's policy might then be a monetary action such as deflation or depreciation. But the question for now is whether there will be a real effect as well.

[1] "An Inaugural Lecture," *Oxford Economic Papers*, V, No. 2 (June 1953), 117–35.

148

Hicks suggested that there might be a real effect if the productivity increases were localized in one sector of the economy or another instead of being spread uniformly throughout the economy. Thus, if the export industry of country 1 were the one that was progressing, one would expect the price of country 1's exports to fall and their quantity to rise. Country 2 benefits because its terms of trade improve. Whether it has a deficit in its balance of payments depends on demand conditions; if its demand for imports were elastic, a deficit would result. But this case is much better for country 2 than the situation where the productivity increase is import-biased, or concentrated in country 1's import-competing industry. In that case the price of country 2's exports would fall, so it would have a terms-of-trade loss as well as having to cope with a deficit. In the following material we shall make a more thorough examination of the causes and effects of import- and export-biased growth.

THE JOHNSON MODEL

For this examination it is customary to ask what is the effect of growth on country 1's demand for imports at the initial terms of trade. This enables one to predict the changes in the terms of trade in the amounts traded. For example, suppose that after growth has occurred the demand for imports has been reduced (at the original terms of trade). Then for equilibrium to be restored, the price of imports must fall; that is, country 1's terms of trade must improve. The extent of the trade changes depends, of course, on the magnitude of the change in the demand for imports and on the elasticity of the offer curve of country 2. We have already met the technique of analyzing problems by investigating how demands shift at the original terms of trade in Chap. 4, footnote 11, and early in Chap. 11.

To answer the question of how growth affects demand, most models begin with the Heckscher–Ohlin approach. They then separate out the consumption and the production effects of economic growth. The production effect is seen in a generally rightward shift of the transformation curve, although various kinds of growth may change the shape of the curve in different ways. The consumption effect comes from the increase in national income that results from growth. Since prices are held constant initially, the consumption effect will depend on the income elasticity of the demand for imports. Different kinds of growth result in different distributions of income, so it is quite likely that the consumption effect will vary from one growth situation to another. The total effect depends on the combination of production and consumption reactions.

Figure 13-1 shows the production and consumption effects in a simple case. As a result of economic growth the transformation curve has shifted from T_0 to T_1, and at constant terms of trade the production equilibrium has shifted from P_0 to P_1. The consumption equilibria are shown as C_0 for the initial trade situation, and C_1 for the position after growth, before any terms of trade change. Since the two production points lie on a straight line through the origin, and so do the two consumption points, they represent a particular kind of growth: Professor Johnson calls it neutral or unbiased growth,

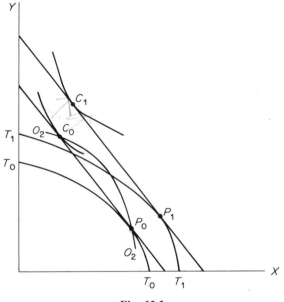

Fig. 13-1

because the demand for imports of Y and the supply of exports of X expand in proportion to the increase in output.[2]

If the transformation curve T_1 had been twisted so that P_1 fell to the southeast of its location in Fig. 13-1, C_1 remaining unchanged, the demand for imports would have increased more than proportionately to the output increase. (In this model the output increase may be measured in terms of Y goods at constant relative prices.) This response to growth is called "protrade"-biased and corresponds to Hick's export bias. Similarly, if C_1 had been located to the northwest of its Fig. 13-1 position, imports would be larger and the consumption effect would be protrade-biased. The opposite production and consumption shifts (P_1 to the northwest, C_1 to the southeast) would have reduced the growth of imports relative to the growth of the national output and the growth effect would be antitrade-biased.

[2] Harry G. Johnson, "Economic Development and International Trade," *Nationaløkonomisk Tidsskrift*, XCVII, Nos. 5–6 (1959), 253–72, reprinted in *Money, Trade and Economic Growth*. Figures 13-1, 13-2, and 13-3 (slightly modified) come from that source.

The offer curve of country 2 is needed to complete the story. This is drawn in Fig. 13-1 between P_0 and C_0 and shows that equilibrium indeed prevailed before growth. After growth the offer curve would be shifted to pass through P_1. It intersects the constant terms-of-trade line to the southeast of C_1, indicating that country 1's demand for imports exceeds country 2's supply. As a result the price of Y rises; that is, P_x/P_y, the slope of the terms-of-trade line, falls in order to restore equilibrium. The knowledge that growth has a particular kind of trade bias is not enough by itself to determine the effects on trade; one also has to know the foreign offer curve. But it remains important to know the trade bias, since it indicates whether growth makes the country more dependent on trade (relatively), whether the market for the exports of other countries is expanding, and whether the supply of the exports of the growth country is expanding.

Now it is time to be a little more specific about the effects of the various kinds of changes that are related to growth, so let us pin down the model more precisely. Using the H–O model, assume that country 1 with its comparative advantage in X is a labor-intensive country. The production function is described by a box diagram such as Fig. 3-3, in which X is the labor-intensive commodity. For the moment forget about consumption effects and concentrate on production effects. There are three types of growth that are much discussed, and we shall look at them in turn: labor supply increase, capital accumulation, and technological change.

The cases of an increase in the supply of the factors of production are handled by the Rybczynski theorem that was developed in Chap. 3. According to that theorem, an increase in the labor supply will increase the production of the labor-intensive good and reduce the output of the capital-intensive good at constant terms of trade (with a constant-returns-to-scale production function). This immediately gives us the simple result that an increase in the working population of our labor-intensive country will give an increased production of X and a decreased production of Y at the initial terms of trade. This is a protrade-biased change according to the classification developed above.

The accumulation of capital is also a simple application of the Rybczynski theorem. By drawing a diagram similar to Fig. 3-7(b), but expanding the capital axis rather than the labor axis, you can show that the output of capital-intensive good Y will expand, while X contracts, at constant terms of trade. The conclusion immediately follows that increased investment in country 1 has an antitrade production effect.

Something has to be done about the consumption effect in order to predict the total effect of growth. It is possible to get some specific results by assuming, for example, that X is a necessary good and Y is a luxury, and also that the owners of capital are wealthier than are the proletarians. This implies that the marginal propensity to consume Y is higher for rentiers than for workers, while the marginal propensity to consume X is higher for workers.[3] Consumption effects then follow easily; if labor is increasing while capital is constant, all the increase in income goes to labor. Why? Because the assumption of constant terms of trade holds the factor proportions constant in each commodity and therefore holds the marginal products constant. Capital's share is a fixed quantity of capital times a fixed marginal product which is clearly a constant. Now if labor is getting all the increased income, with a higher marginal propensity to consume X, the community as a whole will spend a larger proportion of its income on X and a smaller proportion on Y. Hence the consumption effect in this case is antitrade-biased, which is the opposite to the production effect. The total effect, reflecting two opposing tendencies, could be determined only on the basis of specific numerical assumptions.

The other case, where capital is increasing, gives the owners of capital goods all the increased income and leads to a larger proportion of the community's income spent on Y. This is a protrade consumption effect that conflicts with the antitrade bias of the production effect.

Of course, other assumptions about the taste patterns of the factor owners may be made. As an exercise, suppose that X is the luxury good and Y is the necessity. How then are the conclusions modified? Or suppose that country 1 is a welfare state so that capitalists are not wealthier than the typical plumber. What conclusions can you draw?

A somewhat more difficult piece of analysis is required for the examination of technological change. The reason is that one industry may progress while another is remaining stagnant; and within the progressing industry, the technological improvement may affect capital more than labor or vice versa.[4] The various possibilities are illustrated in Fig. 13-2. This is an isoquant diagram with typical isoquants for good X and Y both shown. Line P_1 is an iso-cost line in the situation before the technological change. Its slope shows the initial P_K/P_L or factor/price ratio. Since it is an iso-cost line, the quantities of X and Y represented by the isoquants have equal cost and value under competition. The factor intensity of each is shown by the slope of the dashed lines from the origin, while the overall factor endowment for the economy is shown by the slope of OO.

The next development is that a technological improvement is made in the productive process of good X, so that the same output can be produced with less capital and labor. In Fig. 13-2 this is shown by the shift of the isoquant to X', which represents the same output as the original X. X' is drawn under the assumption of neutral technical change, defined as a change

---

[3] This is Johnson's assumption, in *Money, Trade and Economic Growth*, p. 87.

[4] A pioneering contribution that sets out these different effects is Ronald Finley and Harry Grubert, "Factor Intensities, Technological Progress, and the Terms of Trade," *Oxford Economic Papers*, XI, No. 1 (February 1959), 111–21.

that does not affect the labor/capital ratio at the initial factor prices.[5] Since we want to know the effects on production at the original terms of trade, it is necessary to restore the costs of production of the given quantities of X and Y to equality, which we do by drawing in the new iso-cost line P_2. Along this line, observe two things: First, labor is now relatively more expensive because the P_K/P_L ratio has fallen. Second, and related to the

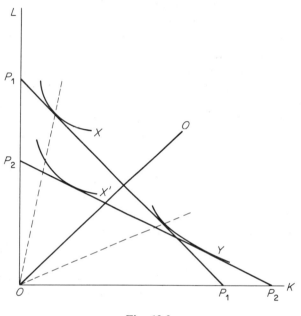

Fig. 13-2

first point, the L/K ratio has fallen in both industries. But this bit of information enables us to determine what has happened to output, because the weighted average method of expressing the overall L/K ratio that we developed in Chap. 5 assures us that the only way to keep a constant L/K ratio for the economy when the ratio drops for both commodities is to expand the output of labor-intensive good X. So the conclusion is established: A neutral innovation in the labor-intensive commodity in the labor-intensive country expands the output of the labor-intensive good and cuts the output of the capital-intensive good. It is obvious that this is a protrade-biased change.

[5] Technical change may twist the isoquant so that at the initial factor/price ratio the labor/capital ratio would be reduced, in which case we would have labor-saving progress; or it may raise the L/K ratio in capital-saving progress. These are only one of the several possible sets of definitions; see F. H. Hahn and R. C. O. Matthews, "The Theory of Economic Growth: A Survey," *Economic Journal*, LXXIV, No. 296 (December 1964), 825–93, for a summary of the literature.

The consumption effects follow readily. Since wages have risen, the demand for X increases under Johnson's assumptions about consumption patterns. The consumption effect in this case is antitrade-biased.

To complete this part of the story, we should sketch the sequence of nonneutral progress. For a labor-saving innovation in good X, the tangency of P_2 and X' would be farther to the right of the original L/K ratio for good X than the Fig. 13-2 result, and the conclusions derived from neutral progress would not be qualitatively changed. Capital-saving progress, however, if sufficiently strong, would change the tangency point to the left of the original L/K ratio. The result would be a rise in the L/K ratio in X and a fall in the L/K ratio in Y. Here the weighted average formula in Chap. 5 gives no guidance in evaluating output changes. Resources may shift in either direction so we cannot tell the trade bias of this particular type of progress.

It would be tedious to work out the effects of progress in Y, or the various cases under the assumption that the country is capital-intensive. It is also unnecessary, since it simply involves a little reshuffling of the relationships just explained.

This model, says Professor Corden, is "simple in conception but is in my view one of the most useful advances in trade theory in recent years."[6] It certainly does enable one to examine a wide variety of growth possibilities. It is, however, based on the same sort of assumptions that gave trouble in the H–O model. Increasing returns, intermediate goods, variable factor supplies, more than two countries, and other modifications will change some of the conclusions. Many of these are indicated in Professor Johnson's article already cited, as well as in his "Effects of Changes in Comparative Costs as Influenced by Technical Change," in *International Trade Theory in a Developing World*, eds. Harrod and Hague (New York: St. Martin's Press, Inc., 1963). Here we shall be satisfied with the basic model, except insofar as changes in the supply of capital is concerned.

CAPITAL, GROWTH, AND TRADE MODELS

Capital theory is an intricate subject. The growth and trade model just examined ignores the intricacies, as a first approximation. Economics is still concerned with developing the second- and higher-order approximations, and advances have been made in the handling of capital theory problems. The combination of newly available techniques and an important problem leads to a new trend in research, so that a number of important studies are

[6] Corden, *Recent Developments in the Theory of International Trade*, p. 39. A thorough investigation of this model in mathematical terms has been provided by Bo Södersten, *A Study of Economic Growth and International Trade* (Stockholm: Almqvist & Wiksell, 1964).

now available that illustrate aspects of the relationships among capital, growth, and trade.

The strategy in this section will be to examine models concocted by Baldwin, Kenen, and Samuelson, in terms of their assumptions and results rather than the detailed models themselves.[7] Each has a somewhat different model, serving to bring out most strikingly the phenomena that concern the author, but each gives new insights into the overall problem.

Baldwin assumes that inputs consist of the capital good and labor, outputs of the capital good and the consumption good, and trade in both goods. Generally the capital-scarce nation will import the capital good, paying for it either by exports of the consumer good or by borrowing from the advanced capital-abundant nation. In his model, which is basically the H–O model with the formation of capital constantly pushing out the transformation curve, the eventual equilibrium involves the same interest rate in both countries—a rate so low that no further saving takes place. With the same rate in both countries, and no net investment taking place, each country has the same capital/labor ratio. Adding the assumption that tastes are the same, the conclusion is that trade will cease. The main point that this model establishes is that there are long-run forces tending to reduce trade. The basis of trade must therefore be found in short-run items such as differences in technology and in tastes.[8]

Samuelson's capital and trade model has labor and capital as inputs, capital and two consumer goods as outputs, and trade in the two consumer goods. It is devoted to uncovering the conditions under which trade will equalize the interest rate. Not surprisingly, these involve the absence of factor-intensity reversals, the production of both goods, and positive capital formation. In contrast to Baldwin's results, in this model sufficient trade must occur to keep the interest rates equalized. The reason for this is that international prices are taken as given; the effects of capital accumulation on output, leading to changes in relative product prices with feedback effects on input prices, are ignored.

A quite different path is explored by Kenen. His suggestion is to treat capital as increasing the productivity of land and labor rather than as a

---

[7] Robert E. Baldwin, "The Role of Capital-Goods Trade in the Theory of International Trade," *American Economic Review*, LVI, No. 4 (September 1966), 841–48. Peter B. Kenen, "Growth Theory, Trade Theory, and International Investment," in *Trade and Development*, eds. Johnson and Kenen, pp. 31–50; and "Nature, Capital and Trade," *Journal of Political Economy*, LXXIII, No. 5 (October 1965), 437–60. Paul A. Samuelson, "Equalization by Trade of the Interest Rate along with the Real Wage," in *Trade, Growth, and the Balance of Payments*, eds. Baldwin et al., pp. 32–52.

[8] It is interesting that other lines of research come to the same conclusion. G. C. Hufbauer, *Synthetic Materials and the Theory of International Trade*, is based on the thesis that trade depends on the existence of a technological gap that is sooner or later closed for a given product but is constantly reopened in other products. See also the discussion of R&D and its relation to comparative advantage in Chap. 8.

separate factor in the production function. An increase in the amount of capital is therefore treated as increasing the amount of labor and land available. With generally H–O assumptions for the rest of the model, and with two traded consumer goods but capital not subject to trade, the result is that goods prices and factor prices are equalized, but not the interest rate. Capital mobility is necessary to achieve interest rate equalization in this model. A major point that emerges from Kenen's study is that it enables him to include estimates of human capital in studying the Leontief paradox of the capital-intensive United States exporting labor-intensive products. Manipulating the data in a fashion suggested by his model, so that skill differences are regarded as being the result of capital invested in the labor force and the higher wages of skilled labor are regarded as a return to capital, he finds that $1 million of U.S. exports use more capital than do $1 million of import replacements (at a 9 per cent return, with human capital deflated by consumer prices).

It is clearly too much to say that the problem of capital, trade, and growth has been solved in light of the very divergent results of the models. Yet each one is helpful and pushes back the frontier a bit.

IMMISERIZING GROWTH

Before closing the subject of trade and growth, it is worth looking at the interesting idea of "immiserizing growth" or "damnification." The idea goes back to Edgeworth, who suggested in the *Economic Journal* in

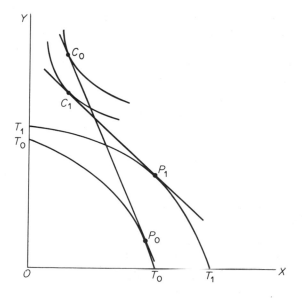

Fig. 13-3

1894 that a reduction in the cost of producing exports might be detrimental. How could this be? Figure 13-3 shows such a case in modern terms. The improvement in the production of the export good X is shown by the shift in the transformation curve from T_0 to T_1. The effect on trade is assumed to be a fall in the terms of trade so that in the final equilibrium C_1 lies on a lower indifference curve than did C_0. The result is that the welfare loss from the adverse terms of trade exceeds the welfare gain from the growth in production capabilities.

The conditions that give this result are either:

1. An inelastic foreign demand for X. Then an increased supply of X reduces the quantity of Y that the other country will offer. Our country will then raise the price of Y, and equilibrium will be achieved because it consumes less Y.

2. The damnification result ensues in the case that Johnson calls "ultra-pro-trade bias," in which more than the whole increase in national income goes to purchase imports. If the domestic output of import-competing goods falls, and if the demand for importables rises, both at constant terms of trade, we have the case of ultra-pro-trade bias. In this case, the damnified country's offer curve may shift so much that its terms of trade turn adverse enough to offset the productivity gain even if its partner's offer curve is elastic.[9]

Are there any real-life cases that illustrate immiserizing growth? The underdeveloped countries sometimes seem to argue that they do; for example, many of the items on the agenda of the 1964 United Nations Conference on Trade and Development stemmed from the position that between 1950 and 1961 the terms of trade between developing and developed countries deteriorated by 17 per cent (excluding the petroleum producers).[10] Apart from the fact that terms-of-trade deterioration by itself does not establish that welfare is diminished—it must be compared to the gains from growth—there is another consideration. Professor Kindleberger points out that the immiserization models such as Fig. 13-3 assume resource movement between industries, whereas in many underdeveloped countries the relevant model is one of increases of factor supply in one sector of the economy together with great obstacles to resource movement into the other sectors. In such a case immiserizing growth is a distinct possibility, but no clear-cut examples have yet come to light.[11]

[9] See Johnson, *Money, Trade, and Economic Growth*, pp. 86–7; also Jagdish Bhagwati, "Immiserizing Growth: a Geometrical Note," *Review of Economic Studies*, XXV, No. 3 (June 1958), 201–5.
[10] United Nations, *Towards a New Trade Policy for Development*, E/Conf. 46/3 (New York: United Nations, 1964), p. 19.
[11] Kindleberger, *Foreign Trade and the National Economy*, pp. 106–8.

CHAPTER **14**

TRADE PROBLEMS
OF DEVELOPING
COUNTRIES

THE CONCERN IN CHAP. 13 was with the relations between trade
and growth, irrespective of whether the country in question was an advanced
or underdeveloped country. There are, in addition, enormous and interesting
special problems of underdeveloped countries in international trade, some
of which we shall now survey.

TRADE THEORY AND DEVELOPMENT THEORY

Many influential writers find the standard theory of trade to be
inadequate for understanding and evaluating the problems of the less-
developed part of the world. For example, Myrdal says that it is an intel-
lectually false procedure to handle the trade policy problems of underdeveloped countries within the framework of theories fitted to advanced
countries. Raúl Prebisch argues that the proposition that because undeveloped
countries have a comparative advantage in primary products they should
therefore put their development efforts into the primary rather than the
industrial sector would result in transferring all the fruits of progress to the
advanced countries.[1]

[1] Gunnar Myrdal, *An International Economy* (New York: Harper & Row, Publishers,
1956), p. 223; Raúl Prebisch, "Commercial Policy in the Underdeveloped Countries,"
American Economic Review Papers and Proceedings, XLIX, No. 2 (May 1959), 252. These
are both very influential spokesmen for underdeveloped countries. Prebisch's views are
also set out forcefully in a United Nations publication, *The Economic Development of
Latin America and Its Principal Problems* (1950). There are many other citations of criticisms
of comparative advantage theory in this connection in Kindleberger, *Economic Development*,
Chap. 16.

It is said, in fact, that the theories of growth in underdeveloped countries either ignore comparative advantage altogether or are interested in trade only as an engine of growth rather than as a way to maximize the productivity of resources.[2] This in turn comes from basic assumptions about the economies of underdeveloped countries that may be different from assumptions used in trade theory. According to Chenery, these include:

1. Factor prices do not necessarily reflect opportunity costs.
2. The quantity and quality of factors of production change over time.
3. Economies of scale are important.
4. Complementarity among commodities dominates producer and consumer demands.

Now while it is true that the simple static models of trade—Ricardian and Heckscher–Ohlin alike—do reflect the converse of these assumptions, it is also true that contemporary trade theory has dealt with all the assumptions. We have already handled the second one in Chap. 13 and the third in Chap. 9.

FACTOR-PRICE DISEQUILIBRIA IN ECONOMIC DEVELOPMENT

The first assumption, about factor prices, means essentially that the markets for the factors of production are not in equilibrium, and this is something we have not paid detailed attention to. (It was noted in Chap. 11, under tariff arguments, as something to be discussed later.) The idea is that in underdeveloped countries there are serious imperfections in the capital and labor markets. The result is that some factors of production get high returns even though their opportunity cost is low (e.g., agricultural labor has a low marginal product) so that the output sacrificed if labor shifts to manufacturing is small. In this case, participating in international trade at prices determined by money costs gives less than an optimum return to the economy, simply because the money costs are distorted compared to the underlying opportunity costs or the slope of the transformation curve.

This argument actually predates the concern with underdeveloped countries, which is essentially a phenomenon of the years after World War II. One of its early suggestions was in the writings of a Rumanian finance minister named Manoilesco.[3] But it did not have much impact until the rising concern with underdeveloped countries after World War II brought interest in such phenomena. The argument has been considerably sharpened and refined, for example, by W. A. Lewis.[4] In Lewis' model, which is supposed to be

[2] Hollis Chenery, "Comparative Advantage and Development Policy," *American Economic Review* LI, No. 1 (March 1961), 20.
[3] *The Theory of Protection and International Trade* (London: P. S. King, 1931).
[4] "Economic Development with Unlimited Supplies of Labor," *Manchester School*, XXII, No. 2 (May 1954), 139–91.

typical of many underdeveloped countries, there are two sectors in the economy. One is the industrial sector, organized along capitalistic lines, and the other is a subsistence agriculture sector. Agriculture has an unlimited, or at least surplus, supply of labor, which may be recognized by the fact that the marginal product of labor in agriculture is zero. Because of the ethics of family peasant life, labor does not get a zero wage and starve to death; instead, sharing gives each one the average product of labor. With a diminishing marginal product of labor, the average product is greater than zero when the marginal product equals zero. To obtain labor, the industrial sector must pay agricultural workers at least the average product in agriculture and probably more (says Professor Lewis, although experience in Brazil and Mexico appears to contradict this). In the industrial sector, operated on a profit-maximizing rather than a family-sharing basis, the wage is equal to the marginal product.

The result is that the marginal product of labor in industry equals the average product of labor in agriculture, which is greater than the marginal product of labor in agriculture. This creates a difference between this model and models such as the isoquant box diagram of Chap. 3, where ratios of factor costs were equal to ratios of marginal products. In Lewis' model equilibrium will not be on the contract curve of the box diagram because the marginal product of labor is different in the two industries even though their wages are the same. Hence the underdeveloped country will not be on its transformation curve, but some place inside it. The implication of the model is that industrial products will be overpriced (the wages in this sector are higher than they would be if equilibrium could be established in the labor market). To correct for this, it is argued, a tariff on industrial products is justified.

The Lewis model is by no means accepted by every student of economic development. For example, Hla Myint criticizes it on the grounds of contemporary experience, claiming that the model is not relevant for many countries; furthermore, in historical experience he says that plantations and mines paid a lower wage than the average return in subsistence agriculture. He also suggests that capital would probably be overpriced in agriculture, compared to industry, which would offset the contrary distortion in labor.[5]

We shall leave it up to the economic development specialists to iron out the relevance of the Lewis model and pass on to another possible labor market distortion that has received considerable attention. By contrast to the Lewis model, where wages are equal even though marginal products are not, this distortion takes the form of unequal wages between the two sectors. Everett E. Hagen suggested that historical data show industrial wages to be

---

[5] "Infant Industry Arguments for Assistance to Industries in the Setting of Dynamic Trade Theory," in *International Trade Theory in a Developing World*, eds. Roy Harrod and D. C. Hague (New York: St. Martin's Press, Inc., 1963), pp. 173–93.

considerably higher than agricultural wages, both in today's advanced countries at the time when they were underdeveloped and in today's under-developed countries. The difference appears to be greater than can be ac-counted for by skill differentials, the cost of urban compared to rural life, or the returns to investment in acquiring skills or in moving.[6] The effect of the wage difference is to make industrial goods overpriced compared to agricul-tural, giving false signals about comparative advantage. A tariff on industrial products would bring the international price ratio into line with the distorted domestic cost ratio. Domestic industry could survive and perhaps improve the real income of the community.

There are a number of plausible reasons for the existence of a wage differential. These include trade unions, prestige pricing of labor by industry, the necessity to pay higher wages to attract labor into the growing sectors, social legislation that prevents child labor in the urban environment, and an excess return to human capital because of imperfections in the capital market.[7]

We can work out the implications of the distortion with the aid of some of the analytical tools of standard trade theory. The assumptions of the model are that there are two products, two factors of production in fixed total supply and always fully employed, a constant-returns-to-scale production function, community or social indifference curves, and competition every-where except in the labor market. Wages are flexible, but as they move up or down there is always a differential in favor of labor hired by the industrial sector (good X) compared to the agricultural sector (good Y). The under-developed country is too small to affect the international terms of trade, which are taken as given.

The first concern is the effect of the wage distortion on the factor market. The proper analytical tool to use here is the box diagram of Fig. 14-1. If there were no distortions, equilibrium would fall along the contract curve at a point such as A. At A, the equilibrium conditions which hold are

$$\frac{P_L}{P_K} = \frac{MPP_{LX}}{MPP_{KX}} = \frac{MPP_{LY}}{MPP_{KY}}, \qquad (14\text{-}1)$$

where MPP_{LX} means the marginal physical product of labor in occupation X, and so on. These conditions by themselves tell us that the slopes of the isoquants are equal (recall from Chap. 3 that the isoquant slopes are the ratios of the marginal products) and are equal to the factor/price ratio. The assumption of full employment guarantees that not only will the isoquant

[6] Hagen, "An Economic Justification of Protectionism," *Quarterly Journal of Economics*, LXXII, No. 4 (November 1958), 496–514.

[7] Hagen, *Quarterly Journal of Economics*, LXXII; Bhagwati and Ramaswami, *Journal of Political Economy*, LXXI; Johnson, in *Trade, Growth, and the Balance of Payments*, eds. Baldwin et al. The following analysis draws on all three of these sources.

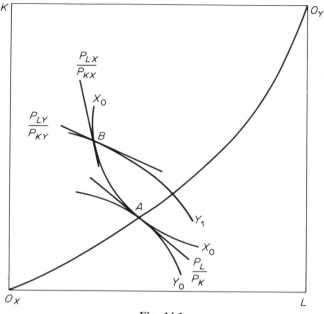

Fig. 14-1

slopes be equal, they will be tangent. Otherwise unemployment would be present (why?).

But because of the distortion in wages, conditions **(14-1)** must be changed to

$$\frac{P_{LX}}{P_{KX}} = \frac{MPP_{LX}}{MPP_{KX}} > \frac{P_{LY}}{P_{KY}} = \frac{MPP_{LY}}{MPP_{KY}}. \tag{14-2}$$

This places equilibrium at some point such as B, where the marginal product ratios are spread out by the necessary amount and full employment still prevails. But B is off the contract curve, since more Y could be produced for the same X. Hence in the transformation curve diagram, Fig. 14-2, the transformation curve corresponding to the Fig. 14-1 contract curve is TT, but the transformation curve along which the economy actually operates is tt. This is the result of the distortion in wages, which gives an incorrect allocation of the factors of production. Any change in demand that changes the economy's outputs will move it along tt, since in equilibrium the isoquant slopes will always be different because of the wage differential.

The wage distortion has a second important implication: The price ratio of the outputs is not equal to the slope of the transformation curve tt. The rigorous proof provided by Hagen is long and involved, but the intuitive idea is that the higher wages make the average cost of inputs greater for X than for Y. As a result the marginal money cost of producing more X

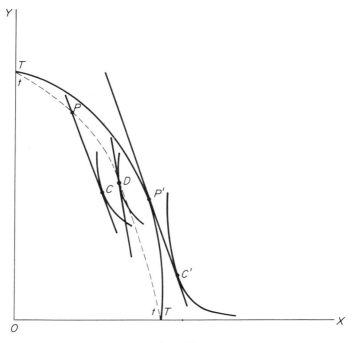

Fig. 14-2

exceeds the actual cost to the economy in terms of foregone Y. Since the ratio of money prices will be equal to the money marginal cost ratio in equilibrium, and since the slope of the transformation curve is the cost of transforming one commodity into the other, the slope of the price line must exceed the slope of the transformation curve. The result of this is that equilibrium without trade might occur at a point such as D, where the marginal money cost ratio equals the price ratio equals the slope of the community indifference curve, but all these ratios exceed the slope of tt.

With trade, production equilibrium might occur at a point such as P, with consumption at C. Since the international terms-of-trade line is less steep than the domestic price ratio before trade, because the relative price of manufactured products is lower abroad, the domestic output of X must be cut in order to reduce the relative money marginal cost of X. In Fig. 14-2 the case is shown where trade brings the economy to a lower indifference curve than before. But it is possible for C to be on a higher indifference curve.

In the case shown in the diagram, it is clear that a prohibitive tariff would return the economy to D and hence improve its real income. This is Hagen's economic justification for protectionism. However, as all the writers cited in footnote 7 point out, such a policy is a second-best one. In terms of the concepts introduced in Chap. 11, the nature of the disequilibrium with trade is that the marginal rate of transformation in foreign trade is equal to the marginal rate of substitution, but neither are equal to the marginal rate of transformation. The prohibitive tariff on the import of X changes the disequilibrium so that none of the marginal rates are equal. To have all three marginal rates equal along the true transformation curve TT, what is called for is a subsidy on the use of labor in X and a tax on the use of labor in Y so that the cost of a marginal unit of labor compared to a marginal unit of capital is the same in both industries. Then the economy would operate along the contract curve in the box diagram.

The economic justification for tariffs in terms of labor market distortions, like so many tariff arguments, does not stand up to analysis as an ideal policy. In terms of the reason given earlier in the chapter for development theory operating from different assumptions than trade theory, we may conclude that it seems likely that factor prices do indeed diverge from opportunity costs, but that the conclusion that therefore either trade theory cannot handle the problem or else that it reaches the wrong conclusion seems strange indeed.

BALANCED GROWTH

The fourth assumption often made in the economic development literature, identified by Chenery as complementarity among commodities in producer and consumer demands, has to do with the question of balanced growth. This is a Pandora's box of formidable dimensions, and for a complete discussion the student should refer to a text on economic development. The notion is that it is a mistake to invest in only one sector, such as the export sector or only one industry in the domestic goods sector. For example, investment in paper will not pay off unless investments are made simultaneously in other industries, because rising incomes are needed for people to be able to afford the purchase of paper. Investment in only one industry, it is thought, will not have the requisite multiplier effect. Also, investment in other industries at a comparable stage of the productive process is needed for the industries to generate external economies for each other. More than that, investment must be forthcoming in supplying industries and in the industries that use the output of the paper industry as an input. Investment is needed every place at once, or so say the balanced growth advocates. Not so, reply the expositors of unbalanced growth. With only a limited amount of entrepreneurial talent available and only limited investment funds, building up one sector to a size where it can achieve economies of scale may use up so much of the scarce resource that a balanced approach is impossible. It may even be undesirable, for technological progress can conceivably be more rapid if attention is focused on one or only a few sectors at a time.

The point of the discussion is that leaving investment decisions to the market may not result in the optimum pattern for economic growth, but it is not clear that a general statement can be made about what sort of pattern of investment should be aimed for. The trade theory set forth in this book is based on leaving the decisions to the market, in general; but both the balanced growth approach and also in unbalanced growth, where decisions are made as to which direction to unbalance the economy, lead to a substantial amount of planning. The planning would, of course, include which industries to protect from competition by imports. In the article by Chenery in *The American Economic Review*, LI, a technique is outlined for combining the insights of growth theory with those of trade theory. It involves the calculation of shadow prices that replace actual market prices in decision making. The shadow prices are designed to allow for wage distortions, for an incorrect level of the foreign exchange rate, for repercussions on the prices of intermediate goods from investment in other sectors, and for the supply-and-demand schedules of the factors of production. The determination of the shadow prices by linear programming techniques goes along with the determination of the social profitability of each investment. From this calculation an idea is obtained of whether to push exports, protect import-competing industries, invest in social overhead capital, or what have you. This approach is still in the early experimental stages.[8]

Historical experience and contemporary planning techniques both show that many combinations of foreign trade with successful growth are possible. In nineteenth-century England and in Puerto Rico in the 1950's and 1960's growth depended on a large and dynamic export sector. By contrast, Latin American development plans and the recent growth of Australia give scant attention to the export sector. The policy chosen partly depends on the size of the country and its resource base; small countries must depend more on trade because it is obviously impossible for them to produce everything. Large countries may ignore the more subtle idea of comparative advantage with the result that, "To most economists, a survey of the procedures actually followed in designing development policy would probably suggest that balance is overemphasized and that the potential gains from trade are often neglected."[9]

THE PREBISCH DOCTRINE

It is obvious that much theoretical work is being done on the subjects where the theory of the underdeveloped countries and trade overlap. At the same time, there is increasing activity in issues of trade policy of

[8] References to some of the experiments are given in Chenery, *American Economic Review*, LI, and also in Richard S. Eckaus, "Appendix on Development Planning," in Kindleberger, *Economic Development*.

[9] Chenery, *American Economic Review*, LI, p. 48.

underdeveloped countries. The high point of the activity so far is the United Nations Conference on Trade and Development (UNCTAD), held in 1964. The intellectual background of the leading figures representing the underdeveloped countries at UNCTAD includes a firm belief in the four points mentioned early in the chapter as typical assumptions in growth theory. But it also is heavily influenced by a particular doctrine known as the Prebisch thesis or Prebisch model—not surprisingly, perhaps, since Raúl Prebisch was the Secretary-General of UNCTAD. What this means is that it is impossible to understand UNCTAD without knowing something about the Prebisch thesis. At the same time the policy demands of the underdeveloped countries are partly a reaction to policies of the advanced nations, and a brief review of these is in order.

To turn to the special theories of Prebisch first, these were formulated a number of years ago, largely on the basis of his Latin American experience. (For many years he was in charge of the United Nations Economic Commission for Latin America.) He has explained his theory in several different guises, so that by now it is so rambling that no simple summary does it complete justice.[10] What follows is only a rough sketch.

The basic model is that of a world composed of an economically advanced center and an underdeveloped periphery. Both experience technological progress but in the center the result is higher wages for labor and higher prices for products, including exports. By contrast, the periphery experiences constant wages and lower prices made possible by technological progress; again exports share the same price trend as domestic products. The result is declining terms of trade for the underdeveloped countries, or what is the same thing from a different perspective, the capture of all the benefits of progress by the advanced countries. The suggested remedy is to form protected manufacturing industries in the periphery so that they can reap the fruits of their own technological progress.

Various reasons are given for this sequence of events. One is that monopolistic markets and labor unions in the center lead to price rises there, with never any price falls. In the periphery, markets are generally more competitive and there is often a labor surplus. This combination leads to stable real wages and falling prices when technological progress occurs. Another point made by Prebisch is that the growing labor supply in the periphery has to be employed in ever-lower productivity pursuits, which also brings pressure on real wages. A third point deals with the structure of international demand. The periphery, it is said, has a high income elasticity of

---

[10] See, in particular, Prebisch, *The Economic Development of Latin America and Its Principal Problems:* "Commercial Policy in the Underdeveloped Countries," *American Economic Review Papers and Proceedings*, XLIX, No. 2 (May 1959), 251–73; and United Nations, *Towards a New Trade Policy for Development*.

demand for imports from the center, while the center's income elasticity of demand for imports from the periphery is low. If both are growing, the exports of the periphery come to lag behind its imports. If the periphery tries to increase its earnings of foreign exchange by cutting its prices, it runs into a low price elasticity of demand from the center, since its exports are typically primary products.

Thus trade brings many problems to underdeveloped countries. Their policy must be to try to overcome these by developing their own manufacturing industries rapidly, to reduce their dependence on imports.

These arguments have been disputed both on factual and on theoretical grounds. On factual grounds, the short-run data used by UNCTAD to show deteriorating terms of trade begin with 1950. This biases the results, since 1950 was the year of the Korean war boom, which raised primary products prices rapidly. For the long-run data, beginning with the 1870's or 1880's, the evidence is mixed. Lipsey finds that while the United Kingdom did enjoy improved terms of trade vis-a-vis the underdeveloped countries over that period, the reverse was true for the United States and for Continental Industrial Europe. On the other hand, Kindleberger concluded that his data showed that in European experience the underdeveloped countries suffered.[11]

The theoretical critiques generally find Prebisch's writings unsatisfactory on the ground of confusion, obscurity, and lack of rigor. Since the main interest at this point is to show the intellectual background of the active spirits at UNCTAD, the details of the criticisms will be passed over.[12] One brief example, however, may be given: In *The Economic Development of Latin America and Its Principal Problems*, Prebisch remarks that the notion of the international division of labor included the proposition that the benefits of technical progress should be distributed equally around the world, no matter where it occurs. Mrs. Flanders points out that if interpreted to mean real wages it will not unless the conditions for the factor-price equalization theorem hold, which as we know is a very questionable thing when applied to the real world with all its monopoly, increasing returns, and other deviance from the assumptions. There is the furthur proposition that increases in productivity from technical progress come from R&D efforts and from the

---

[11] Robert E. Lipsey, *Price and Quantity Trends in the Foreign Trade of the United States*, a study by the National Bureau of Economic Research (Princeton, N.J.: Princeton University Press, 1963), p. 17; Kindleberger, *The Terms of Trade: A European Case Study*, p. 239.

[12] The best one is probably M. June Flanders, "Prebisch on Protectionism: an Evaluation," *Economic Journal*, LXXIV, No. 294 (June 1964), 305–26. Cf. Södersten, *A Study of Economic Growth and International Trade*, pp. 158–81; and, for a more sympathetic treatment, Werner Baer, "The Economics of Prebisch and ECLA," *Economic Development and Cultural Change*, X, No. 2, Part 1 (January 1962), 169–82.

accumulation of physical and human capital; the rewards from this effort are not a fund of unearned increment available for distribution around the world. Even if they were, the question of whether they should be equally distributed would be an ethical question, not the conclusion of the theory of comparative advantage.

UNCTAD

It might be said that while doctrines of the Prebisch variety were the background of UNCTAD, the foreground was the attacks by the underdeveloped countries on existing commercial policy arrangements. In the recent thinking of this group, protection of import-competing industries is not enough; they wish to expand their exports as well. In part the wish is based on a sheer need for more foreign exchange to meet development programs; in part it is an extension of the infant-industry argument. Since the domestic market tends to be quite narrow, the full benefits of the learning process can be obtained only by widening the market to include some exports. But the rules of commercial policy, as codified in the General Agreement on Tariffs and Trade, inhibit the push for exports.

The basic rules of GATT may be summarized as the most-favored-nation clause and the principle of reciprocity in bargaining for tariff reductions. The first one means no discrimination (except for customs unions)— each nation must be treated as well as the most favored nation in any country's tariff laws. The second rule historically has meant that if the advanced countries lowered their tariffs on industrial products of the underdeveloped countries, in order to encourage their exports, the latter would have to make some tariff concession in return. This they were extremely reluctant to do. However, in 1964 the GATT rules were amended by adoption of the principle that the underdeveloped countries would not be expected to make reciprocal concessions in return for lower trade barriers in advanced nations.[13]

The UNCTAD demands were:

1. To eliminate the most-favored-nation clause in favor of tariff preferences given by advanced countries to imports of manufactured products from less-developed nations.
2. To ease nontariff barriers, such as quotas and "voluntary" export restrictions of textiles forced by the threat of overt actions of trade restriction if the "voluntary" restriction did not materialize.
3. The repetition of a long-standing demand that trade in primary products be handled through commodity agreements designed to smooth out

---

[13] This provision is described in Gerard Curzon, *Multilateral Commercial Diplomacy: The General Agreement on Tariffs and Trade and Its Impact on National Commercial Policies and Techniques* (New York: Frederick A. Praeger, Inc., 1966), 247. This is a first-class reference for all topics connected with GATT.

fluctuating prices and to raise the long-run price trend. (The relation of this demand to the Prebisch terms-of-trade thesis is immediately obvious.)[14]

The equally long-standing objections to commodity agreements are basically two: In most cases they don't work, because if prices are initially raised the quantity supplied comes to exceed the quantity demanded, and it is usually impossible to prevent the price from falling again. In the rare cases where they do work, or could be made to work with more cooperation in enforcing them and financing them from advanced countries, they amount to an undesirable kind of income transfer from the advanced countries. The higher prices come from consumers in the advanced countries, and the incidence of these higher prices may not correspond to a desirable distribution of the burden.[15] However, the continued demand by underdeveloped countries and the fact that the United States and only five other developed nations voted against the principle of increasing and stabilizing the earnings of primary commodity exports at UNCTAD shows that the problem cannot be left there. Interesting alternatives to commodity agreements either exist or have been suggested, and the objections to commodity agreements show that the alternatives ought to be intensively explored. Prominent among these are the stabilization measures of the International Monetary Fund, established in 1963, which allows developing countries to borrow from the IMF if their export earnings fall below their recent average. Interestingly, the IMF in its 1966 *Annual Report* (p. 8) noted that these downward fluctuations have not been as numerous or as severe as had been anticipated. For the price-raising aspects of commodity demand by less-developed countries, it has been urged that an explicit tax on developed countries for use by underdeveloped countries is more efficient than attempts to raise the price of commodities by marketing or production quotas, or by purchase and sale from buffer stocks.[16]

The newest idea at UNCTAD was for trade preferences to be given by advanced countries. It would work something like this: If the United States has a 10 per cent tariff on commodity X, which is or could be produced in an underdeveloped country, it would continue to charge 10 per cent on imports from advanced countries but allow duty-free entry from the less-developed source. Assuming that the costs in the underdeveloped country are less than in the United States, it could then take advantage of what is

[14] An excellent brief summary of the setting and the results of UNCTAD may be found in Sidney Weintraub, *The Foreign Exchange Gap of the Developing Countries*, Essays in International Finance No. 48 (Princeton, N.J.: International Finance Section, Princeton University, 1965).

[15] See Charles E. Staley, "An Evaluation of Some Recent Contributions to the Political Economy of the Stabilization of International Price and Commodity Fluctuations," *Weltwirtschaftliches Archiv*, XCIV, No. 2 (1965), 337–47.

[16] See, in particular, Boris Swerling, *Current Issues in Commodity Policy*, Essays in International Finance No. 38 (Princeton, N.J.: International Finance Section, Princeton University, 1962).

in effect trade creation. Its manufacturing industry, expanding because of exports, could reap scale economies and infant-industry learning benefits, if any exist. This is particularly the case because giving a preference on the output without reducing tariffs on the inputs makes the U.S. producer pay a tax, in effect.[17] This is easily established from Eq. **(7-5)**:

$$T_j = \frac{t_j - \sum_i a_{ij} t_i}{v_j}. \tag{14-3}$$

When t_j, the nominal tariff rate, is zero, T_j, the effective tariff rate, must be negative if there are any tariffs on inputs.

There are several issues here. In the first place it is the case that the underdeveloped countries have a justifiable ground for complaint. The effective tariff structures of the advanced countries discriminate against manufacturing commodities in which underdeveloped countries are interested (textiles, processing of primary products, and light manufacturing).[18] That is, the effective rates on these products tend to be higher than they are on the more complex goods. In the next place, does it follow that preferences on these products are justified? In general, as we have seen, the best policy is a subsidy to the infants when the preferences are justified on infant-industry grounds. This remains true even when the alternative to the subsidy is not an infant-industry tariff in the less-developed country but is a preference in the advanced country. The subsidy accomplishes the desired goal of making the marginal rate of transformation in foreign trade equal to the marginal rate of transformation in domestic production. The preferences, on the other hand, are based on industries that the advanced countries happen to protect, not on attempts to choose industries that are likely to progress past the infant stage.[19] Even during the discussion stage it has been very difficult to get agreement among the proponents of the preference idea on issues such as whether preferences to some underdeveloped countries should be generalized to all, or what to do about the fact that some of the less-developed countries have a much better industrial base than others. The political aspects of these frictions have impressed one student of UNCTAD as likely to involve a high political cost in terms of world cooperation if the attempt is made to

[17] Harry G. Johnson, *Economic Policies Toward Less Developed Countries*, p. 173.

[18] Johnson, *Economic Policies Toward Less Developed Countries*, pp. 96–104, which draws on the studies by Balassa, *Journal of Political Economy*, LXXIII, and Basevi, *Review of Economics and Statistics*, XLVIII.

[19] Johnson, *Economic Policies Toward Less Developed Countries*, pp. 182–84. As Johnson points out, the best solution for the trade problems of underdeveloped countries, in theory, is for the advanced countries to pursue a free-trade policy, using adjustment assistance for their injured industries, and providing untied foreign aid to cover the foreign exchange gap of the underdeveloped countries. The latter could assist themselves greatly by eliminating currency overvaluation and uneconomical import substitution policies (op. cit., p. 244). Each of these points seems indeed a Utopian suggestion!

implement the program.[20] The feature that benefits are likely to be concentrated in a few countries has led to the suggestion that quotas on the imports from these favored few would be the next logical step to try to get the benefits spread more evenly. But quotas lead to their own political problems (who gets them, how they are set) as well as compounding the misallocation of resources.[21]

Still, the preference idea has captured the imagination of the underdeveloped world, and it was supported at UNCTAD by a number of advanced countries (including France and Germany, but not the United States and the United Kingdom). Continued pressure on this point is inevitable, and much attention was devoted to it at the generally abortive 1968 UNCTAD meeting. This meeting produced a resolution that a generalized system of tariff preferences for the exports of developing countries should be put into effect as soon as possible, but no progress was reported on the detailed problems of the scheme. It promises to be an issue for years to come.

[20] Gardner Patterson, *Discrimination in International Trade, The Policy Issues: 1945–1965* (Princeton, N.J.: Princeton University Press, 1966), Chap. VII.

[21] The suggestion that tariff preferences would lead on to quotas is made by R. E. Baldwin, "A New Trade Policy For Developing Countries," *Review of Social Economy*, XXIV, No. 1 (March 1966), 49–66.

Part Two

THE BALANCE
OF PAYMENTS

CHAPTER 15

THE
BALANCE OF PAYMENTS

THE STUDY OF INTERNATIONAL FINANCE involves the monetary relations of countries. It is largely concerned with the problem of equilibrium in the balance of payments and the way equilibrium is achieved or disequilibrium is allowed to persist. The first order of business is to become familiar with the concepts involved in the balance of payments.

One of the most intractable problems in international economics for years has been the balance of payments. The British have had repeated crises; the Germans had a surplus for years; the United States had first a dollar shortage and then a dollar surplus—the list could go on. The discussions of these problems get complicated by the fact that the phrase "the balance of payments" has more than one meaning. When it is said that the problem of the United States today is dollar surplus or a weak balance of payments, what is meant is that the desired payments from the United States exceed the desired payments to the United States (at the current exchange rates and interest rates, price levels, and national incomes of the United States and other countries). This meaning is to be contrasted to the balance of payments as a statistical record of the payments and receipts that actually were made during a given period. The distinction between the two concepts is similar to the different meanings of "national income" met with in macroeconomics. On the one hand, national income is defined as a system of accounts that measures the actual output or income in a given period. On the other hand, it is regarded as a flow of payments that may or may not be in equilibrium. The relation between the two meanings is that the statistical record is part of the raw material used by the analyst who tries to understand the balance of payments in the other (perhaps we could call it the economic) sense.[1]

---

[1] Professor Machlup calls the latter the market balance. See his "Three Concepts of the Balance of Payments and the So-Called Dollar Shortage," *Economic Journal*, LX, No. 237 (March 1950), 46–68.

Much of Part II of this book is concerned with the economic aspects of the balance of payments. In this chapter the focus is on the statistical record.

BALANCE-OF-PAYMENTS BOOKKEEPING

Balance-of-payments data are published in a peculiar form of double-entry bookkeeping. It is peculiar from the point of view of business accounting because it mixes together in one statement sales and changes in assets and liabilities. Business accounting scrupulously keeps its sales and purchase records on one account, the income statement, and its assets and liabilities on another, the balance sheet. But nations mix them indiscriminately together. The double-entry feature of conventional bookkeeping is maintained, since it is so convenient. Each transaction in principle gives rise to two entries, one on the credit side and one on the debit side of the balance of payments. (In practice, it may be feasible to gather data only on one side of the transaction.) When both sides are summed they must be equal—the balance of payments always balances, just as recorded investment always equals recorded saving in the national income accounts. For example, an import is recorded as a debit. It must have as an offsetting entry a credit of equal amount. The credit may be a reduction in the importer's holding of foreign currency, an increase in the other's holding of the importer's currency, an account payable, or any of the many ways of payment concocted by the ingenuity of traders and bankers. But a credit there must be.

The basic rule is that exports are credits (also called receipts or simply "+"), and imports are debits (or payments or "−"). For a simple illustration of this principle, suppose the United States exports $100 of products and imports $50 of products during the year. Payments are made in this example by the importer writing a check in favor of the exporter, who deposits it in a bank in the importers' country. These payments in the form of checks are the offsetting entries to the merchandise transactions, and they must therefore

Table 15-1

U.S. BALANCE OF PAYMENTS
(DOLLARS)

	Credits	Debits
Exports	100	
Imports		50
Short-term capital[a]	50	100

[a] Notice that since the $50 credit on short-term capital offsets part of the debit, it would be just as correct to enter only the net movement of short-term capital, a debit of $50. Both entries are shown here for completeness.

appear on the opposite side of the balance of payments from the entries for which they pay. The name of the account in which they appear is short-term capital. The balance of payments for these transactions is shown in Table 15-1.

BALANCE-OF-PAYMENTS TRANSACTIONS

The rules for other classes of transactions are derived from appropriate modifications and extensions of the export equals credit/import equals debit rule. These transactions and the appropriate rules include:[2]

1. *Transportation, travel, and other services such as motion picture rentals, insurance, consulting fees, patent royalties, embassy operation, and so on.* Payments made by a country for these items are debits; they are in fact imports of services. Receipts on these accounts must then be credits. The importance of this part of the balance of payments varies from one country to another. In 1964 in the United States the credit for services was about $11 billion compared to merchandise exports of $25 billion, while the debit entry was about $7 billion, with merchandise imports having a debit of about $19 billion. Obviously, services play a major role in the U.S. balance of payments.

2. *Military items.* This is a complicated and, as the world runs today, a sizable matter. The U.S. Department of Commerce reports military transactions in three parts. One is goods and services transferred under military grants. These are credits, and the offsetting debit appears under government grants. In size, they run $1 billion or so a year. Another part is military expenditure, which is a debit of about $3 billion. It includes spending by military personnel and their dependents stationed abroad, military supplies purchased abroad, and the like. The third part is military receipts, which are credits. The transactions include goods and services sold abroad by U.S. military agencies; the total is about $1 billion per year.

3. *Income on investments.* This item is really part of the general category of services, since the earnings of capital can be regarded as a payment for the service of the use of capital. The rules are that income earned on U.S. capital abroad is a credit, while income earned on foreign investment in the United States is a debit. In 1964 the credits were about $5 billion, while the debits were about $1 billion.

4. *Private remittances.* These include gifts of goods; transfers of money, for example, by immigrants to their families at home; and charitable institutions' gifts abroad. Remittances sent abroad are a debit; the offsetting

---

[2] The student will find it very helpful to get a copy of the March, June, September, or December issue of the *Survey of Current Business* (Office of Business Economics, U.S. Department of Commerce) for any recent year in order to get a feel for the detailed way in which the data are presented.

entries are a credit in the export account if the gift takes the form of goods, or in the short-term capital account if money is sent. It is a small item, $500 million or so for the United States; but at times remittances have been very important in the balance of payments of such countries as Israel, Italy, Ireland, and so on.

5. *Government grants.* Like private gifts, government grants are a debit for the country making them and a credit for the country receiving them. Today they include the programs for economic development administered by the Agency for International Development; technical assistance programs; and relief grants such as aid sent to Chile to assist the victims of earthquakes. The volume involved is about $2 billion.

These five items, plus merchandise transaction, are often put in one section of the balance of payments called the current account. The practice varies; sometimes the remittances and government grants are excluded from the current account and put by themselves in a section called the unilateral transfers account. Fundamentally, the current account shows the movements of goods and services among nations. This immediately puts current account transactions into the national income, since national income accounting measures the output of goods and services produced by a country in a given time period. Exports of goods and services are obviously part of the nation's production, while the purchase of imported goods and services must be excluded from the measure of total spending since it is not spent on local production. In national income accounting, total exports minus total imports minus net unilateral transfers is called "net foreign investment"; this is added to consumption, domestic investment, and government spending to obtain the gross national product.[3]

6. *Capital flows.* Capital is a word with many meanings; in the balance of payments it is taken to mean international claims or assets payable in money—bank accounts, bonds, notes accounts payable, corporate stocks, and so on—as well as ownership equity and currency itself. The basic rule is that an increase in claims is a debit, while a reduction in claims is a credit. This rule can be justified and remembered by a reference to Table 15-1. There the debit item of $100 for short-term capital (the counterpart of the export credit) represents an increase in U.S. ownership of bank accounts abroad, which is an increase in the claims of Americans on a foreign country. Since an increase in claims has the same effect on net worth as a reduction in liabilities, the rules are completed by adding that a reduction in liabilities

---

[3] In the United States the national income statisticians and the balance-of-payments statisticians fail to agree on how to handle some of the transactions, which leads to some confusion between the two sets of statistics. For comments on reconciling the accounts, see *The Balance of Payments Statistics of the United States*, Report of the Review Committee for Balance of Payments Statistics to the Bureau of the Budget (Washington, D.C.: U.S. Government Printing Office, 1965), pp. 177–80.

is a debit and an increase in liabilities is a credit. Thus, in Table 15-1 the payment for exports could have taken the form of a check written by the importer against his account in a U.S. bank. The debit would then have arisen from a reduction in U.S. liabilities to foreign residents.

Increases in assets and reductions in liabilities are called capital outflows; by symmetry, capital inflows are reductions in claims and increases in liabilities. So the rules boil down to debits for capital outflows and credits for capital inflows. We may illustrate by Table 15-2. Suppose that a U.S. corporation sells a 10-year $1,000 bond that is purchased by a Canadian citizen. He pays for it by writing a check on his bank account in New York.

Table 15-2

**U.S. BALANCE OF PAYMENTS
(DOLLARS)**

	Credits	Debits
Long-term capital	1,000	
Short-term capital		1,000

The bond is an increase in liabilities and hence is a capital inflow; it is credited. The transfer of the ownership of the bank account from the Canadian to the U.S. corporation is a reduction in U.S. liabilities; thus it is a capital outflow and is debited.

There are several ways to classify capital movements.

A. *Long-term versus short-term capital flows.* The long-term capital account includes equities as well as assets and liabilities whose maturity date is more than one year from the date of issue. Short-term capital is either demand instruments (bank accounts, currency) or paper with a maturity date less than one year from the time of issue.

B. *Private versus government capital movements.* It is a private capital movement unless the government takes an active part. A foreign purchase of a U.S. government bond would be a private capital inflow; the U.S. government is not considered to take an active part in the transaction. But a U.S. government loan to Brazil under an economic development program would be a government capital outflow, since the government does play an active role.

C. *Direct versus portfolio investment.* Direct investment refers to the equity (i.e., ownership) of citizens in one country in foreign-incorporated companies whenever the equity gives the investors "an important voice in management." As a rule of thumb, 25 per cent of the stock is considered to carry the requisite important voice. If a U.S. company does business abroad through branches, the equity in the branch is considered a direct investment. On the other hand, portfolio investment is long-term private investment other than direct investment—items such as bonds and stocks that do not give an important role to the investor.

7. *Errors and omissions.* When the data have all been gathered and the debits are compared with the credits, it always turns out that the totals are not equal. The statisticians fail to record some transactions; for others, the entry may have a different value than the actual payment for them. Since we know that the debits and credits must be equal, we make them so by the entry "errors and omissions." Before 1960 this item was usually a credit; then it took an abrupt swing to the debit side. It is usually thought that the unrecorded transactions must have been capital flows—specifically, capital inflows before 1960 and capital outflows thereafter. The reason is that the timing for the change coincided with a period of strength for the European economies and of stagnant growth and balance-of-payments problems for the United States, which would have induced capital to leave the United States. This seems plausible, but, of course, no one can be positive about it. If they could, this account would not be needed.[4]

8. *Reserve items.* Under the international monetary system currently in use, countries employ several things as reserves. The function of reserves is, broadly, to maintain the value of the country's currency in the foreign exchange markets. For example, suppose the only transactions for the year were those shown in Table 15-1—U.S. exports of $100, with the U.S. exporter acquiring $100 of a foreign currency (e.g., francs), and U.S. imports of $50, with a French merchant acquiring $50. If the American did not wish to hold francs and the Frenchman had no use for dollars, they could each sell the foreign currency in the foreign exchange market. But since the supply of francs would exceed the demand for them, the dollar/franc exchange rate would fall. If the French monetary authorities wish to maintain the dollar/franc exchange rate at its previous level, they will have to demand more francs (or what is the same thing, supply more dollars) in the foreign exchange market. They may acquire the additional dollars by selling gold to the U.S. Treasury. The outcome of these various transactions is that the U.S. sales of francs and the French sales of dollars simply reverse the short-term capital movements shown in Table 15-1, and the United States has imported gold. Like any import, the gold inflow is a debit. The balance of payments would then appear as in Table 15-3. Here gold has been used as the reserve item.

As the international monetary system has evolved over recent years, there are three items that the United States employs as reserves. These are gold owned by the U.S. Treasury, convertible currency owned by the U.S. Treasury and the Federal Reserve System, and what is called the IMF gold-tranche position. Convertible currency is deposits held in a country that has agreed to convert them to dollars on demand, or the short-term

---

[4] Other possible sources of error are discussed in *The Balance of Payments Statistics of the United States*, Chap. 7.

Table 15-3

**U.S. BALANCE OF PAYMENTS
(DOLLARS)**

	Credits	Debits
Exports	100	
Imports		50
Gold		50

government debt of such a country. The gold-tranche position is rather more difficult to explain. Each country makes a subscription on joining the International Monetary Fund, 25 per cent in gold and 75 per cent in its local currency. (The subscription for the United States is $4.12 billion.) It may then borrow other currencies from the fund, depositing its own currency in exchange; or other countries may borrow its currency from the fund.[5] Consequently, the IMF holdings of a given currency are always changing. The IMF's loan policy depends on its holdings of a country's currency. It will more or less automatically loan enough to bring its holdings of a member's currency up to 100 per cent of its subscription quota. For example, if Panama had a quota of 100 balboas, its gold tranche (or share) would be 25 balboas. If no transactions involving balboas had occurred, Panama could count on borrowing 25 balboas of other currencies at any time. For larger loans, the IMF could require various conditions—sound domestic monetary and fiscal policies, perhaps devaluation or tariffs.

Suppose another country had purchased 10 balboas from the fund; then Panama could count on borrowing 35 balboas of other currencies. Or if Panama had already borrowed 10 balboas of foreign exchange, its automatic loan would be cut to 15 balboas. Hence the logic of the definition of the gold-tranche position. "A member's quota minus the fund's holdings of its currency."

The rules for entering reserve asset transactions are that increases are debits and decreases are credits; this may be remembered by a simple example such as Table 15-3. In most recent years for the United States, reserve assets have decreased. The gold-tranche position and gold have been showing credits, while the convertible currency account has been increasing.

Another side of reserve transactions is the changes in liabilities to foreign monetary officials. These do the same job that changes in reserve assets do. In the case of the French transactions that gave rise to the gold flow in Table 15-3, suppose that the French authorities do not own any gold

---

[5] The transactions are a purchase of the other currency, with an obligation to re-purchase your own currency with a convertible currency within a given time period. Clearly, it amounts to a loan.

but that they do have an account with the Federal Reserve Bank of New York. The extra dollars that they supply to the foreign exchange market in order to maintain the exchange rate would be obtained by a reduction in their dollar bank account. Since this is a reduction in U.S. liabilities to foreign residents, it is a debit. Table 15-3 would be modified by replacing the gold debit with a $50 debit to "Short-term official liabilities." In many years these transactions are larger than the reserve asset transactions, reflecting the role of the United States as a principal supplier of currency used in international settlements.

One other notable transaction that appears on the U.S. balance of payments in recent years is labeled "U.S. government nonmarketable medium-term securities." These were designed to reduce the gold outflow by inducing foreign central banks to purchase them rather than gold. They are often put in a special category, along with accelerated payment of debts by foreign governments, since it is recognized that these are measures to disguise the deteriorating reserve position of the United States.

The various current, capital, and reserve transactions we have been discussing are the standard accounts, and the debit-credit rules are the standard ways of keeping score. What is not standard are the ways the accounts are combined into a balance-of-payments table. Sometimes current and capital accounts are separated, with a separate balance shown for each. Sometimes all debit transactions are shown together, whether on current or capital account, and all credit transactions are put together, in order to show the sources and the uses of foreign exchange. Both ways are useful. The controversy in the arrangement of accounts comes in the definition of surplus or deficit. On the one hand, the total of debits and of credits must be equal. But at the same time we do know that it is rare for the balance of payments to be in equilibrium in the economic sense. Is it possible to separate out some of the accounts that will indicate the direction and extent of disequilibrium?[6] Over the years many attempts have been made to find the most useful and accurate arrangement of accounts that would define the surplus or deficit. Professor Machlup has rounded up some 20 sources that give different estimates of the U.S. balance in 1951, varying from a surplus of $5 billion to a deficit of $1 billion.[7] The variance comes from the definitions of surplus or deficit used, not from the data itself.

[6] Do not make the mistake of thinking that the balance-of-payments disequilibrium can be determined on the basis of the balance-of-payments accounts by themselves. The state of the domestic economy—trends in income, employment, prices, interest rates, and so on—and of the exchange markets is important. Richard N. Cooper argues that the goals of policy should be considered; see his article, "The Balance of Payments in Review," *Journal of Political Economy*, LXXIV, No. 4 (August 1966), 379–95.

[7] *International Payments, Debts, and Gold* (New York: Charles Scribner's Sons, 1964), pp. 140–66.

BASIC BALANCE

Fortunately for us, many of these 20 definitions are not seriously considered by balance-of-payments experts. In fact, discussion centers around three definitions. The first is called the balance on basic transactions. According to this idea, transactions in goods and services, remittances, U.S. government capital flows, and private long-term capital flows are the items that are fairly stable in the short-run but reflect the basic, long-run forces at work in the economy. The other accounts show much more short-run variation, responding quickly to short-run changes in monetary policy and speculative influences, or simply serve to finance the balance on the other items (changes in reserve assets or liabilities). The organization of a balance-of-payments statement constructed to show the basic balance is given in Table 15-4. Note that for each transaction the net debit or credit is to be entered; thus if goods and services showed a $200 credit and a $100 debit, the entry on this summary statement would be +$100. The balance is the net credit or debit resulting from the sum of the first four items; if a credit, the balance of payments shows a surplus, or if a debit, it shows a deficit. The five items below the balance line must be equal in amount but opposite in sign to the items above the line, from our double-entry bookkeeping.

This particular way of computing deficits or surpluses is favored by some writers because it groups together below the balance line items that are either directly under the control of monetary authorities or are heavily influenced by monetary policies (such as short-term capital movements, which respond to changes in the rate of interest). The items above the line reflect basic economics forces—goods and services respond to the demand,

Table 15-4

BALANCE ON BASIC TRANSACTIONS[a]

Goods and services
Remittances
U.S. government grants and loans
Private long-term capital (direct and portfolio)

———

Balance

———

Errors and omissions
Private short-term capital
Foreign holdings of U.S. government securities
Foreign official short-term capital
U.S. reserves: gold, convertible currency, IMF gold-tranche position

[a] This table follows *The Balance of Payments Statistics of the United States*, p. 104.

technological, transportation, and other forces discussed in Part I, for example—or basic political decisions such as affect government grant and loan policy.[8] The claim is that a deficit measured in this way would be an indication of the size of the problem posed for the country's policy tools (apart from monetary policy, whose effects are shown below the line). Other writers employ the balance on basic transaction because they are interested in longer-run trends and feel that this balance excludes the transitory elements in the balance of payments.[9] However, professional enthusiasm for this definition has greatly diminished. The trouble is that there are trends in short-term capital movements and transitory elements in some of the basic accounts—for example, there may be disruptions due to strikes or harvest failures. Furthermore, changes in merchandise trade lead directly to changes in accounts payable and accounts receivable, which means that the same forces affect a "basic" transaction and a short-term capital transaction. And changes in monetary policy may affect the "basic" items as well as the items below the line.[10]

LIQUIDITY BALANCE

The second major approach to a statistical definition of surplus or deficit is called the liquidity concept. Its focus is on the liquidity position of the U.S. authorities: What are the changes in claims on the United States that are subject to sudden withdrawal, and what assets do the authorities have to meet these claims? The arrangement of the balance of payments that answers these questions is presented in Table 15-5. Notice that by contrast with the balance on basic transactions some short-term items appear above the line, if they are regarded as not affecting the liquidity position of the United States. These include private claims on foreigners by U.S. residents, commercial credits, and errors and omissions (which as mentioned earlier, presumably are mostly short-term capital flows.)

Since they are defined differently, the basic and liquidity balances differ: The 1964 balance on basic transactions was a deficit of $359 million, while the liquidity balance in that year was a $2.98 billion deficit. Clearly they give very different impressions of the course of events.

Why would one use the liquidity rather than the basic concept?: According to its proponents, because U.S. policy-makers must pay close attention to all foreign claims that could be quickly withdrawn at the expense of U.S. reserves. To meet these claims the authorities can count only on their official reserve assets, not on claims against foreigners held by private U.S. citizens. Hence, private short-term U.S. capital movements are excluded

---

[8] Lary, *Problems of the United States as World Trader and Banker*, pp. 148–60.
[9] Salant et al., *The United States Balance of Payments in 1968*, pp. 2–9.
[10] *The Balance of Payments Statistics of the United States*, p. 106.

Table 15-5

BALANCE ON LIQUIDITY CONCEPT[a]

Goods and services
Remittances
U.S. government loans and grants
Private long-term capital (direct and portfolio)
U.S. private short-term capital
Foreign commercial credits
Errors and omissions

Balance

Foreign private short-term capital (other than commercial credits)
Foreign holdings of U.S. government securities
Foreign official short-term capital
U.S. reserves: gold, convertible currency, IMF gold-tranche position

[a] This table follows *The Balance of Payments Statistics of The United States*, p. 104.

from the balancing items. And commercial credits are excluded because they are not likely to be quickly withdrawn.

The trouble with this definition is that it leads to such weird results as a deficit in one country without a corresponding surplus in the rest of the world. For example, suppose there are two countries computing their balances of payments according to Table 15-5. Country 1's citizens buy some short-term government bonds in country 2, using gold to pay for them. The entries in country 1 are a credit to gold and a debit to private short-term capital; the first entry is below the line, the second above it. In country 2 there is a debit to gold and a credit to foreign holdings of government securities, but both entries occur below the line and are offsetting. Country 1 has a deficit; country 2 has a balance in its accounts. Hence this measure is not symmetrical. This is an often-cited weakness of the measure. Another is that a flight of domestic capital can give trouble to the reserve position; it is misleading to consider that liquidity depends only on foreign short-term capital compared to reserve assets.[11] It was, however, the definition long used in the official publication of U.S. balance-of-payments data, the *Survey of Current Business*, and it is still presented along with the third of our trio of measures, the balance on the basis of official reserve transactions.

[11] The concept is defended in Walther Lederer, *The Balance on Foreign Transactions: Problems of Definition and Measurement*, Special Papers in International Economics No. 5 (Princeton, N.J.: International Finance Section, Princeton University, 1963). Critics include, inter alia, Charles P. Kindleberger, *Balance-of-Payments Deficits and the International Market for Liquidity*, Essays in International Finance No. 46 (Princeton, N.J.: International Finance Section, Princeton University, 1965); Walter R. Gardner, "An Exchange-Market Analysis of the U.S. Balance of Payments," *International Monetary Fund Staff Papers*, VIII, No. 1 (May 1961), 195–211; and Poul Host-Madsen, "Asymmetries Between Balance of Payments Surpluses and Deficits," *International Monetary Fund Staff Papers*, IX, No. 2 (July 1962), 182–99.

OFFICIAL SETTLEMENTS BALANCE

The concept of a balance on official settlements is the one proposed and favored by the Review Committee for Balance of Payments Statistics. It is an attempt to measure surpluses and deficits by transactions in reserve items on the theory that these transactions measure the amount of official intervention that has been necessary to keep exchange rates stable. The computation of the balance is summarized in Table 15-6. The important difference between this and the liquidity balance is that all private foreign short-term capital items and all foreign official short-term capital except that of monetary authorities goes above the balance line. The effect of this change in organization is to reduce the measured deficit when these items are credited.[12]

In this approach the asymmetries that give one country a deficit without giving another a surplus are not present. And clearly this definition comes closer to describing the events that have required official action than do the other measures. As to its effects on the measurement of the deficit, in 1964 the balance on the official settlements basis was a deficit of $1.224 billion, something less than half the balance on the liquidity basis.

Professional opinion has been somewhat divided about just how good the balance on the official settlements basis is, however. It is very close to the measure suggested by Walter Gardner in his influential work on the exchange-market analysis of the balance of payments.[13] On the other hand,

[12] For example: We have three transactions, a $100 debit in goods and services; a $50 credit in foreign private short-term capital, representing an increase in the foreign ownership of U.S. bank accounts; and a $50 credit in gold, representing the gold outflow necessary to maintain the dollar at a stable foreign exchange rate. Under the two different ways of organizing the accounts, the result in the case of the liquidity concept is:

Goods and services	− $100
Balance	(− $100)
Foreign private short-term capital	+ $50
Gold	+ $50

The balance using the official settlements concept is:

Goods and services	− $100
Foreign private short-term capital	+ $50
Balance	(− $50)
Gold	+ $50

[13] *International Monetary Fund Staff Papers*, VIII. The difference is that Gardner puts below the line U.S. government loans to other governments to compensate for their weak balances of payments. However, *The Balance of Payments Statistics of the United States*, p. 109, does put "special intergovernmental transactions" below the line in some cases, such as advance repayment of loans.

Table 15-6

BALANCE ON OFFICIAL SETTLEMENTS CONCEPT[a]

Goods and services
Remittances
U.S. government loans and grants
U.S. private short-term capital
Foreign commercial credits
Errors and omissions
Foreign private short-term capital (other than commercial credits)
Foreign holdings of U.S. government securities (other than those of official monetary authorities)
Foreign official short-term capital (except that of official monetary authorities)

Balance

Foreign official monetary authorities' holdings of U.S. government securities
Foreign official monetary authorities' short-term capital
U.S. reserves: gold, convertible currency, IMF gold-tranche position

[a] This table follows *The Balance of Payments Statistics of the United States*, p. 104.

a number of distinguished critics find it inadequate. While full understanding of their objections depends on some topics we have not covered yet, a brief reference is not out of place.

One approach is to claim that the organization of a country's balance of payments should depend on the role it plays in international finance. Some currencies—the dollar and the pound—are widely used for payments among countries and are held as part of the reserves of firms and governments around the world. The United States is thus a banker in a sense. And the business of a banker is to provide short-term liabilities (which are assets for his customers) that become the means of payment. Issuing these liabilities does not put a banker in deficit, although it would if international balance-of-payments concepts were applied to his business. Therefore a country that functions as a banker should be treated the same way. Specifically, all foreign short-term capital, including that of foreign monetary authorities, should go above the line—unless by some criterion it is judged that an excessive amount of liabilities to foreigners has been generated. Then the excess would go below the line as a deficit.[14]

A somewhat related interpretation of the United States' role in international finance is the suggestion that the United States has been fulfilling the role of a financial intermediary, exchanging short-term liabilities for

[14] This suggestion is advanced by Lorie Tarshis' book review of *The Balance of Payments Statistics of the United States*, *American Economic Review*, LVI, No. 1 (March 1966), 247–52.

long-term assets. The reason is that in many foreign countries (Europe, Canada, and Japan) businesses wish to issue long-term obligations while savers wish to acquire short-term assets. American savers have no objection to long-term assets, so they buy the long-term obligations of the foreign corporations (which yield a high rate of return). The foreigners in turn put the dollars so acquired into short-term U.S. liabilities. The result and purpose of these capital flows is not to transfer real capital but to balance portfolios. The real capital used by foreign investors is provided by foreign savers; the U.S. capital market is used to provide the desired maturities for savers and investors. Following out this line of thought, capital flows induced by portfolio-balance considerations should go below the line. In this view, the balance of official settlements distinction between official monetary authorities and others is not important.[15] While this is a valuable conception, it is certainly not an easy one to put into statistical practice.

There is, finally, the position that no statistical concept for defining the surplus or deficit can be satisfactory. This is because the statistics measure the transactions that have occurred, while (as in national income analysis) the notion of a surplus or deficit disequilibrium depends on desired spending compared to desired receipts. In theory, the distinction is between autonomous and accommodating payments: autonomous payments that take place no matter the size of other items on the balance of payments and accommodating payments whose function is to fill the gap between autonomous payments and receipts.[16] In practice, the distinction between autonomous and accommodating transactions is so imprecise that it cannot be captured by an arbitrary accounting classification. The result of this position is the attitude that no deficits should be computed or else that all the available concepts should be put forth to the public to indicate just how complicated the matter really is.[17]

APPENDIX: f.o.b. versus c.i.f.

Each of the balance-of-payments accounts presents its own problems of consistent definition and of accurate data collecting; *The Balance of Payments Statistics of the United States* is a gold-mine of information about these problems, how they are presently handled, and how they could be improved. One notable problem in making comparisons between countries should be especially mentioned: the valuation of imports. If one uses, for example the International Monetary Fund's *Balance of Payments*

---

[15] Charles P. Kindleberger, *Balance-of-Payments Deficits and the International Market for Liquidity.*

[16] J. E. Meade, *The Balance of Payments* (New York, Oxford University Press, 1951), Chap. I.

[17] Cooper, *Journal of Political Economy*, LXXIV, 388–90.

Yearbook, he notices that some countries list "imports f.o.b." and others report "imports c.i.f." In the first case, imports are valued at their cost before shipment—that is, free on board the means of transportation. The c.i.f. basis means that the value of imports includes the transportation cost to the importer's port of entry. The c.i.f. basis leads to the anomaly that the world's total of imports is recorded as being greater than the world's total of exports. With sufficient data on transportation it is possible to subtract freight and insurance charges to arrive at an accurate value for imports. Unfortunately these data are difficult to find for many countries that use c.i.f. reporting. In such cases it is necessary to use a rule of thumb such as freight costs are about 10 per cent of the value of imports. For an accurate picture of international trade it would clearly be preferable to put only the f.o.b. cost of imports in the merchandise account and to put freight charges in the service account. More countries currently use the f.o.b. method than was once the case, although some major traders such as Germany still use c.i.f. data.

CHAPTER 16

BALANCE
OF PAYMENTS
ADJUSTMENT

THE BEST WAY TO MEASURE a deficit or surplus in the balance of payments remains in dispute. The fact that these exist and pose problems does not. The next few chapters are devoted to analyzing various aspects of achieving equilibrium in the balance of payments; this chapter covers some preliminary matters.

ECONOMIC MEANING OF BALANCE-OF-PAYMENTS EQUILIBRIUM

To begin with, exactly what does equilibrium in the balance of payments mean? The usual practice in the theory of the subject is to follow the lead of James Meade in the distinction between autonomous transactions and accommodating ones, as explained at the end of Chap. 15. The accommodating transactions are those induced by the state of the balance of payments or are made strictly to fill up gaps between debits and credits in the autonomous items. Equilibrium requires:

1. Putting the accommodating payments below the balance line.
2. Setting the balance at zero.

Otherwise equilibrium cannot exist, for reasons that vary depending on what sort of monetary arrangements prevail. If fixed exchange rates prevail, as is usually the case, an excess of autonomous payments compared to autonomous receipts implies an excess demand for foreign currency. To maintain the existing price of foreign exchange, the official monetary authorities must make an accommodating payment, that is, use some of the country's reserves of gold or foreign exchange, or borrow foreign exchange from someone, or induce someone to hold the excess supply of local currency without putting it on the foreign exchange market. It is the limited availability of these options that makes for disequilibrium. Lacking unlimited gold, other reserves, or borrowing power, something will have to change so that the excess demand for foreign exchange is eliminated. In the more rare case of flexible exchange rates, excess supplies or demands in the foreign exchange market are eliminated by changes in the rate itself. Under the "adjustable peg" regime, the rate may sometimes be changed, but usually attempts are made to change autonomous payments or receipts. And with the gold standard and other rigidly fixed rate schemes, the latter policy is followed exclusively.

It should be made explicit that this formulation of disequilibrium and equilibrium, with its emphasis on policy, is in accord with the theoretical developments stemming from Meade's *Balance of Payments* rather than with the older automatic mechanism of adjustment literature. Although detailed work on this subject is held in abeyance until Chap. 17, the approach of that body of thought may be briefly characterized. An excess of autonomous payments over receipts, for example, was thought of as leading to gold flows or reserve changes on a fixed exchange standard. This in turn led to monetary changes; price level changes; interest rate, investment, and national income changes of a sort that restored equilibrium automatically. But the automatic changes are no longer forthcoming, or are at least attenuated, since the money supply is now generally regulated for the best functioning of the internal economy rather than left to fluctuate according to the state of the balance of payments. The automatic mechanism is of less interest than formerly; it is the policy responses of governments that need analysis.[1]

The simple notion that equilibrium requires a balance of autonomous payments with autonomous receipts has been qualified in various ways. For example, if we are dealing with a deficit, it might be possible to restore payments-receipts equality by imposing import quotas. But some writers would still consider this a disequilibrium situation because quotas (as well as tariffs for balance-of-payments protection) are inefficient, second-best policies. Another possibility would be to restore equality between receipts and payments by reducing the national income, cutting spending on everything including imports. Again, this is sometimes called a disequilibrium situation if the national income is cut below full employment. This usage

---

[1] See, in particular, Robert A. Mundell, "The International Disequilibrium System," *Kyklos*, XIV, No. 2 (1961), pp. 154–72. The famous Brookings Institution study, Salant et al., *The United States Balance of Payments in 1968*, in large part is an exercise in the response of the balance of payments to income and price trends. But it is done in the context of given policies and with the motive of indicating what other policies might be needed.

is often met with but is not universally accepted.[2] An alternative approach is to distinguish between policies and goals. The policy goals are "internal balance"—full employment without inflation—and "external balance"— autonomous payments equal autonomous receipts. The alternative policies, in the broadest generalization, are expenditure-reducing policies and expenditure-switching ones when the current account is the problem. Switching policies change the direction of spending from foreign to domestic goods; reducing policies change the total amount of spending, including that on foreign goods. The problem then is one of choosing the optimum combination of policies. When the capital account is added to the picture, questions of the optimum size of the capital inflow or outflow become important. It then is necessary to look into the ways in which the current account and the capital account adjust to changes in each other, and into the policies—such as controls and interest rates—that influence the size of the capital flows.[3]

So far only the existence of disequilibrium has been assumed, without any attempt to gauge the seriousness of it. But there certainly is a difference in the problem posed by $1 billion deficit if it results on the one hand from a temporary boom in inventory demand or on the other from a permanent replacement of exports by a newly developed substitute abroad. Evaluating the proper policy requires looking into the cause of the external imbalance. The experiences generated by many deficits are summed up in this handy classification of conditions leading to external problems:

1. Long-term changes in real supply or demand conditions, from changes in technology, tastes, factor supplies, and the like. In Part I we assumed that a new equilibrium would be reached, but often it is not easy to do so.

2. Long-term changes in monetary conditions, such as a rapid and continuing inflation in one country.

3. Temporary or short-term changes such as crop failures or changes in demand associated with business cycles.[4]

Each of these cases gives rise to a different type of problem even though the size of the resulting deficits might be comparable. In the case of the short-term problem, it might be preferable to "finance the deficit" rather than adjust

[2] Ragnar Nurkse, *Conditions of International Monetary Equilibrium*, Essays in International Finance No. 4 (Princeton, N.J.: International Finance Section, Princeton University, 1945), is a classic source for these qualifications. They are hotly disputed by Fritz Machlup, "Equilibrium and Disequilibrium: Misplaced Concreteness and Disguised Politics," *Economic Journal*, LXVIII, No. 269 (March 1958), 1–24. Nurkse drew on Germany in the 1920's to illustrate the use of controls and England in the late 1920's and 1930's as a case study in guiding the balance of payments at the expense of a depressed economy.

[3] Meade deals at length with internal and external balance in *The Balance of Payments*. Johnson, *International Trade and Economic Growth*, pp. 153–68, is the source of the expenditure-switching and expenditure-reducing distinctions.

[4] This classification of types of disequilibria is used in *International Monetary Arrangements: The Problem of Choice* (Princeton, N.J.: International Finance Section, Princeton University, 1964), pp. 43–48.

to it and then have to readjust later. Financing a deficit means to use up reserves or to borrow from official monetary authorities or others abroad. It is the long-run cases that pose the severe adjustment problems.

POLICY INSTRUMENTS AND POLICY TARGETS

A final important point for a preliminary survey of balance-of-payments theory is this: The work on policy models has developed the important proposition that in general the number of policy instruments used

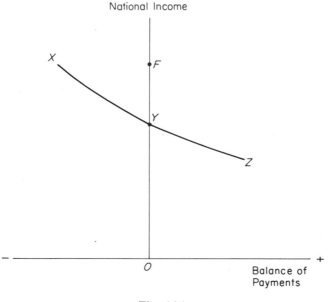

Fig. 16-1

must be equal to the number of policy goals, or else there is a good chance that some of the policy goals will not be fulfilled. To illustrate the problems involved, suppose that the goals are internal and external balance. These are shown in Fig. 16-1 as zero on the balance-of-payments axis and *F* (for full employment) on the national income axis. If the only available tool is monetary policy, the outcome might be illustrated by the line *XYZ*. At full employment, there is a balance-of-payments deficit, shown by point *X*. The appropriate monetary policy to correct the deficit is a tight-money policy; higher interest rates improve the capital account and, by reducing the national income, discourage spending on imports. But the return to equilibrium in the balance of payments by this technique is deflationary. At point *Y*, then, meeting the external balance goal has moved the country away from its internal balance target. What is needed is another policy tool to shift the XYZ line up. Exchange depreciation or tariffs, for example, would reduce the deficit at full employment, and both targets could be met. In general, as many policy instruments are needed as there are policy targets.[5]

[5] See Jan Tinbergen, *On the Theory of Economic Policy* (Amsterdam: North-Holland Publishing Company, 1952).

CHAPTER 17

BALANCE-OF-PAYMENTS ADJUSTMENT WITH FIXED EXCHANGE RATES

THE SIZE AND SIGN of the balance in the balance of payments depends on many things—the national income, prices of exports relative to imports and domestic goods, interest rates, wages, productivities, exchange rates, commercial policies, and so on. To make sense out of these, it is necessary to start with simple models incorporating only a few of the variables. In particular, this chapter is concerned with situations where exchange rates are held fixed. This is the most realistic, if not the most desirable, treatment of exchange rates, since there is great reluctance to change the rate in most countries today.

CLASSICAL MECHANISM

The grandfather of theories about balance-of-payments adjustment under fixed exchange rates was the classical price-specie flow mechanism. (This is sometimes called Hume's Law, from David Hume's early presentation of the idea in *Political Discourses*, 1752.) In the simplest formulation, a deficit in the balance of payments causes an outflow of gold. The money supply is reduced, which sets up corrective forces. These are sometimes summarized as a fall in prices in the deficit country and a rise in the surplus country, but one has to be careful not to fall into the error of interpreting this to mean that commodity X will sell at lower prices in the deficit country. Arbitrage keeps the price the same in both countries (or keeps it spread apart by the total of transport costs and tariffs). It is preferable to be more specific and to identify the corrective forces:

1. A fall in aggregate demand in the gold-losing country and a rise in the gold-gaining one, induced by changes in cash balances, interest rates, and other macroeconomic influences that are the subject of this chapter.

195

    2. Changes in wages and the prices of other inputs (which, again, can be at different levels in the two countries only if there is no migration or capital flows).

With a fixed exchange rate, this changes the comparative advantage limits along the lines of the model we discussed in the section on money wages and exchange rates in Chap. 2. In the terms of that Ricardian example, suppose that the exchange rate is 1 escudo/pound, with Portuguese wages at 2,000 escudos/year, British wages at 1,000 pounds/year, and Ricardo's men per year requirements for each good for the production functions. From the resulting prices, as shown in Table 2-1, Portugal would be running a deficit. Wages might be sticky in Portugal and resist decreases in response to unemployment in the wine industry specifically as well as the economy generally. But British wages are pretty sure to rise, at least to the point where Portugal can sell her wine in England. That requires the cost of production of English wine to rise to at least 160,000 pounds. Using the equations of Chap. 2, we have $P_W^E = 160,000 = 120$ men/year $\cdot$ wages^E. Solving for the unknown wages yields wages$^E = 160,000/120 = 1,333\frac{1}{3}$ pounds/year. When British wages have risen at least that far, the Portuguese can again be shipping wine and are on the way to solving their payments problems.

    More complicated formulations do not destroy the essence of the model. For example, the fall in the money supply at home affects the rate of interest as well as other prices. It leads to a rise in the rate of interest, which attracts a corrective inflow of capital. Or another angle to work with is the effects on the money supply when the fixed exchange rates do not depend on the gold standard. We shall see that the result is still a fall in the money supply. However, this model is now mostly of historical interest. Other methods of adjustment came to be emphasized because of the downward stickiness of prices and wages and the reluctance of governments to accept either deflation or inflation caused by the balance of payments. And the great impact of the Keynesian revolution in economics generally was reflected in the development of models of national income/balance-of-payments relations. These models may be used in either automatic adjustment or policy-oriented theory; we begin with the former.

SIMPLE KEYNESIAN MECHANISM

    In the simplest model, drastic assumptions are made that will later be relaxed. These are:

    1. Prices and wages are rigid.
    2. The interest rate does not change.
    3. The exchange rate is fixed.

4. There are no autonomous capital flows, but the country has enough reserves that it may make any amount of accommodating payments to settle balance-of-payments deficits.

5. The country is too small to affect incomes abroad to any significant degree, so that it is possible to ignore feedback effects from abroad.

Assumptions 1 and 2 might be regarded as applying to an extreme depression where the liquidity trap is operative. The others are simply for convenience at this point.

The first step is to define the real net national product, Y, in terms of the groups that purchase the goods and services:

$$Y = C + I + G + X. \tag{17-1}$$

In this formulation, C, I, G, and X have the usual meanings of real consumption, net investment, government spending, and exports. The first three refer to the spending by these groups on domestic goods and services; any spending by consumers, investors, or the government on foreign products (denoted by M for imports) does not add to our net national product (NNP) and so is excluded from Eq. **(17-1)**.[1] Exports include not only shipments of products and payments for services such as transportation but also payments received from abroad by our factors of production in the form of wages, interest, dividends, and so on.

The next question is what do the component parts of NNP depend on? Generally, C and I depend on national income, the interest rate, and relative prices at home and abroad; G is usually taken as autonomous but sometimes may be plausibly thought of as a function of national income; and X depends on national incomes abroad and relative prices. For the initial development of the model, however, it is permissible to assume that I, G, and X are fixed autonomously and that consumption is a function only of income. Imports also depend on income; a rise in the NNP typically leads to more spending on everything, including imports.

Of course, the incomes earned in producing the net national product are spent by the income earners on various things: consumption, imports, saving (denoted by S), and taxes (denoted by T). In equilibrium, the amount produced by the economy has to equal the desired amounts purchased by the various groups, and this in turn has to equal the desired disposition of their incomes by the income earners. This is expressed by:

$$Y = C + I + G + X = C + S + T + M. \tag{17-2}$$

By subtracting C from both sides of the right-hand equation in **(17-2)**, the

---

[1] Sometimes an alternative formulation is used wherein C, I, and G stand for *total* spending by these groups. To show domestic net national product, it is necessary to subtract M; generally it is subtracted from X to give a term called net foreign investment. Net national product is then expressed as $Y = C + I + G + (X - M)$.

familiar proposition that equilibrium requires equality between the injections into the circular flow of income and leakages away from it results.

$$I + G + X = S + T + M. \tag{17-3}$$

The left-hand side represents additions to the spending on domestic output, and the right-hand side is subtractions from the flow of spending. The flow can be constant only if the subtractions are exactly offset by the additions.

Another useful way to view this equilibrium condition is to rearrange it with all the foreign-trade items on one side and all the domestic items on the other:

$$X - M = S + (T - G) - I. \tag{17-4}$$

Since taxes minus government spending is really government saving, the equilibrium condition says that the balance on current account (equals the balance of payments under our assumptions) equals total saving minus domestic investment. Any imbalance on current account must have its counterpart in a divergence between saving and domestic investment; if there is an export surplus, saving will exceed domestic investment, and the converse for deficits. In Chap. 18 this notion is developed into the "absorption approach."

The balance-of-payments/national income relationships can be visualized as going in the direction of either a change in the NNP (from, for example, a change in I or G) to a change in the balance of payments, or a change in the balance of payments leading to a change in national income. If I rises, Y must rise far enough to induce a new, higher level of saving and imports to offset the higher investment. The balance of payments worsens in this case. Or if X rises autonomously, Y is increased until the newly induced leakages of S and M equal the new injection of X. The rise in M cuts into the balance-of-payments surplus, bringing some adjustment. More precisely, to find the effects of a rise in domestic investment, differentiate Eq. (17-1), holding G and X constant:

$$dY/dI = (dC/dY \ dY/dI) + 1. \tag{17-5}$$

This gives the familiar multiplier, $dY/dI = 1/(1 - dC/dY)$. But since any change in income must be disposed of either in consumption, saving, or imports (assuming taxes are fixed), an equivalent version of the multiplier is $dY/dI = 1/(dS/dY + dM/dY)$. Expressed in the jargon of marginal propensities, the multiplier in this case is $1/(MPM + MPS)$, where MPS is the marginal propensity to save and MPM is the marginal propensity to import. Finally, the change in imports resulting from the increase in domestic investment is given by the marginal propensity to import multiplied by the change in income, that is, by $dM/dI = dM/dY \ dY/dI$.

For example, suppose that the marginal propensity to save is 1/10 and the marginal propensity to import is 2/10. The multiplier is $1/(3/10) = 3\frac{1}{3}$. If investment increased by 10, income rises by $33\frac{1}{3}$. Imports increase by $2/10 \times 33\frac{1}{3} = 6.6$, approximately, and the balance of payments deteriorates by that much. If exports had increased by 10 instead of investment, the multiplier and the change in imports would have been the same. In this case the rise in imports would have gone part way toward correcting the surplus in the balance of payments.

Three basic ideas emerge from this simple analysis. In the first place, there is a corrective mechanism at work when incomes rise because of a rise in exports. By changing the signs in the example above, it is easy to see that the mechanism also works if exports fall; the resulting deficit is partly eliminated by an induced fall in imports. But in the next place, this mechanism does not work if the movements in national income are caused by domestic spending changes; income changes can be a cause of balance-of-payments deficits, just as much as changes in comparative advantage, factor supplies, and the like. Finally, notice that income changes can be used as a tool to correct the balance of payments. If there is a deficit of about 6.6, a fiscal policy of cutting government spending by 10 would reduce Y by $33\frac{1}{3}$, which in turn would eliminate the deficit. Or the interest rate could be raised to cut I, or taxes could be increased to cut C, with the same effect.

While these are fundamental propositions, they are by no means the only ones contained in the national income models. Indeed, some of them—in particular the result of incomplete adjustment—do not carry over to more complete models where some of the simplifying assumptions are modified.

REFINEMENTS: FOREIGN REPERCUSSIONS

One of the important developments comes from modifying assumption 5 above. Suppose, on the contrary, that developments in one country do affect conditions in others significantly. If the United States imports more from France, the French NNP rises. With a higher income, the French import more. To the extent that these extra imports are derived from the United States, the U.S. income rises and in turn its imports increase. These feedback ideas are a prominent part of contemporary balance-of-payments studies; for example, the Brookings Institution study to which we have so often referred puts heavy emphasis on feedback considerations.

Models incorporating feedback must be a little more complicated than the previous one because the national income of all countries concerned must be included. For simplicity, a two-country model can be presented. No longer are exports fixed autonomously; they vary with the national income of the trading partner. Using subscripts 1 and 2 to identify the variables of countries 1 and 2, the national income model becomes

$$Y_1 = C_1(Y_1) + I_1 + G_1 + X_1(Y_2) + a_1$$
$$Y_2 = C_2(Y_2) + I_2 + G_2 + X_2(Y_1).$$

(17-6)

The terms involving parentheses are functional relations—C_1 is a function of Y, and so on. The term a_1 is what is called a shift parameter. It is given the value of zero initially; then if one of the spending schedules of country 1 changes—I increases, or any of the schedules—it can be represented by a change in a_1. What we want to do is see how the incomes in both countries respond to the change in a_1, and also what the effect is on the balance of payments.

The answer is found, of course, by differentiating Eqs. **(17-6)** with respect to a_1. This gives

$$\frac{dY_1}{da_1} = \frac{dC_1}{dY_1}\frac{dY_1}{da_1} + \frac{dX_1}{dY_2}\frac{dY_2}{da_1} + 1$$
$$\frac{dY_2}{da_1} = \frac{dC_2}{dY_2}\frac{dY_2}{da_1} + \frac{dX_2}{dY_1}\frac{dY_1}{da_1}.$$

(17-7)

These two equations in two unknowns can be solved by substitution or by Cramer's rule for dY_1/da_1 and dY_2/da_1. The result is

$$\frac{dY_1}{da_1} = \frac{1 - C_2'}{(1 - C_1')(1 - C_2') - X_1'X_2'}$$
$$\frac{dY_2}{da_1} = \frac{X_2'}{(1 - C_1')(1 - C_2') - X_1'X_2'}.$$

(17-8)

(To simplify the notation, primes are used to indicate derivatives; of course thése derivatives are the marginal propensities.) A shift in one of country 1's spending schedules affects both countries' incomes in ways that depend on all the marginal propensities. This is the characteristic of open economies: One's national income depends on happenings abroad.

Since imports depend on income, the balance of payments is bound to be affected. It is easy to find out exactly how by writing country 1's balance of payments as

$$BP_1 = X_1(Y_2) - X_2(Y_1)$$

(17-9)

and differentiating with respect to a_1:

$$\frac{d(BP_1)}{da_1} = \frac{dX_1}{dY_2}\frac{dY_2}{da_1} - \frac{dX_2}{dY_1}\frac{dY_1}{da_1} = \frac{X_1'X_2' - X_2'(1 - C_2')}{(1 - C_1')(1 - C_2') - X_1'X_2'}.$$

(17-10)

The change in the balance of payments depends on the national income changes and the marginal propensity to import in each country.

·   For a numerical example of how this works, suppose that $C_1' = .6$, $X_2' = .2$, $C_2' = .5$, and $X_1' = .3$. By substituting in the appropriate equations, the values of the unknowns can be found to be approximately $dY_1/da_1 = 3.6$, $dY_2/da_1 = 1.4$, and $d(BP_1)/da_1 = -.3$. The rise in spending in country 1 leads to a multiple rise in income at home and abroad and brings a deterioration in country 1's balance of payments. For comparison with the case where there are no feedback effects, the multiplier in the original simple model is 2.5, yielding a balance-of-payments effect of $-.5$. Clearly it makes quite a difference to take account of foreign repercussions.

A good source of empirical examples of the way these ideas work is research done at the International Monetary Fund.[2] On the basis of recent data fitted to a somewhat more complex model than the one just worked out (three "countries" are used—the United States, Western Europe, and the rest of the world), it is estimated that a $1 billion increase in the U.S. GNP would worsen the current account by $34 million, holding everything else constant. And if the rise in GNP took place in Western Europe, the U.S current account would improve by $55 million.

REFINEMENTS: THE MONEY SUPPLY AND THE RATE OF INTEREST

Changes in the real value of national income are of major importance, but they seldom occur by themselves. One of the things that is bound to change is the money supply, and this has implications for the rate of interest and for capital flows. Under fixed exchange rate systems a deficit reduces the domestic money supply, while a surplus increases it. The exact mechanism depends on the institutional arrangements of each country's monetary system, and many sequences are possible. For example, suppose the only international transaction is a U.S. import from France, paid by the importer writing a check on his bank account. (Notice that this is a capital inflow for the United States, and a reduction in the domestic money supply.) The French exporter then sells the dollars for francs, which tends to lower the franc price of dollars in the French foreign exchange market. The French monetary authorities have to buy the dollars in order to support the fixed exchange rate, which increases the French domestic money supply. The French authorities may then sell the dollars to the U.S. Treasury for gold, if they wish, which will change the short-term capital inflow into a gold outflow. The gold outflow reduces the reserves of the U.S. banking authorities, and may, if carried far enough, force a further contraction of the domestic

---

[2] R. R. Rhomberg and L. Boissonneault, "Effects of Income and Price Changes on the U.S. Balance of Payments," *Staff Papers*, XI, No. 1 (March 1964), 59–124.

money supply. At the same time, either the dollars (if not converted) or the gold can serve as the basis for a further expansion of the French money supply. Of course, if the authorities wish to they can offset or sterilize the effects on the money supplies—the United States by open-market purchases and France by open-market sales, for example. As a matter of fact, they often wish to, but this is a problem that should be saved for a moment.[3]

The changed money supply ordinarily changes the rate of interest. Circumstances in which the rate of interest would remain constant do occur: Keynesian liquidity traps, central bank pegging of the rate, or international capital mobility so perfect that it prevents the country from deviating from the world rate of interest. Now, however, we are going to follow up the implications of changing rates of interest.

Two effects follow from changing the rate of interest. Unless the investment demand curve is very inelastic, a higher rate of interest reduces domestic investment, with a multiplier effect on income and a reduction in imports. Second, foreign capital may be attracted by the higher interest rates, and our capital exports reduced by the prospects of higher interest at home. Both effects improve the balance of payments.

A convenient way to handle the relations among trade, income, the balance of payments, and the interest rate is to use a generalization of the *IS-LM* diagrams of macroeconomics. In a closed economy, with no foreign trade, the *IS* curve shows the combinations of the rate of interest and the level of national income that maintain equilibrium in the market for goods and services. For example, point *A* in Fig. 17-1(a) shows one equilibrium point at a high rate of interest and a low level of national income. Equilibrium requires, of course, that $S = I$. *B* is another possible equilibrium point; here the higher level of *Y* has induced more saving, and to maintain equilibrium the interest rate must fall to induce more investment. Point *C*, by contrast, is a disequilibrium point. Here $S > I$, and at a constant interest rate *Y* will fall to restore equilibrium at a lower level of *S*.

The two variables, the interest rate and income, also determine equilibrium in another important market, the market for money and assets. The demand for money depends on the level of national income, which governs the transactions demand, and the interest rate, which determines how much money is demanded for liquidity purposes. Equilibrium requires that the supply of money equals the demand for it. If point *A* in Fig. 17-1(b) is one

---

[3] A good exercise is to recast the steps in this paragraph into T-accounts, assuming some convenient reserve ratio and noticing that the transfer of ownership of dollar bank accounts to the French authorities may reduce U.S. commercial bank reserves if the French prefer to check the dollars out of the commercial banks and redeposit them in the Federal Reserve bank. *Examples of other exercises:* Suppose the U.S. importer pays with francs that he buys for dollars in the New York foreign exchange market; or suppose he pays with a kind of promissory note called a bill of exchange that the French exporter sells to his bank.

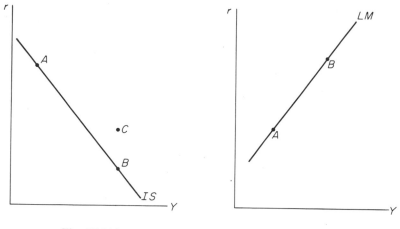

Fig. 17-1(a)   Fig. 17-1(b)

equilibrium position, another equilibrium with the same supply of money
could be found at a higher level of national income. But, as point *B* indicates.
a higher interest rate would be needed. The higher income increases the
transactions demand for money, and to keep the total demand equal to the
given money supply, the interest rate must be higher to reduce the liquidity
demand.

Considering the money market and the goods and services markets
together, as in Fig. 17-1(c), there is one interest rate and level of income
that brings equilibrium in both markets. This is point *A*. Another combination of variables, such as *B*, might gave equilibrium in one market, but
since the other is out of equilibrium the interest rate and the level of income
will change to restore both markets simultaneously to equilibrium.

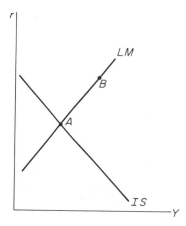

Fig. 17-1(c)

In the open economy, Eq. (17-3) tells us that the $I = S$ equilibrium condition is to be modified into $I + X + G = S + T + M$. Correspondingly, the IS curve must be changed into an XIG-MST curve, along which the injections equal the leakages. This is shown with a negative slope in Fig. 17-2, for this reason: Suppose equilibrium prevails at point A. Then if income increases for some reason, imports, saving, and taxes would all increase. More injections are needed to restore equilibrium. A fall in the rate of interest, which increases investment, is called for.

The conditions of monetary equilibrium remain the same as in the closed economy, so the LM curve is unchanged. But with the open economy there is a third market to worry about: the foreign exchange market. Equilibrium here requires external balance in the sense of Chap. 16—the balance on autonomous trade and capital items equal to zero. The interest rate—national income combinations that give external balance are shown along line BB in Fig. 17-2. Like the LM curve, this curve is upward sloping: A rise in income at a constant interest rate increases imports, giving a negative balance. To correct this, a rise in the rate of interest is needed with its corrective effect on the capital account.

Overall equilibrium requires that all three curves intersect at the same point—point A in the diagram.[4]

To see how the diagram works, suppose that the home country has an autonomous increase in imports because of the development of new products abroad. The BB line shifts to the left; external balance requires that income must fall in order to induce a drop in imports to offset the autonomous increase in imports. (This is shown by the dashed $B'B'$ line in Fig. 17-2.) For the same reason, XIG-MST must also shift to the left, to a new position such as XIG'-MST'. Point A is now a disequilibrium point; there is both a balance-of-payments deficit and a deflationary gap. Now we know that with a fixed exchange rate system, the balance-of-payments deficit reduces the money supply. LM accordingly shifts to the left; it has to shift so that the transactions demand for money will be cut down to equal the reduced money supply. This shift continues as long as there is a balance-of-payments deficit. Finally, general equilibrium is restored at A', with a lower national

[4] Versions of this type of diagram are given in Jaroslav Vanek, *International Trade: Theory and Economic Policy* (Homewood, Ill.: Richard D. Irwin, Inc., 1962), and in Mundell, *Kyklos*, XIV. Note that in the literature Y is sometimes regarded as money income and sometimes as the volume of domestic output at constant prices. So far in this chapter prices are held rigid by assumption, but the distinction will become relevant later on. If Y is interpreted as referring to money income, the spending schedules shift around when prices change unless money illusion is present. For example, if prices fall, the Pigou effect may come into play; the real value of monetary assets is increased, so people consume more. This implies that XIG-MST would shift to the right. On the other hand, if Y is interpreted as real income, all variables are deflated by a price index, including the money supply. The LM curve then shifts around as prices change, since the LM curve as drawn applies to a fixed supply of money. Furthermore, in this case equilibrium at more than full employment is not possible.

income and a changed rate of interest. A policy of sterilization of the gold or reserves outflow, which would maintain a constant money supply and hence result in no change in *LM*, would give an equilibrium in the products market at *A''*, still leaving some deficit in the balance of payments to be corrected or financed by some means.

This analysis shows the dilemma of fixed exchange rate systems. If *A* is at full employment income, both *A'* and *A''* involve the sacrifice of some

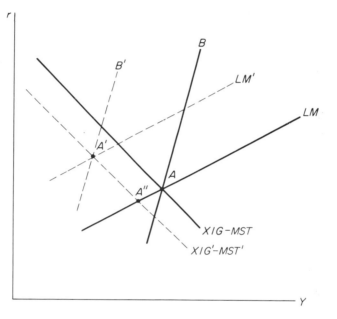

Fig. 17-2

income and employment. At *A'* external balance is restored but internal balance is missing. At *A''* neither external nor internal balance exists; equilibrium in the products market is there, but internal balance as defined in Chap. 16 means equilibrium at full employment without inflation. Internal balance would mean a still bigger deficit in the balance of payments. There is indeed a conflict between the requirements of internal and external balance in the model as developed so far.

The response of the balance of payments to the rate of interest is of considerable importance. If a rise in the interest rate did not attract more foreign capital or reduce the outflow of domestic capital, the *BB* line would be vertical. A rise in income would cause a deficit, but this could not be corrected by a rise in the interest rate. The deficit could be closed only by again cutting the national income (ignoring for the moment commercial policy, exchange rate changes, or other devices). The different components of the capital account probably are not all affected in the same way by a change in the interest rate. Short-term capital movements might be much more quickly affected by international interest rate differentials than long-term ones, which respond to general profitability considerations as well as being heavily influenced by institutional considerations.[5]

A considerable amount of empirical knowledge has been developed on the statistical relations between capital flows and interest rates, stimulated by attempts to find causes and remedies for dollar surplus.[6] The evidence is that different types of capital movements do indeed display quite different degrees of responsiveness. Items such as bank loans to foreign official institutions, to foreign commercial banks, and to other foreigners seem to be related to the flows of trade as far as underdeveloped countries are concerned, but to show a significant relation to interest rates as far as Europe and Canada are involved. This has not been a large quantity, however; Cohen's estimate was that perhaps $50 million to $150 million of these items could be influenced by interest rates. The short-term dollar claims of U.S. nonfinancial corporations were quite sensitive to interest rate changes and showed a large increase of nearly $1 billion after 1960. By contrast, the foreign currency claims of banks and nonfinancial corporations seemed dominated by speculation on the course of exchange rates. Overall, interest rate changes did change capital flows and the balance of payments. Stein's regression analysis, covering 1958–1962, led him to conclude that at equal interest rates in the United States and the United Kingdom there would be a capital inflow into the United States of $691 million per year, which would fall by $462 million if the U.S. interest rate were to become 1 per cent less than the U.K. rate. Speculation was eliminated statistically in this calculation. We

[5] Professor Kindleberger's analogy is that long-term capital flows in deep ditches rather than broad rivers. *International Economics*, p. 386. Recently a number of writers have applied portfolio balance theory to international finance; their analysis suggests that the *BB* line may not be very responsive to interest rate changes. The reason is that in this approach an interest rate change does not induce a continuing flow of capital; rather, the effect is to change the desired proportions of holdings of domestic and of foreign securities. The interest rate differential between countries is only one factor influencing the desired proportions. Others are total wealth, risk differentials, correlation of returns, and tastes. When one variable—such as the interest rate differential—changes, the desired composition of the portfolio changes. Capital will flow internationally until the desired portfolio holdings are achieved and will then stop (or in a dynamic model will return to previous levels). See H. G. Grubel, "Internationally Diversified Portfolios," *American Economic Review*, LVIII (December 1968), 1299–1314.

[6] Philip W. Bell, "Private Capital Movements and the U.S. Balance-of-Payments Position," in Joint Economic Committee, *Factors Affecting the United States Balance of Payments*, 87th Congress, 2nd Session (Washington, D.C.: U.S. Government Printing Office, 1962); Peter B. Kenen, "Short-Term Capital Movements and the U.S. Balance of Payments," in Joint Economic Committee, *Hearings: The United States Balance of Payments*," Part I, 88th Congress, 1st Session (Washington, D.C.: U.S. Government Printing Office, 1963); Benjamin J. Cohen, "A Survey of Capital Movements and Findings Regarding Their Interest Sensitivity," in *ibid.*; and Jerome L. Stein, "International Short-Term Capital Movements," *American Economic Review*, LV, No. 1 (March 1965), 40–66.

are thus justified in drawing the *BB* line as we did. The fact that the balance of payments does respond to the interest rate means that interest rate changes are a tool that policy-makers may use to try to achieve their goals; the implications of this are saved for Chap. 18.

For some countries, such as perhaps Canada vis-a-vis the United States, it is not possible for the domestic interest rate to vary independently because capital markets are tightly integrated. A small fall in the domestic rate below that of the world or the dominant capital market would set off a capital outflow, and a small rise, an inflow.[7] In this case the *BB* line is horizontal, as in Fig. 17-3. That is, balance-of-payments equilibrium must be consistent with the world level of interest rates—higher or lower domestic rates cause a capital flow that continues until the rate is changed. Suppose, for example, that the authorities believe that the level of national income shown by the equilibrium at *E* is too low and consequently expand the money supply, shifting *LM* to *LM'*. At *E'* there is a balance-of-payments deficit caused by the capital outflow seeking higher interest abroad. The deficit reduces the money supply, as we have seen, and *LM'* shifts back to *LM*. The authorities

---

[7] It has been urged that integration of capital markets should be actively fostered in the interest of easier achievement of equilibrium by James C. Ingram, "A Proposal for Financial Integration in the Atlantic Community," in Joint Economic Committee, *Factors Affecting the United States Balance of Payments.* A prediction that European and American capital markets will become increasingly integrated is found in Charles P. Kindleberger, "European Economic Integration and the Development of a Single Financial Center for European Capital," *Weltwirtschaftliches Archiv,* XC, No. 2 (July 1963), 189–209. This development is being slowed down by the attempts of the United States to control capital outflow through the interest equalization tax (an excise tax on U.S. purchases of new or outstanding foreign stocks and bonds, imposed in 1963) and the "voluntary restraint" program that since 1965 has asked banks, financial institutions, and nonfinancial corporations to limit their capital outflows. These programs are discussed in papers by A. F. Brimmer and Jack N. Behrman in *The Journal of Finance,* XXI, No. 2 (May 1966). A development that has had considerable influence in tying interest rates closer together is the "Euro-dollar market." This consists of a complicated network of deposits and loans denominated in dollars but handled through Canadian, U.K., and European banks (including foreign branches of U.S. banks.) A corporation in Belgium earns dollars through exports; rather than converting these into Belgian francs or holding the dollars in New York, it deposits dollars in a Belgian bank. The bank now has an equal dollar asset and a dollar liability. It may in turn lend dollars to other corporations for financing trade or investment or it may lend them to other banks who need the dollars for liquidity. The original depositor earns interest, which he could not do on demand deposits in the United States, and which is likely to be higher than could be earned on short-term investments in the United States. The bank, of course, earns interest on its loans. Note that the bank's lending involves creating Euro-dollars. The point of importance for us is that the depositors and lenders in the market come from many countries, determining the interest rates in the market on the basis of supply-and-demand forces from all the countries, and in turn reducing the interest rate differentials in all the countries participating in the market. A clear textbook discussion of Euro-dollars is in Leland B. Yeager, *International Monetary Relations* (New York: Harper & Row, Publishers, 1966); a series of descriptions and analyses of the development of the market is given by Oscar L. Altman in articles in *Staff Papers,* VIII, IX, X, and XII; and annual data are to be found in the *Annual Reports* of the Bank for International Settlements (Basle, Switzerland). Their 38th *Annual Report* for 1967–1968, p. 154, estimates that $16 billion circulated through the market in 1967.

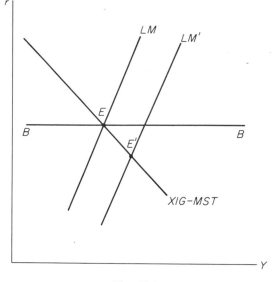

Fig. 17-3

can continue to expand the money supply as long as they have any foreign currency reserves to sell to cover the deficit, of course, but under fixed exchange rates with capital moving freely monetary policy is not a potent device to influence the national income.[8]

REFINEMENTS: THE PRICE LEVEL

Among the assumptions made early in the chapter was the hypothesis that prices did not vary when the national income changed. As a matter of fact, the real value of NNP and the general price level are related to one another, as work on the Phillips curve has shown. It is also true that changes in prices are one of the causes of deficits and may be used as a policy device to try to correct deficits.[9]

One particularly appealing approach to the analysis of the combination of income changes and price changes is to make relative prices a determinant of consumption and imports in Eq. **(17-6)**, along with national income. Then it is possible to work out the effects of price changes on national incomes and the balance of payments.[10] The effects depend on both marginal

[8] See Robert A. Mundell, "Capital Mobility and Stabilization Policy under Fixed and Flexible Exchange Rates," *Canadian Journal of Economics and Political Science,* XXIX, No. 4 (November 1963), 475–85.

[9] "Continued price stability at home, contrasted with the upward trend in prices abroad, will create an increasingly favorable climate for American exports . . . ." President John F. Kennedy, *Message to Congress on the U.S. Balance of Payments,* July 18, 1963.

[10] See, for example, Vanek, *International Trade: Theory and Economic Policy,* pp. 124–30, for a complete exposition.

propensities and price elasticities, as becomes apparent in the following example: Suppose that the price level in the United States rises relative to European prices. In the best Hume's Law tradition, Americans should increase their purchases in Europe, while Europeans buy fewer U.S. goods. If the levels of national income are provisionally held constant for a moment, the effects on the balance of payments depends on the elasticities of demand for the other countries' products—a result that comes from the stability analysis of Chap. 3. In the example at hand, the U.S. balance of payments deteriorates in stable trading situations. But this in turn changes the levels of national income—down in the United States, up in Europe. Then U.S. imports fall and Europe's rise, so some correction is brought to the adverse balance of payments.[11]

The heavy weight given to price changes in recent thought about the balance of payments is illustrated in The Brookings Institution's report, *The United States Balance of Payments in 1968*. Their projection was based on:

1. First calculating what the response of imports to national income changes and to changes in domestic prices relative to foreign export prices had been in recent years.

2. Then projecting likely price changes, based on an assumed growth of national income and on recent trends in productivity, labor forces, and the like.

3. Finally applying the national income and price data to the elasticities and marginal propensities found in the first step.

The results of this research are illustrated by some of the data that are reported in the book: for example, the calculation that a $1 billion increase in real U.S. GNP leads to a rise in imports from Europe of $15.5 million; or that a doubling of U.S. prices, while prices in the rest of the world (excluding Europe) remain constant, would raise U.S. imports by $2.69 billion.[12] A more recent study, along much the same lines, shows that in recent experience a 1 per cent rise in U.S. domestic prices worsens the current account by $91 million, while a 1 per cent rise in U.S. export prices worsens the current account by $55 million.[13]

The effects of price changes are complicated by several additional but

[11] This sort of sequential analysis helps make clear the fact that income and price changes are interrelated and is used, for example, by Sidney S. Alexander, "Effects of a Devaluation: A Simplified Synthesis of Elasticities and Absorption Approaches," *American Economic Review*, XLIX, No. 1 (March 1959), 22–42. It is sometimes difficult to know when to end the sequence in a verbal exposition, however. For example, both Europe and the United States might be imagined to have a Phillips curve relating income and prices—the higher the national income, the faster the rate of increase in the price level. Then the income changes lead to price changes in the same direction, giving a further correction to the adverse balance of payments. In Vanek's model, referred to in footnote 10, simultaneous rather than sequential interactions of price and income changes are analyzed, and the results are not a simple addition of the effects of elasticities and marginal propensities.

[12] Salant et al., *The United States Balance of Payments in 1968*, pp. 267–68.

[13] Rhomberg and Boissonneault, *Staff Papers*, XI.

familiar factors that can be mentioned without dwelling on them at length. One is that elasticities are lower in the short run than in the long run, so that price effects may take several years to work themselves out. Another is that general price deflation is out of the question in today's industrial economies, while price inflation may be more or less successfully resisted. General price level changes between countries may therefore be fairly limited, but there may be significant changes in specific prices—caused by tariffs, for example, or by discriminating monopolists who engage in dumping in the export market. A point not so familiar in general economics, but the subject of much discussion in international finance, is the relation of the propensity to consume to the terms of trade. A change in country 1's price level occurs, for example; let us suppose that as a result its export prices rise and the terms of trade improve. The "real" income corresponding to a given volume of domestic output therefore is increased; since foreign products may be purchased relatively more cheaply, a given amount of domestic output exchanges for more foreign products. It has been argued that since people save more at higher real incomes, the propensity to consume would shift down in country 1 and up in country 2. Presumably the propensities to import are affected the same way, so that these spending changes improve country 1's balance of payments.[14]

Finally, the student of balance-of-payments adjustment has to pay some attention to microeconomic reactions as well as the macroeconomic variables that bulk so large in the theory. Most of the reactions contemplated by the theory of comparative advantage fit in this category. For example, suppose a deficit develops because technological progress abroad has changed comparative advantage so that a product formerly exported is now on the import list. If the domestic industry can innovate in its turn, it may recapture the market; or if displaced resources move into other lines where comparative advantages exist, the deficit can be eliminated. A very obvious example of this kind of response is the development of the U.S. compact car in response to the success of small European cars. The development of pecan-shelling machinery to compete with imported hand-shelled pecans, the stimulus to the U.S. semiconductor industry (a branch of electronics) of Japanese competition, and U.S. production of lightweight bicycles are other examples.[15] The hope of the pro-Common Market groups in the United Kingdom that exposure to competition from Europe would stimulate U.K. industry is

---

[14] See Svend Laursen and L. A. Metzler, "Flexible Exchange Rates and the Theory of Employment," *Review of Economics and Statistics*, XXXII, No. 4 (November 1950), 281–99, for the paper that started a long debate on the existence and importance of this effect. The current judgment is that it is not very important; see Corden, *Recent Developments in the Theory of International Trade*, p. 22.

[15] The pecan example is described in Kindleberger, *Foreign Trade and the National Economy*, p. 114; the semiconductor case comes from Lary, *Problems of the United States as World Trade and Banker*, p. 116.

based on experiences such as these. The microeconomic responses, however, are bound to be rather slow and uncertain, since they depend on the agility and ability of entrepreneurs as well as on the social capacity for change on the part of the labor force. The relationships between export experience of various industries and the R&D efforts of the firms, described in Chap. 8, suggest that "competitive response" should be important even if it is slow.

CHAPTER **18**

ADJUSTMENT
WITH FIXED RATES

POLICY MODELS

THE BASIC IDEA OF CHAP. 17 is that the economy responds in certain ways to balance-of-payments change, ways that help restore equilibrium. But widespread and long-continued disequilibrium shows that the responses are insufficient, work slowly, or are frustrated by the actions of policy-makers. In the discussion of these problems the idea of policy models has developed: models that are concerned with policies rather than automatic responses. They show the effects of various policies, as well as giving ideas about why the automatic mechanisms find the difficulties they do.

The most extreme level of generalization in policy models is the proposition that the number of policy instruments has to equal the number of policy goals, a topic dealt with in Chap. 16. At a somewhat lower level on the scale of generalization is the distinction sometimes made between types of policies, a distinction that classifies policies into expenditure-reducing and expenditure-switching policies. Expenditure reduction, through monetary or fiscal policy, affects the level of national income as well as the balance of payments via the marginal propensity to import and the multiplier. Expenditure-switching policies operate to change the direction of spending from foreign to domestic products or from domestic to foreign. They include policies that change the relative prices of foreign and domestic goods, such as devaluation, tariffs, quotas, or exchange restrictions. There is some overlap among the policies; an interest rate increase will reduce domestic spending but also switch the direction of capital flows, and an expenditure reduction in an inflationary economy can change relative prices by reducing the general price level (or more realistically by stopping the rise in domestic prices, while foreign prices continue to edge up). At this level of generality one could say that with two goals a switching and a reducing policy are both needed.[1]

THE ABSORPTION APPROACH

The close link between the national income and the balance on current account has been exploited in policy models under the name of "the absorption approach." It will be seen that the expenditure-reducing and expenditure-switching notions fit neatly into the absorption concept, which was originally introduced in the study of exchange rate changes but can be applied to other policies as well.[2] It starts from the idea developed in Chap. 17 [Eqs. **(17-3)** and **(17-4)**] that $X - M = S - I$, where S is interpreted as total savings in the economy. In the jargon of the absorption approach, $S - I$ is termed "hoarding." An improvement in the current account, it is obvious, must be the counterpart of an increase in hoarding. From another point of view, the production of national income is $C + I + G + X$. The "absorption" is the amount purchased by domestic users, $C + I + G + M$. If absorption is subtracted from output, the difference is $X - M$. It follows that another way to view the problem of adjusting the balance of payments is to say that an improvement in the current account requires a reduction of absorption relative to output and income.

To illustrate, suppose that there is a deficit while the economy is producing a full-employment level of output. Since real output cannot be increased, absorption must be reduced to improve the trade balance. We might try doing this via an increase in the interest rate. This will cut I, with a multiplier effect on Y. In the simple national income models, at least, $\Delta I = \Delta S + \Delta M$; S and M both fall, but since I falls more than S, hoarding increases and the $X - M$ balance is improved. However, with only one policy it is not possible to maintain full employment simultaneously.

An expenditure-switching policy, such as a tariff, would run into trouble in the postulated circumstances because switching spending from M to C would be inflationary. If we had started out with less than full employment, the increase in C would increase output, with a multiplier effect on Y that would lead to increased savings. In this case, hoarding would increase, and equivalently output would increase relative to absorption, so the balance of payments would be improved. But at full employment the switching policy would need to be accompanied by a reducing policy to prevent inflation.

---

[1] The distinction between switching and reducing policies was introduced by Harry G. Johnson, *International Trade and Economic Growth*, Chap. VI.

[2] The originator was Sidney Alexander, "The Effects of a Devaluation on a Trade Balance," *Staff Papers*, II (April 1952), 263–78.

The absorption idea has not had an easy life, but it has had considerable influence.[3] For example, it figured prominently in one of the criticisms of the Brookings Institution report, *The United States Balance of Payments in 1968*. That report made a projection that the U.S. balance would improve because of greater European inflation compared to U.S. inflation; the effect was essentially switching from spending on European goods to spending on U.S. goods, increasing U.S. exports compared to imports. But the report was criticized for failing to investigate the implied improvement in hoarding to see what factors would lead to the increase in domestic saving relative to domestic investment. It apparently accepted without question that savings would automatically change in the desired direction.[4]

SOME ILLUSTRATIONS OF POLICY THEORY

Moving down to a still lower level of generality, we can use the model of Fig. 17-2 to analyze a number of important problems in balance-of-payments policy making. The strategy will be to discuss some hypothetical problems that illustrate the range of possibilities of the model, leaving it to the student to fill in the details for the rest.

The first case is shown in Fig. 18-1. The horizontal axis represents real income (money NNP/price index). The vertical axis is the rate of interest, and the schedules representing income-interest rate combinations at which equilibrium occurs in the three macro markets are *BB* for the balance of payments, *LM* for the money-assets market, and *XIG-MST* for the market in goods and services. The two policy goals, as in all these cases, will be balance-of-payments equilibrium anywhere along *BB* and full employment.

If we are currently at point *A*, two of the markets display equilibrium at full employment, but there is a balance-of-payments deficit. Fiscal policy would shift *XIG-MST* downward and to the left if it involved higher taxes or lower government spending. This would restore equilibrium in all three markets at *A'* but at the cost of the full-employment goal. An alternative policy is tight money, which shifts *LM* upward and would bring all markets into equilibrium at *A"*—again at the cost of a lapse from full employment. Clearly one policy tool of the expenditure-reduction variety is insufficient.

---

[3] It was thoroughly criticized by Fritz Machlup, "Relative Prices and Aggregate Spending in the Analysis of Devaluation," *American Economic Review*, XLV, No. 3 (June 1955), 255–78; reformulated by Alexander, "Effects of a Devaluation: A Simplified Synthesis of Elasticities and Absorption Approaches," *American Economic Review*, XLIX, No. 1 (March 1959), 22–42; and thoroughly exposited by M. O. Clement, Richard L. Phister, and Kenneth J. Rothwell, *Theoretical Issues in International Economics* (Boston: Houghton Mifflin Company, 1967).

[4] See Harry G. Johnson, "The International Competitive Position of the United States and the Balance of Payments Prospect for 1968," *Review of Economics and Statistics*, XLVI, No. 1 (February 1964), 14–32.

Another possibility is to experiment with switching devices whose initial impact is on the balance of payments. Tariffs, quotas, or a restriction on the capital outflow shift *BB* to the right; and the first two also shift *XIG-MST* to the right. It would indeed be a coincidence if the shifting of both lines brought their intersection to the full-employment income level. Typically monetary and/or fiscal policy would be needed as well in order to bring the *XIG-MST* schedule to intersect the (shifted) *BB* schedule at full employment.

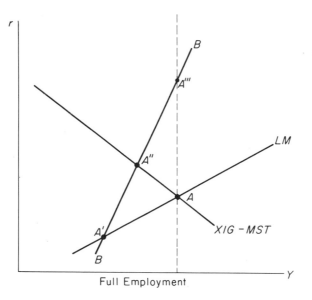

Fig. 18-1

Still another possibility is suggested by point *A'''*: Would it be possible to concoct policies that would allow all three curves to intersect there? *XIG-MST* could be shifted up by a big increase in government spending or a big tax reduction. *LM* could be shifted up by a tight-money policy, which would reduce investment spending as a counterbalance to the inflationary effects of fiscal policy. The combinations of these policies would give the two policies needed to accommodate the two goals.[5] (Notice that if a high rate of investment and of economic growth is a third goal, we are again in trouble; a third tool of some sort is called for.)

A second case for a work-out of the policy analysis we are developing arises by assuming that the economy starts at point *A'''*, with *LM* intersecting *BB* there (not drawn, to avoid clutter). Here the balance of payments is in

---

[5] See Robert A. Mundell, "The Appropriate Use of Monetary and Fiscal Policy for Internal and External Stability," *Staff Papers*, IX, No. 1 (March 1962), 70–77, for a more extended discussion.

equilibrium but the economy faces a deflationary gap. That this is the situation follows from the fact that to restore equilibrium in the products market a cut in the interest rate bringing a rise in investment is needed; hence at A''' leakages from the income stream must exceed injections. Indeed, if the interest rate is held constant, the deflationary gap will force the economy to a very low level of employment and the balance of payments into surplus.[6] What combinations of fiscal, monetary, and switching policies would be appropriate in this case?

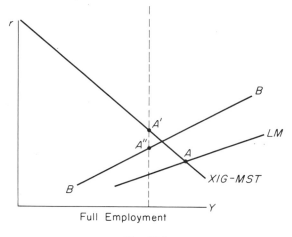

Fig. 18-2

A third, very realistic case is that of inflation and a balance-of-payments deficit. Figure 18-2 shows this case, with point A the current position of the economy. Since A is to the right of both the full-employment line and the BB schedule, it is clear that the economy has problems of both an inflationary gap and a balance-of-payments deficit. Two possible equilibria that meet both the external and the internal goals are A' and A''. A' could be reached by a combination of reducing the money supply, to shift LM up, and tariffs or quotas, to shift BB up. A'' requires reducing the money supply and also shifting $XIG\text{-}MST$ down by fiscal policy.

There are many other possible cases, such as inflation/surplus, deflation/deficit, and cases involving disequilibrium in only one market rather than two. In each case the possibilities for policy combinations follow the same considerations we have been using. The important thing is that these cases are not just hypothetical; they occur all the time. Beginning with equilibrium

[6] More advanced analysis deals with issues of potential instabilities, cobweb responses, and cyclical approaches to equilibrium. Those interested in such problems should read Robert A. Mundell, "The Monetary Dynamics of International Adjustment Under Fixed and Flexible Exchange Rates," *Quarterly Journal of Economics*, LXXIV, No. 2 (May 1960), 227–57.

in all three markets, for example, a loss in export markets may occur because of technological progress abroad, which would shift *BB* to the left, *XIG-MST* down, and generate the depression/deficit case, as some observers contend has been the problem in the United Kingdom for many years. Or the loss in export markets may result from a rapid rise in money wages (recall the discussion in Chap. 2 about the relations among wage rates, exchange rates, and comparative advantage). This can result in the inflation/deficit case, as in Italy in the early 1960's. In the 1930's the typical experience was a business

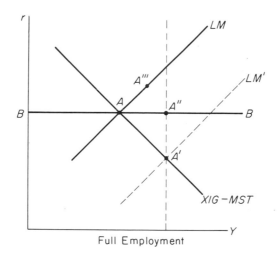

Fig. 18-3

cycle abroad leading to a loss of exports at home, with the depression/surplus case in the country originating the cycle and the depression/deficit case in its trading partners.

The special case, mentioned in Chap. 17, where international capital movements are so responsive to interest rate changes that *BB* becomes a horizontal line, gives some interesting policy consequences. In Fig. 18-3 point *A* indicates a depression with balance-of-payments equilibrium. An attempt to use monetary policy to restore full employment shifts the economy to *A'*, but the lower domestic interest rate compared to the world rate leads to a capital outflow and a balance-of-payments deficit. As we saw in Chap. 17, the deficit leads to a fall in the money supply that would continue until *LM'* is shifted back to the original *LM*, so that a "one-shot" expansion of the money supply would have no lasting effect on national income. However, the monetary authorities could continue to feed more money into the economy by open-market purchases to offset the deficit-caused loss of domestic monetary balances—as long as they had any international reserves to use in the foreign exchange market to maintain the fixed exchange rate. When their reserves are exhausted, this alley will be closed to them.

The alternative is to use fiscal policy. An expansion of government spending will shift *XIG-MST* up to intersect *BB* at *A″*. If no simultaneous action is taken about the money supply, there would be an intermediate stage where *LM* intersected the new internal balance schedule at *A‴*; this would involve a relatively high domestic interest rate, a capital inflow, a balance-of-payments surplus with its automatic increase in the money supply, and a shift to the right of *LM* until all three markets are in equilibrium at *A″*. On this showing, fiscal policy rather than monetary policy is the appropriate device for restoring full employment when the exchange rate is fixed and there is a high degree of capital mobility.[7]

The various cases we have looked at are designed to illustrate the point that generally the number of tools should equal the number of targets. Sometimes for one reason or another the number of tools is less than the policy-makers' targets, however, and then compromises in reaching the goals must be accepted. One reason for the discrepancy is that the number of goals may be expanded. The case of adding a high rate of growth as a goal was mentioned earlier; this adds a goal and usually preempts the interest rate as a tool, since a low level of interest is needed unless the economy is highly planned. Others may believe in domestic self-sufficiency or have a desire for industrial development, adopting tariffs for that purpose and removing or attenuating one of the switching devices. In the case of the United States, foreign aid and defense lending are goals of the government; reducing them in the interests of shifting the *BB* line then becomes undesirable. Or a country may have free trade as a goal, as in nineteenth-century England after the repeal of the Corn Laws.

CASES: ENGLAND AND THE UNITED STATES

On the other hand, a prominent feature of current international monetary economics is that a major tool—exchange rate changes—has been eliminated from the picture. In Chap. 19 we shall see how this tool works; so far it has been ignored because many countries do not regard it as a potential policy.[8] The United Kingdom experience between the middle of the 1950's and 1967 is a classic example. The pound remained in bad shape for years, and one expedient after another—short of devaluation—was tried. There was a low rate of economic growth after 1955, since an expenditure-increasing policy to raise growth rates would have given a larger deficit. Sterling crises, when there was a run on the pound and the necessity for IMF

[7] This case is analyzed by Mundell, *Canadian Journal of Economics and Political Science*, XXIX; and, on the basis of a more comprehensive model, by Anne O. Krueger, "The Impact of Alternative Government Policies under Varying Exchange Systems," *Quarterly Journal of Economics*, LXXIX, No. 2 (May 1965), 195–208.

[8] A good discussion of the changing attitudes toward exchange rate adjustments is R. S. Sayers, "Co-operation between Central Banks," *The Three Banks Review*, No. 59 (September 1963), 3–25.

and other aid, occurred in 1955, 1956, and 1957. Finally in 1959 the government decided to try to increase domestic growth, but the resulting deficit led to a 1961 crisis, followed by expenditure-reducing policies and trade and capital controls. A return to expansionary policies in 1963 was followed by a crisis in 1964, more controls, more rescue operations, more monetary restraint, and in spite of all that another crisis in 1966.[9] So for more than a decade a major country confronted a major problem without use of one of the potent policy weapons, before finally and reluctantly being forced to use it.

The policies of the United States during the dollar surplus period since 1958 is a good illustration of the tools-goals dilemmas in which countries may find themselves. During the early part of this period unemployment of up to 7 per cent and a fall below potential GNP of some $35 billion was the experience; at the same time there was a deficit on most ways of computing the balance of payments.[10] However, many tools were considered either ineligible or of very limited usefulness. Tariffs and quotas were eliminated because they conflicted with the United States' leadership since the 1930's in the movement to liberalize trade. Capital restrictions were eliminated because they were originally regarded as incompatible with liberal trade ideals and because the United States, as the most developed country, was a natural source of capital for the world. Exchange rate changes were unthinkable, since they were incompatible with the U.S. role of chief supplier of world liquidity (a topic taken up in Chap. 22). Attempts to lower domestic wages and prices, as a switching policy, are not possible under contemporary conditions of downward wage rigidity. Full employment with its accompanying larger deficit was not regarded as possible because it would precipitate a rush of conversion of outstanding dollar balances in the hands of foreigners into gold. The possibility covered in the theoretical models of using a combination of a big government deficit and tight monetary policy was not regarded as politically feasible. So apparently all avenues were blocked. As the situation developed, the goals were compromised: For some years neither full employment nor balance-of-payments equilibrium was achieved, and eventually some of the other goals were compromised by the adoption of various illiberal trade and capital restrictions.[11]

[9] Bank for International Settlements, *Thirty-Eighth Annual Report* (April 1967–March 1968), pp. 7–19, has an excellent short history of sterling since 1949. It lays major emphasis on faulty wage policies and the lack of adequate cost restraint.

[10] Seymour E. Harris, ed., *The Dollar in Crisis* (New York: Harcourt, Brace & World, Inc., 1961), is a good source for discussions during the early part of the dollar surplus period. For discussion of the minority view that there was not really a balance-of-payments deficit, but rather appropriate behavior for a banking country, see the references in our Chap. 15.

[11] References discussing these dilemmas are Warren L. Smith, "Are There Enough Policy Tools?," *American Economic Review Papers and Proceedings*, LV, No. 2 (May 1965), 208–20; and Harry G. Johnson, "An Overview of Price Levels, Employment, and the Balance of Payments," *Journal of Business*, XXXVI, (July 1963), 279–89.

Much of the policy effort was devoted to handling the liquidity and confidence aspects of the deficit, which are not of concern at the moment but will be discussed in later chapters. As far as adjustment goes, the concession was to abandon the posture of liberal policies in many lines, starting with a reduction in the duty-free allowance for items brought back by returning tourists, with a tightening of the requirements that the recipients of foreign aid spend the aid funds only in the United States, and with a return of servicemen's dependents from overseas. As the deficit wore on, controls on private capital outflow were instituted. The initial one was the Interest Equalization Tax of 1963, an excise tax on U.S. purchases of foreign stocks and bonds, which was intended to reduce the outflow of long-term portfolio capital. The deficit persisting, additional restrictions on other parts of the capital account were introduced in 1965 in the form of guidelines. These limited the outflows of capital from commercial banks and of direct capital from large corporations. These guidelines were to be voluntary; in the case of banks, the Federal Reserve Board set the amount of capital outflow; in the case of corporations, the guidelines were set on the basis of individual meetings between the corporation and the Department of Commerce.

While these programs continued on to date, detailed objective evaluations of them are not plentiful. Experience with the first year of the voluntary program on bank loans abroad showed that the capital outflow from bank lending abroad increased much less rapidly than in previous years—but also that there was a much bigger capital outflow from a reduction in bank liabilities to foreigners. The combination of asset and liability changes gave the banking sector more of a contribution to the balance-of-payments deficit with the guidelines than without them. The unanswered question is, what was the contribution of the guidelines to a capital outflow via a reduction in foreign short-term claims on the United States?[12] No matter what the answer to this question, critics of the guideline approach in both the banking and the corporate sectors point to the inefficiencies that capital controls bring (similar in nature to those brought by trade controls) and to dangers implicit in business doing favors for the government and thereby building up a reservoir of good will from which return favors can be drawn. (This criticism apparently does not take the "What have you done for me lately?" joke seriously.[13])

Certainly events showed that these guidelines were no match for the pressures operating in the domestic and the international economy during

[12] See Allan H. Meltzer, "The Regulation of Bank Credits Abroad: Another Failure for the Government's Balance of Payments Program?," in *Guidelines, Informal Controls, and the Market Place*, eds. George P. Shultz and Robert Z. Aliber (Chicago: The University of Chicago Press, 1966), pp. 183–206.

[13] In addition to the Meltzer paper cited in the previous footnote, Harry G. Johnson has criticized the guidelines in "Balance-of-Payments Controls and Guidelines for Trade and Investment," in *Guidelines, Informal Controls, and the Market Place*, eds. Shultz and Aliber, pp. 165–81.

1967. The rise in GNP associated with the Vietnam war had its predictable consequence of reducing the balance on current account; there was also an increase in the capital outflow through banking and portfolio capital transactions. Internationally, the U.K. devaluation of the pound from $2.80 to $2.40 in November was the major event. The devaluation was brought on by years of inability to adjust the balance of payments by other means in spite of repeated efforts, culminating in a loss of confidence in sterling and a speculative flight from the pound.

This event had severe repercussions on the confidence aspect of dollar dealings, since it was associated with widespread speculation that the United States would devalue in its turn. The speculation showed up in the balance of payments partly in the form of a $1 billion gold outflow during the last quarter of 1967 as gold was fed into private markets to keep the price there close to the official $35 per ounce.[14] This was approximately matched by a rise in U.S. holdings of convertible currencies as the United States swapped currencies with the United Kingdom in order to provide them with dollars to help support the pound at its new level. But speculation also showed up in a rise of $1.3 billion in liabilities to foreign official agencies; these agencies acquired dollars by selling gold as their share of the gold pool price support effort and by buying dollars from private individuals abroad who were trying to get into what they regarded as safer currencies.[15]

The short-term developments piled on years of past deficits caused Washington policy-makers to stiffen the informal controls into formal ones. The 1968 capital controls put ceilings on the amount of direct investment, varied according to the status of the country receiving the investment: For less-developed countries, new capital transfers plus reinvested earnings were to be 110 per cent of the 1965–1966 average; for developed countries outside continental Europe, the ceiling was 65 per cent; and for continental Europe, no new capital at all but reinvestment equal to the percentage of earnings reinvested in 1964–1966 was allowed. Furthermore, the guidelines for bank lending were tightened; government spending abroad was reduced; and an abortive proposal for a tax on foreign travel was suggested. Not until much later in 1968 did the fiscal policy tool come into play in the form of a 10 per cent tax surcharge coupled with a reduction in government spending.

Clearly, policy action has been much less neat than the models, partly because of preoccupation with other issues (an unpopular war, poverty, urban crises). And the policies have tended toward the direct control form of expenditure shifting in spite of its inefficiencies. Deep political divisions,

[14] A renewed gold run in 1968 led the authorities to experiment with a "two-price" system in which the links between official and private markets were severed; central bankers pledged themselves not to buy or sell in the London or other private gold markets. This was designed to halt the drain of gold from official stocks to meet speculators' demands.

[15] Data from Office of Business Economics, U.S. Department of Commerce, *Survey of Current Business*, XLVIII, No. 3 (March 1968), 15–34.

however, have made fiscal policy sluggish, and so that important tool has been pretty much out of contention.

Before experimenting with informal and formal controls, the U.S. Treasury and the Federal Reserve System made an attempt beginning in 1961 to exploit the effects of a higher interest rate on the balance of payments without simultaneously reducing domestic investment by "Operation Twist." Based on the notion that the important rate for the balance of payments is the short-term rate and for domestic investment is the long-term rate, the attempt was made to twist the interest rate structure so that the short-term rate was raised relative to the long-term rate. The process involved both increasing the supply of short-term government debt compared to long-term debt (thereby lowering the price of short-term debt and hence raising the interest rate) as well as raising the ceiling on interest rates on time deposits. Short-term interest rates did increase relative to long-term rates, as a matter of fact. But a careful study of the experience suggests that this usually happens during business cycle upturns away, so that Operation Twist had only a moderate effect.[16]

The troubles of deficit countries in matching goals with tools, illustrated by the United States' experience, is often repeated by surplus countries who demonstrate that other goals are given priorities over balance-of-payments equilibrium. European countries whose surpluses were the counterpart of the U.S. deficit preferred not to cut trade barriers, expand aid programs, reduce interest rates, or use other tools to the extent needed to restore equilibrium. Sheer nationalism is often suggested as the overriding goal in this case.[17]

The United States' experience also illustrates a typical response of deficit countries, although most of them lack the large volume of reserves of the United States and therefore must move much more quickly in the direction of trade and capital restrictions. Some examples: Canada used "import surcharges" in 1962, and the British imposed tariffs in 1964 for balance-of-payments reasons, much to the distress of their partners in the European Free Trade Area. France announced higher tariffs in 1968 in anticipation of a probable forthcoming deficit. One authority claims that quantitative import restrictions have probably been the main balance-of-payments tool used in recent years.[18] There are three theoretical points about the use of trade controls. The first is well-known to us: They are a switching device; they shift BB to the right and $XIG\text{-}MST$ upward; and they can be used in conjunction with another tool to achieve the internal and external balance goals.

---

[16] Franco Modigliani and Richard Sutch, "Innovations in Interest Rate Policy," *American Economic Review Papers and Proceedings*, LVI, No. 2 (May 1966), 178–97. Their econometric model is too complicated to be summarized here.

[17] By, for example, James Tobin, "Europe and the Dollar," *Review of Economics and Statistics*, XLVI, No. 2 (May 1964), 123–26.

[18] Corden, *Recent Developments in the Theory of International Trade*, p. 19.

The second point goes back to the section on the optimal tariff in Chap. 11. There it was pointed out that there are circumstances under which a tariff will raise welfare—in effect, if a country is not optimally exploiting its monopoly powers in using the tariff to improve the terms of trade. These conditions do not have anything to do with the state of its balance of payments, so that it would be a coincidence if trade restrictions for balance-of-payments reasons turned out to give the optimum tariff. Hence the general suspicion with which theorists eye trade—as well as capital—controls.

The third proposition begins with the assumption that restrictions are going to be used and proceeds by asking to what extent they should discriminate by countries. Meade formulates it this way: Suppose two countries are maintaining external balance by restricting trade with one another. In each country the marginal social value of imports (measured by exporter's price plus the tariff) is higher than the marginal social cost (measured by exporter's price alone). If each reduces its tariffs in such a way that equilibrium is maintained in the balance of payments, there will be a welfare gain. The extra imports have a higher marginal social value than do the exports that pay for them. The reduction should continue until one of the two has eliminated its tariffs. When generalized into a multicountry model, the result of this process is that countries with weak balances of payments are discriminating against countries with strong ones.[19] GATT rules are that tariffs for balance-of-payments reasons should be nondiscriminatory; the theory suggests that well-devised discrimination might be superior.

Trade restrictions and other switching devices are not the only tools that have an impact on the terms of trade. Expenditure-reduction policies, by moving the offer curve, also affect the terms of trade. The choice among alternative policies may therefore be influenced by the way in which the terms of trade are changed and by where the country is located on its utility possibilities curve. Another, perhaps secondary consideration is what does each tool do to the distribution of income and how does this strike the policy-maker. Tariffs, for example, have a definite income redistribution effect, and so will other switching devices that change the relative prices of foreign and domestic goods. Balance-of-payments policy is obviously not one of life's simplest problems.

[19] Meade, *Trade and Welfare*, Chap. XXXIV; J. M. Fleming, "On Making the Best of Balance of Payments Restrictions on Imports," *Economic Journal*, LXI, No. 241 (March 1951), 48–71.

CHAPTER 19

ADJUSTMENT UNDER FLEXIBLE EXCHANGE RATES

SOMETIMES THE VIEWS of a sizable number of economists conflict with the attitudes of practical men of affairs. One case in point is the role of flexible exchange rates—or even devaluation where a currency is nominally on an "adjustable peg" basis. Many eminent economists have urged a switch to flexible rates,[1] but actually very little use has been made of this approach. Indeed, there is great reluctance to adjust rates even occasionally on the part of advanced industrial countries, although less-developed countries depreciate quite frequently. In this chapter we shall look at some of the issues involved.

THE FOREIGN EXCHANGE MARKET

The fundamental basis of the flexible exchange rate system is that equilibrium in the balance of payments is maintained through exchange rate changes, and the changes are brought about by the unimpeded working of supply-and-demand changes in the foreign exchange market. Foreign exchange itself is an instrument used to transfer the ownership of funds from one country to another; the instrument may be currency, bank accounts, drafts, bills of exchange, or some other instrument. The supply of foreign exchange comes from exports, capital inflows, transportation service rendered, and the other credit transactions in the balance of payments. The demand

[1] Fritz Machlup gives references to 25 of them on pp. 79–81 of *Plans for Reform of the International Monetary System*, Special Papers in International Economics No. 3 (rev. ed.) (Princeton, N.J.: International Finance Section, Princeton University, 1964).

is for exchange to pay for imports, capital outflow, tourism, and the other debit items. The market where the forces of supply and demand meet consists of the dealers—usually the foreign exchange departments of commercial banks and brokers—and their customers. All countries where the foreign exchange is traded are linked together to form the total market.[2]

For a preliminary analysis of the foreign exchange market, it is possible to start with the partial-equilibrium supply-and-demand curves for foreign exchange drawn in Fig. 19-1. The pound sterling is the illustrative foreign currency traded in this market, and the exchange rate is quoted as dollars

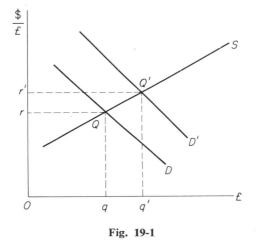

Fig. 19-1

per pound. Initially the balance of payments is in equilibrium at rate *r*, with the total quantity of pounds demanded equal to the total quantity supplied (or *oq*). Then something changes so that the demand for the pound increases—a new product is developed abroad or a higher rate of interest abroad leads to a capital outflow. At rate *r* there is a deficit in the balance of payments, but with flexible rates the excess demand for sterling increases the exchange rate (depreciates the dollar). As the price of sterling rises, the excess demand is gradually eliminated until the deficit is corrected at the new rate *r'*.

This simple analysis is suggestive but leaves many questions unanswered. What about the national income and domestic price levels during all this? What are the roles of other policy instruments? Will depreciation always work to correct deficits? For these questions a more general analysis is needed.

[2] An excellent institutional description of foreign exchange markets is in Alan R. Holmes and Francis H. Schott, *The New York Foreign Exchange Market* (New York: Federal Reserve Bank of New York, 1965).

COMMODITY TRADE AND THE EXCHANGE RATE

A first step has traditionally been to investigate the effects of exchange rate changes on the components of the balance of payments, particularly in the commodity markets involved in the export and import sectors. Initially we simplify by assuming that national income effects are negligible and that no capital movements take place. The balance of payments is then exports minus imports, and their value may be expressed in either dollars or pounds (i.e., in domestic or in foreign currency). The analysis is

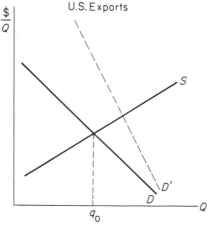

Fig. 19-2(a)

laid out in Fig. 19-2. Fig. 19-2(a) and 19-2(c) show the quantities of U.S. exports and imports, respectively, as a function of their dollar prices; Figs. 19-2(b) and 19-2(d) show the markets for the same products as viewed in the United Kingdom, where supplies and demands are a function of the prices in pounds. The solid line supply-and-demand curves show the situation at the initial exchange rate. Then the dollar is depreciated. The effect of this is to shift one of the curves in each diagram, and from the shift the effects on the balance of payments and the foreign exchange market may be determined. For example, the demand curve must shift up in Fig. 19-2(a) because it is based on tastes, incomes, and prices in the U.K. economy. Since by assumption none of these change, the United Kingdom wishes to pay the same number of pounds for a given quantity of U.S. exports, no matter what the exchange rate. If, for example, the U.K. price was £1 per unit for quantity q_0 of U.S. exports, the price in the United States would be $1 when the exchange rate is $1/pound. After a depreciation, when the rate goes to, for example, $2/pound, the United Kingdom still wishes to pay £1 per unit of U.S. exports, but this translates into $2 per unit in the United States. Since the same translation occurs for each possible volume of exports, the effect is to shift up the demand curve as seen in the United States. The supply curve, however, remains fixed, since it is based on dollar costs, which by assumption have not changed.

When the same market is viewed in terms of pounds in Fig. 19-2(b), the U.K. demand curve remains fixed for the reason noted in the last paragraph. But the supply curve shifts down. Using the same illustrative numbers, quantity q_0 has a supply price of \$1, which translates into £1 at the initial

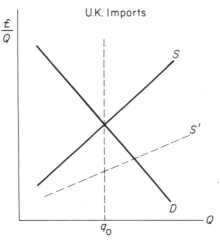

Fig. 19-2(b)

\$1/pound exchange rate. After the depreciation to \$2/pound, the \$1 supply price has a U.K. equivalent of £$\frac{1}{2}$. Using similar reasoning for each possible quantity of U.S. exports, it is obvious that the supply curve must shift down and to the right. In all cases, the shift depends on the percentage by which the currency is devalued; and the higher the price of the commodity, the bigger the absolute value of the shift in the curve.

It should be unnecessary to repeat the reasoning in order to establish that the supply curve shifts up in Fig. 19-2(c) and the demand curve down in Fig. 19-2(d).

The price impact of depreciation is now immediately apparent. Given a positive slope to the supply curve, the home price of both exports and imports rises. This guides more resources into the export industry, reduces the quantity of imports demanded, and induces more resources into import-competing lines. Abroad, the price of both imports and exports falls, which stimulates the consumption of U.S. products and pushes resources out of the industry that supplies U.S. imports. These price and resource movements are the way in which the balance of payments adjusts.

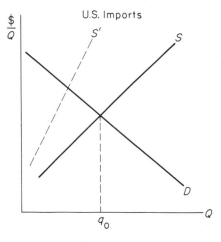

Fig. 19-2(c)

Thus depreciation changes the quantities traded in the desired directions. But the balance of payments depends on the total values of imports and exports, and the way total values change with quantities depends on the elasticities of the curves. Assuming that the United States is interested in the foreign exchange earned and spent, we can concentrate on Fig. 19-2(b) and 19-2(d). Obviously the amount of pounds spent on imports will fall. The diagram for U.K. imports shows that the amount of pounds earned rises if the U.K. demand is elastic and falls if it is inelastic. If export earnings do fall, they may fall by more or less than import spending, depending on the elasticities. The crucial nature of the elasticities in determining whether or

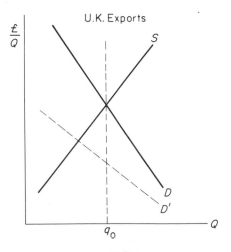

Fig. 19-2(d)

not depreciation will be successful in improving the balance of payments has earned this type of theory the name of "the elasticities approach," in distinction to the reliance on national income concepts of the absorption approach explained in Chap. 18.[2a]

THE MARSHALL–LERNER CONDITION

There is a long literature devoted to the algebraic formulation of devaluation conditions that essentially translates the diagrams into precise definitions of what is needed for depreciation to improve the balance of payments. The most famous of these is the Marshall–Lerner condition: Given infinite supply elasticities, so that the prices of exports in domestic currencies are constant, and given that exports equal imports at the initial exchange rate, the balance of payments will be improved under depreciation if the sum of the elasticities of import demand in each country is greater than 1. If either assumption fails to hold, it is still possible to express the conditions for devaluation to be successful in terms of elasticities, but the expressions become very involved.[3] In the case of less than infinite elasticities of supply, the important thing is that the demand requirements become less stringent, as is suggested by the limiting case where each supply curve is vertical. By modifying Figs. 19-2(b) and 19-2(d) to show vertical supply curves, the reader may quickly show that depreciation improves the balance of payments no matter how low the elasticities of demand.

In spite of the fact that the Marshall–Lerner condition is considerably weakened by less than infinitely elastic supply curves, there was an important body of opinion in the years after 1945 that depreciations should be avoided because the elasticities were so low that the balance of payments would not be helped much. This general opinion, which was shared by an influential group including Balogh, Harrod, and others,[4] has been dubbed "elasticity pessimism." Before commenting on elasticity pessimism, however, it is in order to show the effects in the foreign exchange market of low elasticities in the product market.

The major result is shown in Fig. 19-3, in particular the neighborhood

[2a] A definitive treatment of the partial-equilibrium analysis is Gottfried Haberler, "The Market for Foreign Exchange and the Stability of the Balance of Payments: A Theoretical Analysis," *Kyklos*, III, No. 3 (1949), 193–218.

[3] For derivations of the Marshall–Lerner condition and related formulas, see Kindleberger, *International Economics* (3rd ed.), Appendix D; or Alexander, *American Economic Review*, XLIX. The technique is similar to that of footnote 7 in Chap. 4: Express the balance of payments in terms of domestic prices, foreign prices, and the exchange rate; then differentiate with respect to the exchange rate and express the result in terms of elasticities.

[4] References to the relevant literature are found in Egon Sohmen, *Flexible Exchange Rates: Theory and Controversy* (Chicago: The University of Chicago Press, 1961), p. 6.

around point *B*. Remembering that depreciation means a rise in the dollar/ pound rate, it is easy to see from Fig. 19-2(d) that depreciation reduces the quantity of pounds demanded (unless the U.S. demand for imports is perfectly inelastic). Hence the demand curve in the foreign exchange market has a negative slope. But if the demand curve of the United Kingdom in Fig. 19-2(b) is inelastic, a rise in the exchange rate reduces the quantity of pounds

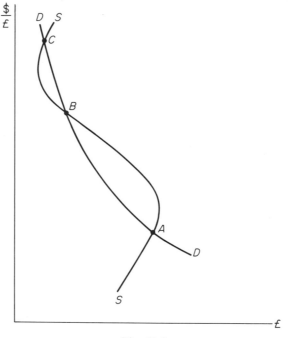

Fig. 19-3

supplied, giving the supply curve of foreign exchange a negative slope also. When the negatively sloping supply curve is flatter than the demand curve, as around point *B*, a rise in the rate increases the excess demand for the pound. This means that *B* is an unstable equilibrium: A small rise in the rate from *B* leads to demand greater than supply and a further rise until equilibrium *C* is reached, or a small fall from *B* makes supply greater than demand and a continued fall until *A* is reached. This instability, it should be noted, has nothing to do with speculation, which may also make exchange markets unstable. Elasticity pessimism is a strong element in the negative reaction to proposals for freely fluctuating exchange rates.

The contention of the elasticity pessimists has led to a lively theoretical and empirical literature. For example, one thing that has to be decided is the precise meaning of the elasticities and of the supply-and-demand curves drawn in Fig. 19-2. If interpreted as supply-and-demand curves usually are, the reference is to situations where money income and the prices of other commodities are constant. But this interpretation is not of much use when the depreciation changes the balance of payments, because that will lead to national income and money supply changes, as we already know. In that case, the diagrams in Figs. 19-2 and 19-3 would have to be interpreted as showing the immediate impact of devaluation, and analysis along absorption lines would be needed to trace out the subsequent chain of events. Alternatively, the diagrams would be given a more general interpretation to include the monetary and national income considerations, in which case the elasticities are called "total elasticities" to distinguish them from the more common Marshallian concepts.[5] The first approach is probably more used. In either case, conclusions based on knowledge of partial-equilibrium supply and demand must be considerably modified.

The empirical basis for rejecting elasticity pessimism is of two sorts. One is the familiar point that long-run elasticities are higher than short-run ones, so that a devaluation that seems to have little impact in the short run may turn out to have a great effect on the balance of payments a few years later. Some of the explanations of the U.S. deficit after 1958 are based on the long-run effects of European devaluation in 1949.[6] For a more recent example there is the short-run effects of the U.K. devaluation of November, 1967. The impact on trade was an increase of £239 million in current account credits for the first quarter of 1968 (seasonally adjusted) and an increase in imports of £325 million, so that the current account actually worsened. As late as May, 1968, imports in terms of pounds were 26 per cent higher in value and 10 per cent more in volume than they were in the middle of 1967. A glance at Fig. 19-2(c) will confirm that this result for imports means that the demand curve has shifted, for otherwise the higher volume figure would not be observed. There is no doubt that such a shift did happen, for total consumer spending rose 4 per cent between October, 1967, and March, 1968.[7] Hence the trade data show a mixture of income (or absorption) and of price effects that need to be sorted out by an econometric study. At the least, however, they are consistent with low short-run elasticities. The second is that although statistical measures of elasticities based on price and quantity trends over a period of several years typically show that elasticities of demand either for total imports or for individual commodities are quite low, often less than 1 in absolute value, various

[5] Alexander, *American Economic Review*, XLIX, adopts the former approach, and Sohmen, *Flexible Exchange Rates*, the latter.

[6] For example, Johnson, *Review of Economics and Statistics*, XLVI, p. 19; Richard N. Cooper, "Dollar Deficits and Postwar Economic Growth," *Review of Economics and Statistics*, XLVI, No. 2 (May 1964), 155–59.

[7] Data from *The Economist*, CCXXVII, No. 6513 (June 22, 1968), 13–14, 65–66.

downward biases in the statistical techniques make it plausible that as a matter of fact the elasticities are fairly high.[8]

THE ABSORPTION APPROACH AGAIN

There are some interesting side issues in the elasticities approach, but because they are rather peripheral they are disposed of in a footnote.[9] The immediate business is to see what additional light the absorption approach

[8] Some samples of the estimates, all covering total imports into the United States: For the 1924–1938 period, elasticity = −.97 [T. C. Chang, *Cyclical Movements in the Balance of Payments* (Cambridge: Cambridge University Press, 1951)]; for the 1922–1929 period, elasticity = −.52 [J. Hans Adler, "U.S. Import Demand during the Interwar Period," *American Economic Review*, XXXV, No. 3 (June, 1945), 418–30]; for 1922–1937, elasticity = −.48 [Randall Hinshaw, "American Prosperity and the British Balance of Payments Problem," *Review of Economics and Statistics*, XXVII, No. 1 (February 1945), 1–9.] Harberger claims that the elasticity of import demand for the "typical country" runs about −.5 to −1.0 or above for the short run, while its elasticity of demand for exports is −2.0 or more [Arnold Harberger, "Some Evidence on the International Price Mechanism," *Review of Economics and Statistics*, XL, No. 1, Part 2 (Supplement: February 1958), 123–32; and "Some Evidence on the International Price Mechanism," *Journal of Political Economy*, LXV, No. 6 (December 1957), 506–21]. A complete survey of this literature is given by H. S. Cheng, "Statistical Estimates of Elasticities and Propensities in International Trade: A Survey of Published Studies," *Staff Papers*, VII, No. 1 (April 1959), 107–58. The criticism that these are biased downward because of the statistical technique is in Guy H. Orcutt, "Measurement of Price Elasticities in International Trade," *Review of Economics and Statistics*, XXXII, No. 2 (May 1950), 117–32.

[9] One intellectual puzzle is whether an unstable equilibrium in the foreign exchange market must be bounded by a stable equilibrium on both sides, as in Fig. 19-3. Egon Sohmen claims that it must be; Bhagwati and Johnson claim that it need not be. See their articles in *Economic Journal*, LXX and LXXI.

An issue often brought up is what happens to the terms of trade when the exchange rate changes. In domestic prices the price of both exports and imports rises; which rises most? Figures 19-2(a) and 19-2(b) indicate that the answer depends on the elasticities; according to Joan Robinson, the terms of trade deteriorate if the product of the supply elasticities exceeds the product of the demand elasticities ["Beggar-my Neighbor Remedies for Unemployment," reprinted in *Readings in the Theory of International Trade* (Philadelphia: The Blakiston Company, 1949), p. 400]. A more complete model in which nontraded goods as well as importables and exportables are included yields a markedly different conclusion: An improvement in the balance of trade requires a reduction in the price of the nontraded goods compared to both exports and imports, and the change in the terms of trade (which may be either an improvement or a fall) will be of little importance compared to the relative cheapening of the domestic goods. See I. F. Pearce, "The Problem of the Balance of Payments," *International Economic Review*, II, No. 1 (January 1961), 1–28.

Reference to Figs. 19-2(a) and 19-2(c) helps establish this point: If a country buys a large number of products abroad and is not a major part of any foreign market, it can be regarded as facing an elastic supply curve; while if it is the major supplier of some export commodity, the foreign demand for this will be rather inelastic in all probability. Countries fitting this description would tend to find their terms of trade deteriorating after devaluation. Michaely found that this pattern of trade concentration was true for 39 of the 44 countries that he studied, but was not true for the United States, the United Kingdom, Japan, and the leading trading nations of Western Europe. See his *Concentration in International Trade*, p. 50. In general, the effects on the terms of trade can be expected to vary from country to country, and dicta that depreciation always worsens the terms of trade should be discarded.

casts on exchange devaluation. As formulated by Alexander, *American Economic Review*, XLIX, it starts with a model such as Fig. 19-2, where the supply-and-demand curves refer to the effects of price changes at a constant money income. Assuming that the exchange market is stable, a depreciation improves the balance of payments and increases the national income. But if the improvement is to remain, hoarding will have to increase. (Starting from $X = M$, and $S = I$, after depreciation $X > M$ and $S > I$.) Output must increase relative to absorption. What effects are likely to be in operation?

Figure 19-2(a) tells us that the quantity and domestic price of exports are likely to rise. Thus demand for output is increased. This generates additional employment if the economy is below full employment, and additional money income in any case. In turn, the additional income leads to more imports through the marginal propensity to import; Alexander calls this a reversal factor that diminishes the impact improvement of the balance of payments. The marginal propensities to invest and consume also lead to an increase in absorption. The amount of income not spent in any of these ways goes into the change in hoarding.

The outcome for the economy is likely to be different, depending on whether the depreciation occurs when the economy is above or below full employment. Indeed, it has been suggested that the depreciation is likely to increase the output from full employment of the labor force because it allows for an improved allocation of resources: Labor and other factors are enabled to shift into industries more in accord with comparative advantage, and if the balance of payments has been policed by inefficient trade controls, these can be lifted.[10] This would automatically increase output relative to absorption.

If the initial situation is one of less than full employment, the reversal factors operate in the fashion of the national income models outlined in Chap. 17; from that analysis comes the presumption that an initial export surplus will be partly but not completely eliminated. Depreciation, however, introduces additional elements into the picture. One possibility, made famous by Laursen and Metzler,[11] arises from the impact of depreciation on the terms of trade (see footnote 9). If depreciation worsens the terms of trade, the real value of money income falls. Making the further assumption that the proportion of income saved depends on real income, it follows that real saving would fall and absorption would increase. Or if the terms of

---

[10] See Fritz Machlup, "Relative Prices and Aggregate Spending in the Analysis of Devaluation," *American Economic Review*, XLV, No. 3 (June 1955), 255–78; and Egon Sohmen, *International Monetary Problems and the Foreign Exchanges*, Special Papers in International Economics No. 4 (Princeton, N.J.: International Finance Section, Princeton University, 1963), p. 44.

[11] Svend Laursen and Lloyd A. Metzler, "Flexible Exchange Rates and the Theory of Employment," *Review of Economics and Statistics*, XXXII, No. 4 (November 1950), 281–99.

trade improve, absorption would decrease. Most commentators think this effect is likely to be negligible. Income redistribution is likely to be more important. Depreciation pulls resources into the foreign trade (export and import-competing) sector and raises incomes there relative to the incomes of factors used more intensively in the domestic goods sector. It also redistributes incomes via price changes: Those with a high consumption of foreign trade goods face higher prices no matter what the state of the economy, and at full employment the general price index rises because of the impact of depreciation. If the rise in money wages lags behind the price increase, there will be an income shift away from wage-earners. This redistribution has an effect on the reversal factors, since the various groups involved may have different marginal propensities to save and to import. The prospect is that non-wage-earners have higher marginal propensities to save and to import than do wage-earners, so that both savings and imports will increase, with the final result for the balance of payments depending on which is more important.[12]

Additional factors in the absorption process come into play when the economy is at or above full employment, for then the increased demand coming from the impact effect of devaluation raises prices rather than output. Imports will probably increase rapidly in that case, giving a reversal effect that eliminates much of the original balance-of-payments improvement. Whether absorption is reduced and hoarding is increased depends on the reaction of the public to price rises at constant real income. In this context macroeconomics deals with two major points: the Pigou effect and money illusion. In the Pigou effect, if prices rise, the real value of the public's stock of money is reduced; and if people wish to rebuild the real value of their cash balances, they will cut expenditure, that is, increase hoarding. Many authorities agree that the Pigou effect is more important in mending a hole in income theory than it is in practice.[13] Under money illusion, with both prices and money incomes rising, consumers pay attention only to the latter. For an illustration of how absorption would be reduced and hence the balance of payments improved in this case, suppose that initially $Y = 100$, $S = 10$, and $MPS = 1/5$. Then prices and wages both double so that money $Y = 200$. A consumer functioning without money illusion would realize that his real income was unchanged and would desire to maintain constant real consumption and saving. Therefore he would double his money saving to 20. However, one laboring under money illusion would regard the 100 increase in

[12] Diaz Alejandro, *Exchange-Rate Devaluation in a Semi-Industrial Country*, has done the most systematic theorizing about income redistribution, in the context of a model in which the terms of trade and the supply of exports are fixed. This model gives price inflation with real income deflation, a result of devaluation that he claims is typical of Argentina and other less-developed countries.

[13] P. A. Samuelson, "A Brief Survey of Post-Keynesian Developments," in *Keynes' General Theory: Reports of Three Decades*, ed. Robert Lekachman (New York: St. Martin's Press, 1964), p. 333.

income as the same as a 100 real income increase and would apply his *MPS* to that, generating additional saving of 20 (to make total $S = 30$). Clearly money illusion increases hoarding.

Finally the interest rate should be brought in as an influence on the amount of hoarding (defined, remember, as $S - I$). The rise in national income coming from the impact effect of devaluation will raise interest rates, according to the standard *IS-LM* analysis; but the improvement in the balance of payments increases the money supply, which shifts the *LM* curve so as to reduce the rate of interest. In some models the money supply continues to increase as long as there is a surplus in the balance of payments, increasing national income, and raising imports until a zero balance results.[14] In Alexander's original absorption presentation the assumption was that the money supply varied so as to keep the rate of interest constant; hence any effect on hoarding through the investment term was eliminated by assumption. Since the money supply is usually not allowed to follow any course *automatically*, it is more suitable to deal with it in the context of policy models; but what is done with the money supply has much to do with the outcome of changing exchange rates.

In summary, the impact of a devaluation has been analyzed as depending in the first instance on the elasticities of supply and demand for imports and exports. Assuming a stable foreign exchange market, the balance of payments is improved. Thereafter a chain of reversal factors may operate, depending on whether the economy is above or below full employment for their exact nature. (Although the exposition dealt with the country whose balance of payments improved, similar and simultaneous reactions may be expected in the partner country.) For a country with a depression, the expectation is that the reversal factors do not completely eliminate the improvement in the balance of payments (barring a monetary reaction such as presented in Kemp's model). However, if the depreciating nation is above full employment, the Pigou effect, money illusion, improved allocation of resources, and income redistribution seem to be the economic forces making for an improvement in hoarding. It is rather more doubtful that these can be relied on to have a substantial effect in reducing absorption, so that this situation typically calls for an expenditure-reducing policy as well as the switching policy that devaluation itself is.

British policy after the 1967 devaluation is a very clear example of this point. To make the devaluation take—that is, to reduce absorption by the necessary amount—the biggest tax increase in U.K. history was passed in March, 1968. Taxes were raised by nearly £1 billion/year from the previous level of £12 billion/year, with the goal of cutting personal consumption by more than 1 per cent per year.[15]

---

[14] Kemp, *The Pure Theory of Foreign Trade*, pp. 231–32.

[15] *The Economist*, CCXXVI, No. 6500 (March 23, 1968), 13–15, 63–65, has a detailed account.

THE FORWARD MARKET

One complication introduced by changing exchange rates is that importers and exporters have to take account of the possibility of rate changes in making their plans. Further, speculators may enter the foreign exchange market, trying to make money on their ability to forecast the changes. Guarding against losses from changes in the rates (called hedging) and speculation both make use of the part of the foreign exchange market known as the forward market.[16]

In the forward market, contracts are made today for purchase or sale of foreign exchange against domestic currency, payment to be made on delivery at the specified future time (often but not necessarily three months) at exchange rates fixed today. For example, an importer might be able to buy sterling exchange for $2.80 (the spot rate, so-called) or buy sterling forward at $2.7795.[17]

The development of the forward market as an institution allows traders to cover in order to reduce the risks of exchange rate changes. If an exporter sells products, anticipating collection in foreign exchange in, for example, 30 days, he would lose if the rate depreciates. He can cover his risk by selling the foreign exchange forward; then no matter what has happened to the spot rate in the meantime he knows how much domestic currency he will get. Or the importer can hedge his risk of possibly having to pay more domestic currency to procure his needed foreign exchange when payment falls due by buying forward exchange. The rule is that the trader is covered when his total spot and forward foreign exchange assets equal his total spot and forward foreign exchange liabilities. This rule also extends to foreign exchange dealers; a bank with an inventory of spot exchange covers by selling forward in order to protect itself against inventory losses.[18] For

---

[16] Speculation does not depend on the existence of a forward market, as the leads and lags that plagued the United Kingdom under sterling controls in the 1950's shows. If it seemed that the pound was under pressure that threatened devaluation, foreign importers would delay payment, hoping to be able to buy pounds more cheaply, while foreign exporters would try to collect as soon as possible in order to get more domestic currency for their pounds. This behavior put pressure on U.K. reserves in a self-justifying way.

[17] The forward rate is often given as a premium or discount from the spot rate; in the example, forward sterling would be at a discount of .0205. Another standard way of quoting the forward rate is to treat the premium or discount as a percentage per year of the spot rate in order to be able to compare it with interest rates. To do this use the formula:

$$\text{percentage premium or discount} = \frac{(\text{forward rate} - \text{spot rate}) \cdot 100}{\text{spot rate}} \cdot \frac{12}{n},$$

where n is the number of months specified in the forward contract. See Holmes and Schott, The New York Foreign Exchange Market, p. 45. For a three-month contract, the example works out to a discount of 2.93 per cent.

[18] Holmes and Schott, The New York Foreign Exchange Market, has considerable detail on the way banks handle their foreign exchange positions.

example, an exporter who has sold £1,000 of products to a U.K. importer when the spot exchange rate is at \$2.80/pound and gives the importer two months before payment is due might find that the pound had depreciated to \$2.79 at the end of two months. He would then take an exchange loss of \$10, certainly not a large sum; but if his shipment had been worth millions of pounds, the loss would not be negligible. On the other hand, if he had covered by selling forward pounds at, for example, \$2.795, his exchange cost of covering would have been only \$5.00.[19] As an alternative, the exporter could borrow abroad, sell his borrowed exchange in the spot market, and repay his foreign debt from the proceeds of his exports. Or an importer with a payment to be made in foreign exchange in the future could eliminate his exchange risk by buying spot exchange and investing it in a short-term instrument abroad, selling that when it is time to make his payment. Hedging does not depend on the forward market, therefore; but it is certainly easier to deal in forward exchange than to go through all the alternative transactions.

SPECULATION

When the forward market is used as a vehicle for speculation, the speculator "takes a position" rather than attempting to remain covered. For example, a speculator thinks that the mark will appreciate. He would then buy marks forward (called going long in the mark), anticipating that when the forward contract matures he can sell the mark for more dollars in the spot market than he has to pay for the forward contract. If he thinks the mark will depreciate, he sells it forward (goes short of the mark), expecting to be able to buy the marks to meet the contract for fewer dollars than he collects on his forward contract. Speculation also takes place in the spot market, since one can go long by buying spot exchange or go short by reducing his inventory of spot exchange below his total foreign exchange liabilities. Indeed, a trader who does not cover is speculating.

Speculation is sometimes a major force in the foreign exchange market, but before pursuing it in detail it is necessary to deal with the phenomenon of covered interest arbitrage. Suppose the short-term London interest rate exceeds the New York rate by 1 per cent per year. People seeking the higher

[19] Professor Sohmen argues that traders are not affected by the level of spot rates; their marketing decisions are governed by the level of the forward rate appropriate to the transaction at hand. It is therefore inappropriate, he states, to regard traders as seeking to avoid risk and to regard the difference between spot and forward rates as a risk premium. See Egon Sohmen, *The Theory of Forward Exchange*, Princeton Studies in International Finance No. 17 (Princeton, N.J.: International Finance Section, Princeton University, 1966), pp. 4, 28–31. Other authorities [e.g., Herbert G. Grubel, *Forward Exchange, Speculation, and the International Flow of Capital* (Stanford, Calif.: Stanford University Press, 1966), pp. 29–33] take the elimination of risk approach to commercial covering.

return buy spot sterling and invest it in London, but to avoid making losses on possible exchange rate changes before they reconvert the pounds to dollars, they cover by selling forward sterling. As a result of these operations, the spot rate tends to rise and the forward rate to fall, so that a discount develops on forward sterling. In equilibrium, the discount, when expressed as a percentage per year, almost equals the interest differential.[20] Or if London has the lower interest rate, forward sterling would develop a premium almost equal to the interest difference. This difference is called the interest parity.

A great deal of model building has been done in this field, beginning with Keynes' *Tract on Monetary Reform* (1922). The major elements of the forward market can be expressed in a version of the back-to-back diagrams used in connection with the analysis of transport costs in Chap. 6, but adapted to the forward market.[21]

In Fig. 19-4, the right-hand side of the back-to-back diagram shows the demand and supply in the spot exchange market, the left-hand side in the forward market. The S and D curves represent the supplies and demands of traders and of covered interest arbitrageurs, with no speculation in the initial situation. The assumption is that there is a discount of AB on the forward exchange because of a higher interest rate abroad. We are interested in the impact of the markets of a speculative flurry, touched off by a belief that the domestic currency will depreciate in the near future. As previously explained, in this case speculators sell the domestic currency forward—or the equivalent, buy forward exchange. This is represented by the shift in the demand curve in the forward market from D to D'. At the equilibrium given by the intersection of S and D' in the forward market, the discount on forward exchange is reduced below the interest parity, so an opportunity for covered interest arbitrage is opened up. Arbitrageurs can make money by buying spot exchange, investing it abroad, and covering by selling forward exchange. These actions shift D in the spot market to D' and S in the forward market to S', which restores the necessary discount (subject to the "almost" clause mentioned when interest arbitrage was explained). If the interest arbitrage is substantial, interest rates may be affected, which would narrow the discount. That is, the extra supply of loanable funds abroad reduces

---

[20] Speculation, transfer charges, and risks are usually cited as reasons interest arbitrage would not make the forward discount exactly equal to the interest difference. Grubel, *Forward Exchange, Speculation, and the International Flow of Capital*, Chap. 2, adapts the theories of portfolio balance and the inventory approach to the holding of assets to explain differences in interest rate differentials and forward discounts. Holmes and Schott, *The New York Foreign Exchange Market*, have lots of examples showing that the forward rates often differ from their interest parities, but the capital flows are in the direction of the higher interest markets.

[21] Paul A. Samuelson, "International Price Equilibrium: A Prologue to the Theory of Speculation," *Weltwirtschaftliches Archiv*, LXXIX, (1957), used back-to-back diagrams to analyze futures markets in general. Sohmen, *Flexible Exchange Rates: Theory and Policy*, applies supply and demand analysis to a variety of exchange market institutional arrangements and circumstances.

their interest rate, while the reduction in loanable funds at home increases the domestic rate. Unless the interest arbitrage is very substantial, however, this effect is likely to be small.

Now we are in a position to review the consequences of the speculation. In the spot market there is a short-term capital outflow of CD. In the forward market, CE is purchased by speculators. But DE represents an excess supply

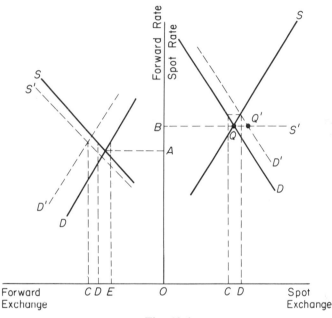

Fig. 19-4

from commercial participants in the market; it means that more exporters at home and importers abroad are covering than importers at home and exporters abroad. Traders are therefore taking a speculative position in favor of the domestic currency. The net speculative position, CD, is the result of a partial offset of the speculative demand by the position taken by the traders. In the final equilibrium we need not only to have the forward rate at its interest parity but also to have the desired capital outflow equal the net speculative position.[22] In this case speculation results in a capital outflow and a rise in both the spot and forward rates.

If the spot rate is fixed, a rather different equilibrium would result. The authorities would have to intervene to prevent the local currency from depreciating. They would have to supply QQ' from their reserves of foreign

[22] See J. M. Fleming and Robert A. Mundell, "Official Intervention in the Foreign Exchange Market," *Staff Papers*, XI, No. 1 (March 1964), 1–17, for the importance of this last condition.

exchange, or sell gold, or buy foreign exchange from foreign authorities who are willing to hold the domestic currency. In this case the forward rate would not change in the absence of repercussion on interest rates. The counterpart of the credit in the balance of payments from the loss in reserves and the counterpart of the net speculative position would be a capital outflow from covered interest arbitrage. Thus speculation in the forward market with fixed rates leads to capital outflows and a weakening of the reserve position.[23] Under the rules of the IMF, members are to keep their currencies within 1 per cent of their par values so that in practice both of the cases might be observed: a rise in the spot rate if it is not already at the upper limit, followed by the loss in reserves.

An alternative policy that is often urged and sometimes followed is for the authorities to sell forward exchange when the speculative demand appears. The effect is to keep the forward rate at a discount so that the covered interest arbitrage would not appear. Such a policy is particularly applicable if the speculative attack seems to be short-run and is expected to reverse itself soon.

The same policy of meeting speculation by selling in the forward market can be useful even though speculation occurs in the spot market in the form of a short-term capital outflow as speculators buy spot exchange to hold. In Fig. 19-5, we start with the D and S curves in each market reflecting trading and interest arbitrage operations, no speculation, and the discount in the forward market equal to the interest differential. Then the first step in the story is for the D curve in the spot market to shift to D' as speculators go long in the spot market. Rather than use QQ' of reserves to hold the spot rate stable, the authorities sell forward exchange, shifting the S curve in the forward market to S' and increasing the forward discount. This in turn starts covered interest arbitrage toward the domestic country; even though it has the lower interest rate, the arbitrage profit by foreigners buying domestic currency spot and selling it forward is greater than the interest difference. The interest arbitrage creates a supply of spot exchange and a demand for forward exchange; the supply of spot exchange to match the excess demand created by speculation is provided by interest arbitrage and the reserves can remain intact. As a matter of fact, both cases—speculation in the spot and in the forward markets—were behind the U.S. authorities' sales of forward exchange during the early 1960's, sales which reached a volume of $1.5 billion during one 14-month period.[24]

[23] Stein, *American Economic Review*, LV, computes from his regression analysis of the years 1958–1962 that speculative pressure that would cause a 1 per cent variance in the forward discount from its normal relation to interest differentials would lead to a $1.7 billion capital outflow.

[24] These sales are described in a series of articles entitled "Treasury and Federal Reserve Foreign Exchange Operations" by Charles A. Coombs, which appear every six months in the *Federal Reserve Bulletin*. The operations, by the way, include swaps of spot currencies by central banks as well as forward exchange transactions.

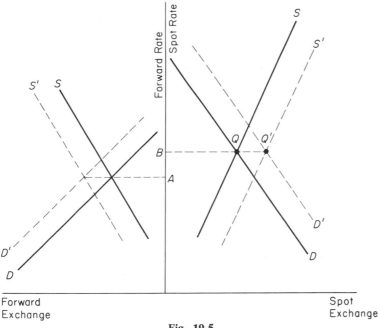

Fig. 19-5

So far the analysis has shown that forward sales by the authorities allow them to meet a speculative demand without drawing on their reserves. But what happens when the forward contract matures after, for example, three months? The answer seems to be that it depends on what has happened to speculators' anticipations in the meantime. If the speculators have given up on the idea that the currency will be devalued, they will sell their holdings of foreign exchange (either the spot exchange they purchased earlier or the exchange they receive when their forward purchase matures) and the authorities can buy this exchange in the spot market to meet their forward obligation. Otherwise they will simply have postponed the loss in reserves.[25]

THE INTEREST RATE

The same sort of analysis is useful in including the effects of the forward market on one of our expenditure-reducing policies: interest rate changes. It is digressing to discuss it at this point, but convenient to do

[25] The students of the problem are not agreed on the likely outcomes. S. C. Tsiang, "The Theory of Forward Exchange and Effects of Government Intervention on the Forward Exchange Market," *Staff Papers*, VII, No. 1 (March 1959), 75–106, is pessimistic; while Peter B. Kenen, "Trade, Speculation, and the Forward Exchange Rate," in *Trade, Growth, and the Balance of Payments*, eds. Baldwin et al., pp. 143–69, is optimistic.

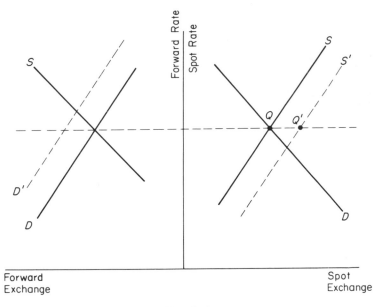

Fig. 19-6

so while the diagrammatic analysis is fresh. In Fig. 19-6 the S and D curves refer to the demands of commercial traders only; interest rates are assumed to be the same in both countries so there is no covered interest arbitrage, and there is no speculation in either market. Then the short-term rate of interest is increased by the authorities in the home country. Covered interest arbitrage sets in, changing the supply of foreign exchange to S' in the spot market and the demand curve to D' in the forward market. If the exchange rates are flexible, the rise in the forward rate and the fall in the spot rate creates the interest parity premium on the forward rate. The appreciation of the spot market generates the import surplus needed to match the covered capital inflow and simultaneously leads to an increase in absorption compared to output. On the other hand, if exchange rates are fixed, the covered capital inflow leads to an increase in reserves as the authorities purchase QQ' of foreign exchange in order to hold the rate stable.[26]

[26] Mundell points out that if the concensus is that the spot rate will not change, speculators will have a perfectly elastic demand curve in the forward market at the spot rate. This means that no forward premium is possible. Raising the interest rate in that case would continue to attract foreign capital until the increased supply of loanable funds forces the interest rate back down to the level abroad. Capital mobility would tie interest rates together. See Robert A. Mundell, "The Exchange Rate Margins and Economic Policy," in *Money in the International Order*, ed. J. Carter Murphy (Dallas: Southern Methodist University Press, 1964), p. 77.

IS SPECULATION STABILIZING?

To return to the main theme after the digression on interest rate changes and the mechanism of the forward market, a great deal of importance is lodged in the precise nature of speculation: Is it stabilizing or destabilizing? The different impacts of the two types can be shown by referring again to Fig. 19-4. In the context of flexible exchange rates, suppose that the spot rate in the very recent past has been above B, although the spot rate today is B, and that speculators believe the rate will return to a higher level. As our analysis showed, the result of the speculation is to force the spot rate above B. The speculation is stabilizing, preventing the exchange rate from moving very far from its original level. On the other hand, if the rate was originally below B, then rose to B, and speculators anticipate that it will rise still further, their purchase of forward exchange forces the spot rate above B. Speculation of this variety makes the spot rate unstable. Clearly, destabilizing speculation would make flexible exchange rates function poorly. It is also hard on the reserves under fixed rates, as the loss' of QQ' of reserves in Fig. 19-4 shows when pegged spot rates are assumed.

The problem of destabilizing speculation can be approached both theoretically and empirically. On the theoretical side, Milton Friedman once suggested that destabilizing speculation must be rare, because under it speculators buy at high prices and sell at low prices—the wrong recipe for making profits.[27] This proposition stimulated ingenuity to show that speculation can be destabilizing and profitable simultaneously; Kemp, in *The Pure Theory of International Trade*, Chap. 19, has concocted an example and gives references to other examples proposed by Baumol, Stein, and Vanek.

A second proposition about destabilizing speculation is that it is likely to be a worse problem under the present IMF rules, where a currency has a fixed rate until fundamental disequilibrium forces it to change with IMF consent, than under flexible rates. The reason is that speculators cannot lose under the IMF rule. If the spot rate is \$2.00/pound and speculators think the dollar is weak and will depreciate to, for example, \$3.00/pound, they can buy spot pounds. If the dollar does depreciate, they reconvert the pounds at a profit; if it does not, they can reconvert at their purchase price and so do not lose. The loser is the authorities who must supply reserves to maintain the original rate as long as they can. Hence it is argued that by contrast with flexible rates where speculators can lose, the adjustable peg generates more speculation and more crises.[28]

---

[27] Milton Friedman, "The Case for Flexible Exchange Rates," in *Essays in Positive Economics* (Chicago: University of Chicago Press, 1953), p. 175.

[28] See W. M. Scammell, *International Monetary Policy* (2nd ed.) (London: Macmillan & Co., Ltd., 1961), pp. 104–5. However, it is also argued that in the event of a crisis under flexible rates the direction of change of the spot rate will be obvious and therefore the "one-way option" will prevail there too. See Donald MacDougall, *The World Dollar Problem: A Study in International Economics* (London: Macmillan & Co., Ltd., 1957), p. 385.

Empirically, there are two famous cases: Europe in the 1920's, particularly France, which demonstrated destabilizing speculation; and Canada in the 1950's, where speculation was stabilizing. In the case of the French franc, the exchange rate went from 17–18 cents/franc in 1919 to 9 cents in 1922; 6 cents in October, 1923; 3 cents in March, 1924; less than 2 cents in July, 1926; and eventual stabilization at nearly 4 cents in December, 1926.[29] The students of the episode all agree that speculation was destabilizing and forced the franc to a level of depreciation much below that required for equilibrium in the balance of payments (the technical jargon is that the franc was undervalued). The disagreement arises in the interpretation of the causes. Nurkse puts it on the psychology of speculators and of traders who began to import more to beat subsequent expected price rises and export less, anticipating higher domestic currency prices later as the depreciation continued. Tsiang puts the cause on monetary mismanagement: There was a highly elastic supply of money as the banks purchased short-term government debt unloaded by the public. This money supply furnished the fuel for speculation and for domestic inflation. Aliber tends to agree more with Nurkse, saying that where government policy failed after 1924 was not so much in handling the money supply as in being unable to halt the speculation that was the cause of the public's conversion of government debt.[30] However, France was the example of destabilizing speculation in flexible exchange systems in Europe at that time; exchange systems of England, Holland, and Switzerland did not seem to exhibit it, and Belgium was a special case because of the close ties of its economy to France.

The more recent example of a fluctuating rate system was Canada in the 1950's, where the exchange rate fluctuated in the range of $1.00 U.S./$1.00 Canadian to $1.06 U.S./$1.00 Canadian, between 1952 and 1960. The stability of the rate over the period until 1958 has been attributed to stabilizing speculation by economists and econometricians alike. If the demand for Canadian dollars increased because of a rise of Canadian exports or because of a long-term capital flow from the United States, the typical reaction was a short-term capital outflow from Canada as speculators bought U.S. dollars while they were temporarily cheap. In more cases than not (15 out of 25 quarters), the short-term capital flows reduced the change in exchange rates that would have resulted from the current and long-term capital accounts. This tendency of speculation to be stabilizing has been attributed to "parity psychology": the notion that the normal U.S./Canadian

---

[29] Data from Robert Z. Aliber, "Speculation in the Foreign Exchanges: The European Experience, 1919–1926," *Yale Economic Essays*, II, No. 1 (1962), 198–99.

[30] *International Currency Experience: Lessons of the Interwar Period* (Geneva: League of Nations, 1944); S. C. Tsiang, "Fluctuating Exchange Rates in Countries with Relatively Stable Economies: Some European Experiences After World War I," *Staff Papers*, VII, No. 2 (October 1959), 244–73; and Aliber, *Yale Economic Essays*, II.

rate is $1.00/$1.00.[31] A fairly elaborate 13-equation econometric model used by Rhomberg gave the result that short-term capital movements, presumably inspired by speculation, were stabilizing in the 1950's: If the Canadian dollar depreciated by 1 cent, a stabilizing capital inflow of $24 million during one quarter was predicted by the model.[32]

After its success in the 1950's, the Canadian experiment with a fluctuating exchange rate fell upon evil days. The troubles are apparently connected with the economic policies followed by the Canadian government and hence fits into the subject matter of Chap. 20.

In summary, this chapter has looked at the economic effects of changing exchange rates. These effects are the same whether the change is one of a series in a system of freely fluctuating rates or is a change in an adjustable peg. We found that a deficit in the balance of payments would be reduced in the first instance by a depreciation if the elasticities of supply and demand behaved properly—the Marshall–Lerner condition or one of its relatives. But the conclusions of the first instance had to be modified to take account of absorption considerations; for a permanent improvement, absorption has to be reduced, relative to output. And finally we saw that the necessary changes in the exchange rate could be greatly modified by speculation, destabilizing speculation magnifying the changes and stabilizing speculation reducing them.

[31] Paul Wonnacott, *The Canadian Dollar, 1948–1962* (Toronto: University of Toronto Press, 1965), pp. 172–79.

[32] Rudolf R. Rhomberg, "Canada's Foreign Exchange Market, A Quarterly Model," *Staff Papers*, VII (April 1960), 439–56.

CHAPTER 20

FLEXIBLE
EXCHANGE RATES

POLICY MODELS

Now that the analytical propositions about changing exchange rates have been developed, it is time to look at policy. The exchange rate is a tool, like monetary and fiscal policy. It affects both the balance of payments and the national income. Sometimes the number of tools falls short of the number of targets, as when a commitment to "sound finance" prevents adequate use of fiscal policy, or when highly integrated capital markets prevent changing the domestic interest rate. In such cases it would be nice to have another tool to turn to.[1]

EXCHANGE RATE/NATIONAL INCOME/BALANCE-OF-PAYMENTS RELATIONS

With another variable added, the two-dimensional policy models of Chap. 18 have to be modified. A convenient way to begin is to suppress the interest rate as a variable, keeping it as a parameter. The exchange rate

[1] A number of writers have pointed out that flexible exchange rates merit consideration as a policy only because domestic product and factor prices are not sufficiently flexible to adjust to an arbitrarily fixed exchange rate. For example, if we go back to the Ricardian model with money wages, prices, and exchange rates, the numerical example of footnote 5, Chap. 2, established that the lower limit of Portuguese wages was 1,500 escudos/year, given the productivity data; British wages of 2,000 pounds/year; and an exchange rate of 1 escudo/pound. If the Portuguese wage is instead 1,000 escudos/year, the price for locally produced wine is 80,000 escudos (imported wine would cost 120,000 escudos) and for domestically produced cloth is 90,000 escudos compared to 100,000 for imports. Adjustment via wage changes would call for a rise in Portuguese wages and prices and a fall in British, in order to allow the British to sell their cloth and eliminate their balance-of-payments deficit. If such adjustment were quick and easy, without lags, stickiness, and inflationary or deflationary consequences on output and employment, then exchange rates could remain fixed indefinitely. In such a case money would be able to function better in its various roles as a medium of exchange, unit of account, and store of purchasing power. See Richard Caves, "Flexible Exchange Rates," *American Economic Review, Papers and Proceedings*, LII, No. 2 (May 1963), 120–29; and Mundell, "Exchange Rate Margins and Economic Policy," in *Money in the International Order*, ed. Murphy, p. 69.

and real income are the variables. Following the lines of the models of Chaps. 17 and 18, it is possible to define an internal and an external balance schedule in Fig. 20-1. Internal balance still requires that the sum of exports, investment, and government spending equals the sum of imports, saving, and taxes. Starting from a point such as *E* on the *XIG-MST* line, where it is assumed that the equilibrium condition holds, suppose that the national

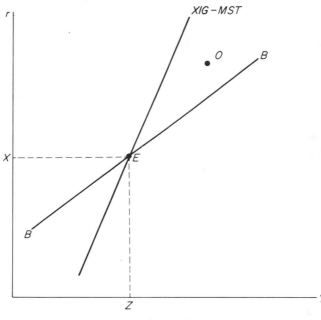

Fig. 20-1

income increases at a constant exchange rate. Then imports, savings, and taxes will increase; and to restore national income equilibrium exports, investment, and government spending must rise, or the leakages must fall. Induced investment may do some of the job, but generally with a constant interest rate the foreign exchange rate will have to depreciate. Assuming that the elasticities are high enough and that there is no destabilizing speculation, the higher exchange rate raises exports and cuts imports, and restores internal balance at a higher national income and a higher exchange rate.

External balance requires that the current account balance equals the capital accounts balance, with opposite sign. At point *E*, for example, this is the case. If the national income rises, imports rise; and to restore balance along the *BB* line, a depreciation is necessary.[2]

[2] Diagrams of this sort are used by Robert Mundell, "Flexible Exchange Rates and Employment Policy," *Canadian Journal of Economics and Political Science*, XXVII, No. 4 (November 1961), 509–17.

To show that the equilibrium in this model is at E, the intersection of the *XIG-MST* and *BB* lines, try the experiment of starting some place else. Suppose that the exchange rate is higher than rate X when national income is at Z. The balance of payments will be in surplus and, with a flexible exchange rate, under our assumptions about the elasticities the rate will appreciate, moving back to X. Or if national income is higher than Z when the exchange rate is at X, there will be a deflationary gap: The sum of imports,

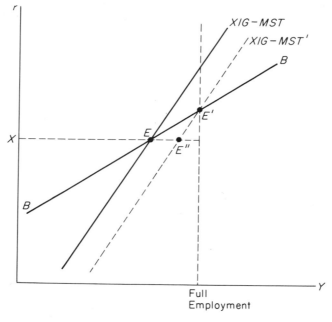

Fig. 20-2

savings, and taxes will exceed the sum of exports, investment, and government spending, so national income will fall back to Z. These considerations explain why the *BB* line is the flatter of the two for a stable equilibrium. If the labels were transposed, so that *BB* were steeper, then from a point like O national income would rise and the exchange rate depreciate, which would lead away from equilibrium.

The model can now be used to work out a few cases. In the first case, suppose that equilibrium is established in Fig. 20-2 at point E, which is less than full employment. Using fiscal policy to increase employment, an increase in government spending, for example, shifts *XIG-MST* to the right. If exchange rates are fixed at level X, the new equilibrium national income will involve a deficit in the balance of payments and a loss of reserves at E''. But if the exchange rate is set free or is deliberately depreciated, the new tool allows equilibrium of both the national income and the balance of payments at E'. Observe the increased potency of fiscal policy with flexible exchange rates; the increased national income at E' compared with E'' results from the impact on national income of the depreciation necessary to restore the balance of payments.[3]

In a similar way we can trace out the effects of monetary policy. If initially in Fig. 20-3 the equilibrium is at less than full employment, a reduction in interest rates would be appropriate. This would shift XIG-MST

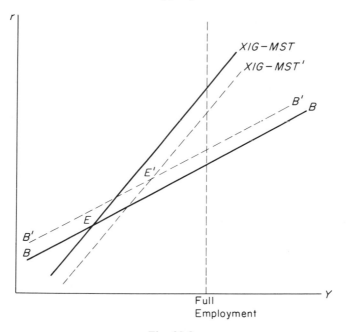

Fig. 20-3

to the right, since the fall in interest rates stimulates investment, which requires a higher national income (generating more leakages) for equilibrium. At the same time, BB shifts up: Lower interest rates cut the capital inflow or increases the outflow, which adds to the debit side of the balance. For equilibrium a higher exchange rate is needed to cut import debits and raise export credits. As drawn, E', the new equilibrium, is closer to full employment, and a further decrease in the interest rate is needed to complete the transition to full employment. Again notice that without the change in exchange rates a deficit would be involved, indicating that both tools are needed to meet two goals—also that the interest rate cut has a bigger impact on national income if the exchange rate is allowed to vary than if it were held constant.

[3] A neat mathematical analysis demonstrating this point is in Krueger, *Quarterly Journal of Economics*, LXXIX, 204.

The cases so far have dealt with domestic policy. But the same model can be used to show adjustment to changed conditions in international trade. In Fig. 20-4, E is the initial equilibrium with the balance-of-payments and the national income equilibrium conditions both satisfied. Postulate a reduction in exports because of technological progress or the formation of a trade-diverting customs union abroad. As a result, both *XIG-MST* and

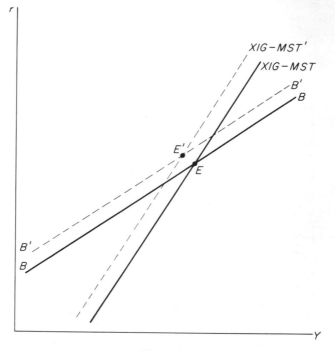

Fig. 20-4

BB must shift to the left: As a result of the fall in exports, national income must fall at a constant exchange rate in order to reduce imports so that equilibrium can be maintained along both lines. The adjustment to the new foreign demand conditions at E' involves both exchange depreciation and a lower level of national income. If this level of national income is unsatisfactory, further exchange adjustments together with monetary or fiscal policy may be called for, along the lines of the previous models.

REFINEMENTS: THE RATE OF INTEREST

This basic model can be supplemented in various ways. One is to relax the assumption that the rate of interest is constant except when it changes as the result of a policy decision. The national income changes will change the interest rate, with effects on domestic investment and absorption and on foreign capital flows. In effect, the *LM* curve is put back in the model.[4] For example, suppose that with less than full employment the money supply is expanded. This lowers the rate of interest, increases national income, and increases imports and the capital outflow. With a flexible exchange rate, the exchange rate depreciates. The depreciation by increasing exports and decreasing imports raises national income still more, increasing the transactions demand for money, and raising the interest rate because the amount of money available to satisfy the liquidity demand for money is reduced. Indeed, it has been suggested that sometimes this latter effect is really overwhelming. Rhomberg, in studying the Canadian economy, analyzes the case where government spending is increased with a constant money supply. The resultant rise in interest rates can attract more capital than can be transferred by the rise in induced imports, so that the balance of payments turns favorable and the rate of foreign exchange appreciates instead of depreciating, as in Fig. 20-2. It has been suggested that Canada in the 1950's exhibited this behavior.[5] In terms of model building, the crucial assumption here is that fiscal policy consists in increasing government spending financed by borrowing from the public and is not accompanied by sufficient monetary expansion to hold the interest rate constant.

REFINEMENTS: FEEDBACK

Another refinement in the model is to consider the impact and feedbacks from the rest of the world. A reduction in interest rates in the home country and the accompanying depreciation improve the local current account at the expense of the rest of the world; their national income is correspondingly reduced by a multiple amount. If the rest of the world had a full-employment policy, they in turn would need to use monetary or fiscal policy, and the feedback in turn would reduce national income in the home country. Flexible exchange rates do not isolate countries from one another as far as employment policy goes.[6]

REFINEMENTS: THE FORWARD MARKET

The discussion of policies under flexible rate systems would be incomplete without looking at the forward market and forward speculation. We can illustrate by this example: Suppose that the balance of payments and the national income are in equilibrium, but at less than full employment,

---

[4] See Mundell, *Canadian Journal of Economics and Political Science*, XXIX, 475–85.

[5] Rudolph R. Rhomberg, "A Model of the Canadian Economy under Fixed and Fluctuating Exchange Rates," *Journal of Political Economy*, LXXII, No. 1 (February 1964), 1–31.

[6] For a mathematical development see Krueger, *Quarterly Journal of Economics*, LXXIX, p. 206.

with interest rates in London and New York both at 6 per cent and the spot and forward rates both at $1.00/pound. To increase domestic employment, the New York interest rate is cut to 4 per cent. We know from the analysis of Fig. 20-3 that the spot rate depreciates and capital outflow is increased. Interest arbitrageurs buy spot pounds, depreciating the spot rate, and sell forward pounds, appreciating the forward rate, until the discount on the forward pound just offsets the gain in interest earnings. So far no modification of Fig. 20-3 is called for; all that has happened is that the capital outflow is covered. But now suppose that speculation is introduced. The effect depends on the position that the speculators take. If they believe that the spot rate will continue to be at its depreciated level, they will buy forward exchange. The consequent rise in the price of forward exchange allows more scope for covered interest arbitrage and shifts BB still higher, giving more of a short-run impact on the exchange rate and on national income from the interest rate change.

The effects of fiscal policy may also be influenced by speculation. In Fig. 20-2 the equilibrium at E' involved constant interest rates but a depreciated spot rate compared to the original equilibrium at E. This should attract a covered capital inflow, with the covering appreciating the forward rate. If speculators buy forward pounds in this situation, the scope for a covered inflow will be increased. Balance-of-payments equilibrium would require a flatter BB line; with speculation generating more capital inflow, a higher national income is required for any exchange rate change in order to call forth the import debits necessary to meet the capital inflow credits. The impact of fiscal policy would thus be reduced. Using Rhomberg's model, where fiscal policy tightens interest rates, the covered capital inflow is still bigger, but the modifications of speculation are the same.

In reviewing the mechanism of adjustment under fixed rates in Chap. 18, the case of extreme capital mobility fixing the local rate of interest at the world level was discussed. It was noted that monetary policy ran into trouble but fiscal policy was effective. When the rates are flexible, however, the situation is reversed: Expanding the money supply and thus temporarily lowering the local rate of interest touches off capital outflows, depreciating the spot rate and hence stimulating national income. Fiscal policy now runs into trouble, though. With less than full employment, suppose government spending is expanded. This tends to raise the interest rate, so capital flows in. The inflow appreciates the exchange rate, worsening the current account balance. XIG-MST shifts to the right from fiscal policy, to the left from the exchange appreciation; and if the money supply is fixed, equilibrium in the assets market with a fixed rate of interest requires no change in the national income when it is all over.[7]

[7] For a diagrammatic analysis, see Mundell, *Canadian Journal of Economics and Political Science*, XXIX. These extreme conclusions are modified when speculation and the forward market are taken into account, for then capital mobility requires that there be

The wide use of tariffs and quotas for balance-of-payments purposes when exchange rates are fixed was discussed in Chap. 18. With flexible exchange rates tariffs are not needed to restore external balance, but of course they might be used for other purposes such as infant-industry protection. Adjustment in the foreign exchange market involves appreciation of the exchange rate, since the demand for imports falls; it has also been contended that with flexible rates the tariff is deflationary—a quite opposite conclusion to the expected effect under the usual Keynesian analysis with fixed rates. The reasoning involves the Laursen–Metzler effect: As a result of the tariffs the terms of trade are improved, which means that real income is increased at a given output. If saving is therefore increased, national income will fall.[8]

THE CASES AGAINST FLEXIBLE RATES

The purpose of all the foregoing models is to illustrate that the exchange rate is a policy tool that can be used in combination with other policy tools to achieve internal and external goals. The interesting question is why is it a tool that is not more used. The prevailing standard is a fixed rate held as long as possible before adjusting. Suggestions that more flexibility be incorporated—either completely free rates or freedom to fluctuate within a band of 5 or 10 per cent on either side of parity—are rejected. Much of the debate takes the form of pro and con arguments. For example, there is the question of the stability of flexible exchange rates—both from the elasticities of nonspeculators and from destabilizing speculation. This possibility of instability is a prominent feature of the criticism of flexible rates,[9] although, as we have seen, the general thrust of empirical research is that the elasticities are high enough for stability and that it is impossible to generalize about destabilizing speculation.

An issue of some prominence has been whether the fixed exchange rate, rather than indicating the absence of a policy tool, has not served to make the monetary policy tool more serviceable. In the eyes of some official groups as well as academic economists, the need to defend a fixed exchange

---

no covered interest differential, giving the possibility that the domestic rate of interest can be changed. Furthermore, some of the impact of capital flows will be handled by changes in the forward rate so that the spot rate is not likely to change as much as indicated in the paragraph. As a result, monetary policy might lose some of its potency but fiscal policy would be likely to gain. For a discussion, see Mundell, "The Exchange Rate Margins and Economic Policy," in ed. Murphy, *Money in the International Order*.

[8] Mundell, *Canadian Journal of Economics and Political Science*, XXVII.

[9] For example, by the staff of the Federal Reserve System Board of Governors in "A System of Fluctuating Exchange Rates: Pro and Con," in Joint Economic Committee, *State of the Economy and Policies for Full Employment*, 87th Congress, 2nd Session, 1962, p. 659.

rate keeps central banks from expanding the money supply in an inflationary manner; the resulting loss of reserves on a fixed rate signals them to slow down monetary expansion, whereas a depreciating rate would not.[10] Professor Kindleberger suggests that, like the problem of destabilizing speculation, this one cannot be generalized about. Some countries with previously difficult experiences with exchange rates will be very sensitive to them, such as Germany.[11] As a general proposition, the signal to tighten money on the fixed rate may come at the wrong time as far as the domestic economy is concerned, as it would when a balance-of-payments deficit developed at less than full employment. Professor Johnson points out that with speculative short-term capital movements taking place vigorously in recent years, many countries have maintained their fixed rate only by the aid of cooperating central banks who have loaned reserves—exacting in return a commitment to "orthodox" economic policies of the sort that appeal to conservative central bankers. In the case of the United States and the United Kingdom, these orthodox policies for years yielded less than full employment or high-level growth.[12]

Another common argument against flexible rates is the inconvenience, increased risk, and increased cost of trade and international investment from the risks of losses due to exchange fluctuations.[13] The trader can achieve certainty of the exchange rate for an individual transaction by resorting to the forward market; Professor Sohmen argues that this does not involve the payment of a premium for risk; since if interest arbitrage is effective, any difference between spot and forward rates does not accrue to risk-bearing speculators but to interest arbitrageurs. Also, since there are both commercial buyers and sellers of foreign exchange, if importers cover by buying forward exchange at more than the spot rate, for example, then exporters also cover by selling at more than the spot rate, and for the class of traders as a whole the gains and losses are offset.[14] Another, rather broader, theoretical answer to the risk objection is to point out that with fixed rates there are also risks of a different sort: of income or domestic price changes or of governmental controls, depending on which tool is used to control the balance of payments.

[10] Staff of the Federal Reserve System Board of Governors in Joint Economic Committee, *State of the Economy and Policies for Full Employment*; Committee on the Working of the Monetary System, *Report*, Cmd. 827 (London: Her Majesty's Stationery Office, 1959), p. 260; Jacob Viner, "Some International Aspects of Economic Stabilization," in *The State of the Social Sciences*, ed. L. D. White (Chicago: University of Chicago Press, 1956), p. 294.

[11] C. P. Kindleberger, "Flexible Exchange Rates," in *Monetary Management*, Research Studies Prepared for the Commission on Money and Credit, eds. Frank M. Tamagna et al. (Englewood Cliffs, N.J.: Prentice-Hall, Inc., 1963), pp. 403–25.

[12] Harry G. Johnson, "Equilibrium under Fixed Exchanges," *American Economic Review Papers and Proceedings*, LIII, No. 2 (May 1963), 117.

[13] See the first two references of footnote 10.

[14] Sohmen, *The Theory of Forward Exchange*, pp. 28–29.

The form of uncertainty is changed, not the fact.[15] Empirically, neither trade nor investment in Canada seemed to be inhibited during their experiment with fluctuating rates.

Another objection to flexible exchange rates is that the depreciation, by raising import prices, leads to a rise in internal costs, prices, and wages. The currency would then have to depreciate again, with the probability of speculation entering to hasten the depreciation.[16] Essentially this is the position that absorption will not be reduced relative to output by a change in the exchange rate at full employment. If it does not, a combination of monetary, fiscal, and exchange policies is needed to maintain both internal and external equilibrium; if monetary and fiscal policy are too easy, internal inflation will indeed lead to a devaluation spiral,[17] but this is not a general argument. Inappropriate monetary and fiscal policies lead to trouble under fixed rates also.

Fluctuating exchange rates have also been attacked as providing an unstable standard by which comparative advantage could be measured, since any growth in productivity would be offset by an appreciation of the exchange rate.[18] As our model of wages, productivities, and exchange rates in Chap. 2 showed, it is indeed the case that exchange rates must fall within limits that depend on domestic productivities and factor costs. If technological progress changes productivity, with fixed factor wage rates, the exchange rate limits must change. But it is equally true that if the exchange rate is fixed, there are limits on the size of the factor costs if equilibrium is to be maintained. No matter whether the rates are fixed or not, a change in productivity changes comparative advantage. The adjustment of the balance of payments to this change will typically involve a change in the terms of trade and in factor rewards, whether the rate changes or not. And there will be no question about where the comparative advantage lies under either system of exchange rates; trade is based on a comparison of domestic with foreign prices, a comparison that does not require a fixed exchange rate for its existence.

The final point concerns difficulties in the transition to a regime of flexible exchange rates if it should be decided that that was desirable. Would it not involve great chaos in the foreign exchange markets? Even though fluctuating rates might work well enough after everyone was familiar with them, when they are first established, many people visualize destabilizing speculation, reluctance to engage in foreign trade, and general disruption. The problem would be particularly acute for the dollar and the pound,

[15] Friedman, *Essays in Positive Economics*, p. 174.

[16] Robert Triffin, *Gold and the Dollar Crisis* (New Haven: Yale University Press, 1960), pp. 82–86.

[17] Described for some European countries after World War I by Nurkse in League of Nations, *International Currency Experience*, pp. 113–16.

[18] Robert V. Roosa, *Monetary Reform for the World Economy* (New York: Harper & Row, Publishers, 1965), p. 28.

currencies that are now held as reserve assets by other countries. Changes in their values, and the fact that the need for international reserves would be greatly reduced if adjustments are made by rate changes, would lead countries holding key currencies to dump them on the market, accentuating rate fluctuations. It is suggested that in that case a great demand for gold would arise, leading to large price rises in the gold market.[19]

Because the chaos argument seems so pervasive, some advocates of flexible rates have suggested that the transition from fixed rates should be done gradually, by widening the limits around parity at which authorities intervene in the exchanges.[20] The IMF rules permit a 1 per cent fluctuation on each side of parity; perhaps 10 or 15 per cent total width of band might allow the exchange rate to function as an equilibrating mechanism without creating chaos.[21]

So the debate goes on. Since Bretton Woods, when the International Monetary Fund was set up, the basic international arrangement has been for fixed exchange rates, to be altered when required by a "fundamental disequilibrium." But it is widely recognized that this original notion has changed into an attitude much less favorable to altering the exchange rate even in very difficult balance-of-payments conditions.[22] The advocates of flexible rates are in the position of the famous academic scribblers described by Keynes at the end of *The General Theory*, whose ideas bear fruit (if at all) only some years later through their effects on those in authority. And if Professor Galbraith is correct, the flexible exchange rate idea has a remarkable handicap to overcome. Galbraith contends that the large, powerful, technologically mature corporation needs stable prices as a basis for the planning of its very large and very long-term projects, and that it attempts to manage the market to assure both the stable prices and stable quantities demanded. If true, it is unlikely that these politically potent organizations would welcome freeing the exchange rate, even if as in the case of Canada for several years the fluctuating rate proved not to be very unstable.[23]

[19] Staff of the Federal Reserve System Board of Governors, in Joint Economic Committee, *State of the Economy and Policies for Full Employment*, p. 657.

[20] Called the "band proposal" in George Halm, *The 'Band' Proposal: The Limits of Permissible Exchange Rate Variations*, Special Papers in International Economics No. 6 (Princeton, N.J.: International Finance Section, Princeton University, 1965).

[21] Professor Machlup thinks that limited flexibility is the reasonable policy for another reason: Governments would have to overcome strong public opposition to either depreciation or appreciation, so it seems doubtful that they would agree to stay out of the exchange market altogether. See "The Report of the Nongovernment Economists' Study Group," *American Economic Review Papers and Proceedings*, LV, No. 2 (May 1965), 176.

[22] R. S. Sayers, "Cooperation Between Central Banks," *The Three Banks Review*, (September 1963), believes that the experience of the European Payments Union, the experience of the perhaps too large devaluations in 1949, and the development of *ad hoc* assistance among central bankers are responsible.

[23] See John Kenneth Galbraith, *The New Industrial State* (Boston: Houghton Mifflin Company, 1967).

Some of the debators point to Canada as a case illustrating the failure of flexible exchange rates after a period of initial success; others claim that Canada illustrates what unsound policies can do to a flexible rate system. Canada experienced high unemployment toward the end of the 1950's, a slowdown in economic growth, a fall in the U.S. dollar price of the Canadian dollar after 1960, then a decision to use official reserve policy to depreciate the Canadian dollar still more, and finally in 1962 a decision to go on a fixed rate at 92.5 cents U.S. to the Canadian dollar. Many authorities trace the difficulties to restrictive monetary policies, including here a lengthening of the public debt maturities as well as restriction of the money supply. Apparently the high Canadian interest rates attracted a large capital inflow, appreciating the Canadian dollar, worsening the current account, and reducing the national income both from the impact on domestic investment and from the international trade sector. The reason for the tight-money policy was a fear of inflation. Attempts were made to combat unemployment by use of fiscal policy, but this also has the effects of raising interest rates unless the money supply is simultaneously expanded. The flexible exchange rate was not the cause of the Canadian difficulties; it simply magnified the effects of the domestic policies.[24]

APPENDIX I: The Theory of Purchasing Power Parity

By developing the idea of the rate of exchange as a policy variable that influences the balance of payments and the national income, we have ignored the famous old doctrine of purchasing power parity, for which PPP is a handy abbreviation. This proposition is often referred to and has been used by some recent empirical workers in spite of often-repeated theoretical questioning,[25] so it is worth working through.

The basic idea of purchasing power parity, which goes back at least to the Napoleonic wars, is that equilibrium exchange rates move proportionately to changes in the domestic price levels of the countries involved.

[24] Analyses of the period are given in Wonnacott, *The Canadian Dollar, 1948–1962;* Harry G. Johnson, *The Canadian Quandary: Economic Problems and Policies* (Toronto: McGraw-Hill Company of Canada Limited, 1963), Chap. 3; Robert A. Mundell, "Problems of Monetary and Exchange Rate Management in Canada," *The National Banking Review* (September 1964), 77–86.

[25] H. S. Houthakker, "Exchange Rate Adjustment," in Joint Economic Committee, *Factors Affecting the U.S. Balance of Payments*, 87th Congress, 2nd Session, 1962, pp. 287–304, used PPP calculations to show that the dollar was overvalued by some 22 per cent compared to the mark at that time. S. C. Tsiang measured speculative activity by the divergence of the exchange rate from PPP in *Staff Papers*, VII, in the course of his study of European foreign exchange experience after World War I. A brief history of thought on the subject of PPP is in Haberler, *A Survey of International Trade Theory*, pp. 45–48.

The *absolute* version says that

$$r = \text{price index of country 1/price index of country 2,}$$

where r is the exchange rate defined as the price of 1 unit of country 2's currency in country 1. Thus, if the U.S. price index were 100 and the U.K. price index 200, the PPP exchange rate would be 50 cents/pound. At that rate, an item costing \$1 in the United States and £2 in the United Kingdom could be imported for \$1, transport costs and tariffs aside. This version is generally regarded as either trivial or wrong. It is trivial if interpreted as applying to a situation where every good moves without cost, for arbitrage will make any rate the correct one. If the actual rate in the example were \$1/pound instead of the PPP 50 cents/pound rate, the United States would stop buying U.K. products and the United Kingdom would buy only U.S. products. British prices would fall, while U.S. prices would rise until the price indexes became equal. It is false if transport costs and tariffs are included, for transport costs create, realistically, the class of domestic goods and services where transport costs are so high that they are not traded. Generally, productivity in the domestic sector relative to the foreign-trade sector differs from country to country, so that the cost of a standard market basket of goods is different in each. The price of services affects the PPP calculation rather than the equilibrium rate.[26]

An alternative formulation of PPP is the *relative* version, where rates of exchange and price indexes for two different periods of time are compared. Using superscripts b for before the change and a for after, the formulation is

$$\frac{r^a}{r^b} = \frac{(\text{price index of country 1})^a/(\text{price index of country 1})^b}{(\text{price index of country 2})^a/(\text{price index of country 2})^b}.$$

The justification for defining this as the PPP formula can be shown by a variant of the earlier example. Suppose that the dollar per pound rate was initially at a level where internal and external balance prevailed, for example, \$1/pound when the price index in each country stood at 100. Then postulate a worldwide inflation that brings the price index to 200 in the United States and 300 in the United Kingdom. Unless the pound depreciates, the United Kingdom will run a deficit from their overpriced merchandise; and PPP says that the new rate should be \$2/3/pound to maintain the original price relationships between the countries.

The relative formulation is obviously not of much help when conditions other than the general price level have changed. Changes in demand or productivity, which shift the offer curves, would require a new rate of exchange unless money wages and other costs shift. A change in capital flows

[26] See Bela Balassa, "The Purchasing-Power Parity Doctrine: A Reappraisal," *Journal of Political Economy*, LXXII, No. 6 (December 1964), 584–96; Samuelson, *Review of Economics and Statistics*, XLVI.

indicates a new equilibrium rate different from PPP. An increase in real national income greater in one country than another, leading to more imports for the growing country, would mean a different equilibrium rate. Even when far-reaching changes in the structure of trade, capital flows, or employment are not present, the empirical data show that productivity changes and wage adjustments differ greatly among countries in regard to their relative impact on domestic goods and on internationally traded goods. Suppose that in the United Kingdom no changes in productivity or cost take place, but that in the United States a greater increase in productivity occurs in manufacturing exportables and importables than in the domestic service industries. Suppose further that money wages rise so that the price of the internationally traded goods does not fall, while the price of services rises. Since the U.S. price index rises, PPP indicates that the dollar should depreciate. To the extent that the rising price of services leads people to substitute foreign-traded goods for them, some depreciation is indeed indicated, but it is coincidence if PPP shows the needed amount.[27]

APPENDIX II: The Theory of Optimum Currency Areas

A recent theoretical development, extending the theory of flexible exchange rates in an interesting way, is the notion of an optimum currency area. Traditionally, each nation has controlled its own currency and monetary policy as part of its political sovereignty. The growth of common market projects has led to the question of whether the nation is indeed the appropriate currency area or whether a larger (or perhaps even smaller) region is more suitable.

As originally developed by Mundell,[28] a currency area is defined as an area within which exchange rates are fixed. It might therefore include a single national currency or more than one. A region is defined as an area within which there is factor mobility; between regions factors are immobile. In this sense, a country that consists of two regions (one agricultural and one industrial, for example) with a single currency is not an optimum currency area. A shift in demand from agriculture to industry leaves unemployment in agriculture and excess demand in industry. If the central bank expands the money supply to combat the unemployment, it worsens the inflation in industry. With flexible exchange rates between the two regions, each having its own currency, however, another tool is created. The central bank in each

[27] See Balassa, *Journal of Political Economy*, LXXII; Lloyd Metzler, "Exchange Rates and International Monetary Fund," in *International Monetary Policies*, Postwar Economic Studies No. 7 (Washington, D.C.: Board of Governors of the Federal Reserve System, 1947).

[28] Robert A. Mundell, "A Theory of Optimum Currency Areas," *American Economic Review*, LI, No. 4 (September 1961), 657–65.

region could take action appropriate to its problem, using the flexible exchange rate as the second tool to meet the internal and external balance goals. Of course, if resources are mobile between agriculture and industry, the shift in demand would pull labor and capital out of agriculture and into industry. The adjustment problem arises because of factor immobility.

On an international scale, the EEC might become an optimum currency area if labor and capital mobility can be achieved. So far the European capital markets are not sufficiently integrated to equalize returns on capital; and while there is a great deal of labor movement from Italy during boom times in Europe, most of the immigrant workers have come from Eastern Germany, North Africa, Portugal, Spain, Greece, and Turkey.[29] Until the institutions promoting factor mobility are achieved, a common currency is not appropriate in this view.[30]

Implicitly, this view of optimum currency areas assumes that the conditions for factor-price equalization do not exist.

The optimum currency concept may be further refined by considering the impact of flexible rates on an open region as compared to a closed one, where an open region is one with a large share of its output in exportables and importables. Another refinement would be to disaggregate and deal with differing degrees of factor mobility among industries. A rather different angle is to explore the differences within a currency area between a single currency and several currencies with fixed exchange rates. The adjustment mechanism may differ between these cases because of differences in the character of monetary reserves and lenders of last resort and because nations typically have special tax, credit, and depressed-area policies for their lagging regions that might not exist if several countries composed the currency area. The interested student may follow up these ideas in Johnson, *American Economic Review*, LIII, and in R. I. McKinnon, "Optimum Currency Areas," *American Economic Review*, LIII, No. 4 (September 1963), 717–25.

---

[29] C. P. Kindleberger, "European Integration and the International Corporation" in *Europe and the Dollar* (Cambridge, Mass.: The M.I.T. Press, 1966) pp. 27–40.

[30] J. E. Meade, "The Balance of Payments Problems of a Free Trade Area," *Economic Journal*, LXVII, No. 267 (September 1957), 379–96, argues for flexible exchange rates between members of a common market when labor mobility does not exist.

CHAPTER 21

THEORY
OF CAPITAL
MOVEMENTS

THE TRANSFER PROBLEM
AND THE OPTIMUM AMOUNT
OF FOREIGN INVESTMENT

PART I CONCENTRATED ON REAL ASPECTS of the current account in the balance of payments; Part II has been concerned with overall problems of the adjustment of the balance of payments. So far slight attention has been paid to the long-run capital account, although there is a considerable literature on the subject. Interest historically has been centered on the transfer problem: If country 1 loans $1 million to country 2, equilibrium requires an export surplus of $1 million for country 1. How is this achieved? The problem comes up for reparations, unilateral aid, and ordinary commercial lending. In the first half of this chapter, some of the theory will be reviewed.

Another problem has attracted attention recently; it is not particularly related to the first except that it deals with international capital movements. The problem is how much capital ought to flow between countries? Will a free market give the optimum results? This question occupies the second half of the chapter.

THE TRANSFER PROBLEM

In 1921 it was decided that Germany should pay reparations to the Allies of 132 billion gold marks ($33,000,000,000) over a 20-year period.[1] What would be involved in generating an export surplus of that much over the coming years? The problem has usually been broken down into a money transfer of converting the payer's money into the receiver's currency and a real transfer, that is, the export surplus. More recently it is common to distinguish between cases where full employment is continuously maintained,

[1] Haberler, *The Theory of International Trade*, gives a summary of the negotiations, the Dawes Plan, the Young Agreement, and the rest of the complicated story.

on the other hand, and cases of less than full employment where output can be expanded with no rise of prices on the other.[2]

A classical gold-standard answer to the problem was that if country 1 had to buy country 2's currency to make a unilateral payment, country 1's currency would depreciate to the gold export point. The loss of gold in country 1, and the gain in country 2, would change money supplies and hence price levels in each country so that country 1 would acquire its export surplus.[3] Or, under freely fluctuating exchanges, the depreciation itself would generate the export surplus. Keynes, in a famous article on German reparations, urged that in the German case the mechanism would not work because Germany would have to increase its exports by 40 per cent in value and the elasticity of demand for these exports was so low that it seemed unlikely that such an expansion could be achieved by price changes; in any event, devaluation was ruled out by the Allies and a gold-standard type of deflation was politically infeasible.[4] Ohlin replied that if the Germans used taxation to raise the money to pay reparations instead of borrowing the foreign exchange from the United States, the public would buy less imports as well as fewer home products. Resources would then shift to the export- and import-competing sectors. In the countries receiving the reparations, purchasing of imports and home products would expand and resources would be pulled away from exports. The balance of trade would thus adjust without the necessity for large changes in the terms of trade or large price cuts for German exports, although relative prices between home goods and foreign-trade goods would change in each country.[5] Keynes thought the transfer was impossible; Ohlin thought it feasible.

This famous debate occurred before the development of modern income theory. Today the analysis typically proceeds in the fashion we have used on previous occasions: The first step is to see what happens on the assumption of constant terms of trade to the demand for imports in each country during the process of raising the reparations or forming the money capital in one country and disposing of it in the other. If the current account has not changed by the amount of the transfer, the next step is to see how the resulting disequilibrium is corrected by a change in the terms of trade, by income changes, or by some policy tool such as tariff changes.

---

[2] Called the classical and the Keynesian transfer problems, respectively, by Harry G. Johnson in "The Transfer Problem and Exchange Stability," *International Trade and Economic Growth*, Chap. VII.

[3] Worked out at length in Taussig, *International Trade*, and tested empirically by a number of his students: Viner in Canada, White in France, Williams in Argentina.

[4] "The German Transfer Problem," *Economic Journal*, XXXIX (March 1929), 1–7, reprinted in American Economic Association, *Readings in the Theory of International Trade*.

[5] "The Reparation Problem: A Discussion—Transfer Difficulties, Real and Imagined," *Economic Journal*, XXXIX (June 1929), 172–78, reprinted in American Economic Association, *Readings in the Theory of International Trade*.

INCOME ANALYSIS IN A CLASSICAL SETTING

The classical full-employment case provides a simple example of this technique. Suppose that the sum to be transferred under a foreign aid program, for example, is raised by an income tax in country 1 and is distributed as a subsidy to the citizens of country 2. With given full employment and constant terms of trade, disposable income falls in country 1 and rises in country 2 by the amount of the transfer. Imports in country 1 fall by MPM_1 times the transfer; the import increase in country 2 is MPM_2 times the transfer. Only if the total of these trade changes equals the amount of the transfer can the real transfer be accomplished at the original terms of trade. These considerations lead to a well-established proposition: Income changes associated with the transfer will complete the real transfer under constant output assumptions if the sum of the marginal propensities to import equals 1. This can be shown in the following way: Country 1's balance of trade, B_1, is equal to the difference between her exports, which are, in fact, country 2's imports, and her own imports:

$$B_1 = M_2 - M_1. \tag{21-1}$$

Denoting disposable income by Y, we can write the change in B_1 as the result of a change in T, the transfer, in this form:

$$dB_1 = \frac{dM_2}{dY_2}\frac{dY_2}{dT}\,dT - \frac{dM_1}{dY_1}\frac{dY_1}{dT}\,dT. \tag{21-2}$$

Making use of the facts that $dM/dY = MPM$, $dY_2/dT = 1$, and $dY_1/dT = -1$, Eq. (21-2) can be rewritten as

$$dB_1 = MPM_2\,dT + MPM_1\,dT = (MPM_2 + MPM_1)\,dT. \tag{21-3}$$

It is now immediately obvious that $dB_1 = dT$ if $MPM_2 + MPM_1 = 1$.

If the sum of the marginal propensities to import is less than 1, an insufficient current account surplus will be developed, and the terms of trade of country 1 will have to fall in order to restore equilibrium. Or if it should happen that the sum is greater than 1, the current account will develop an excessively large surplus and the terms of trade will improve as a corrective device. The size of the change in the terms of trade depends on the elasticities of the offer curves, as indicated by this consideration: Starting from an initial equilibrium where the two offer curves intersect, the transfer can be regarded in real terms as the payment of a certain quantity of goods from country 1. But this payment changes the origin of the offer curves and gives a new equilibrium. Part of the transition to the new equilibrium is accomplished by the income changes; how much of a terms-of-trade change is needed to complete the transition depends on the elasticities.[6]

[6] See Mundell, *American Economic Review*, L, for mathematical and geometrical analysis.

The tradition in economics has it that the classical or orthodox view is that the terms of trade will have to decline. Our analysis shows that there is no "have to" involved; it all depends on the size of the marginal propensities. For the classical view to hold, the sum of the marginal propensities of the paying country and the rest of the world would have to be less than 1, and there is no a priori ground for believing that has to be the case.[7]

As we know from earlier chapters, tariffs and transport costs can make a difference in some of the theoretical conclusions. This happens also in the case of the transfer mechanism. Take the case of the tariff first. The standard assumption of analysis is that tariff proceeds are redistributed to the public in the form of a reduction of their income taxes, and that the public disposes of the extra disposable income in accordance with their marginal propensities. A smaller volume of trade, conversely, bringing lower tariff revenue to the government, is connected to a fall in disposable income because the government is assumed to increase income taxes to hold its revenues constant. The meaning of this for the transfer problem is that in the payer, country 1, disposable income and hence imports are cut because of the transfer. The fall in imports reduces tariff proceeds; hence disposable income is reduced as just explained and imports will fall still more. The converse sequence goes on in country 2. A given transfer is therefore associated with a bigger current account change at constant terms of trade with tariffs present than in the free-trade case. It follows that if $MPM_1 + MPM_2 = 1$ with tariffs, the real transfer will be more than accomplished. The criterion for accomplishing the transfer with no change in the terms of trade must then be $MPM_1 + MPM_2 < 1$.[8]

When transport costs are included in the analysis, the crucial point is that the shipment of goods uses up resources and therefore can be regarded as an indirect demand for the products and labor of the country supplying the transportation services. An extra dollar spent on imports will worsen the balance of payments by more than \$1, in debits for transportation if it is supplied by the exporter, or by tying up resources that otherwise would go to exportables if transportation is supplied by the importer. Since the balance-of-payments impacts are greater than the simple MPM's, the transfer can again be completed without terms-of-trade changes if $MPM_1 + MPM_2 < 1$.[9]

Why the concern about the values of the marginal propensities necessary

[7] Paul A. Samuelson, "The Transfer Problem and Transport Costs: The Terms of Trade When Impediments are Absent," *Economic Journal*, LXII, No. 246 (June 1952), 278–304.

[8] Johnson, *International Trade and Economic Growth*, p. 173, works out the exact conditions involving tariff rates and marginal propensities.

[9] See Johnson, *International Trade and Economic Growth*, p. 174. Samuelson works out the tariff and transportation cost effects in the context of the real barter model using offer curves and indifference curves in "The Transfer Problem and Transport Costs, II: Analysis of Effects of Trade Impediments," *Economic Journal*, LXIV, No. 254 (June 1954), 264–88.

to accommodate the transfer without changing the terms of trade? Partly the desire to be able to make predictions, but also partly a reflection of welfare analysis. The transfer will be a burden to the paying country in any case, since it means a transfer of products to consumers in other countries; deteriorating terms of trade implies a secondary burden to it. Of course, if the sums of the *MPM*'s work out so that transfer is overaccomplished, the improvement of the terms of trade eases the primary burden. Could the terms of trade possibly improve so much that the original burden was wiped out and the payer was actually better off after the transfer? Yes, but only if the elasticities of reciprocal demand are so low that the international trade equilibrium is unstable.[10]

As for how this would all work out in practice, econometric studies show that anything is possible, although Professor Kindleberger believes that the two-country model is too unlike the real world to allow any confidence in statistics and that long-run changes are more important than the short-run ones dealt with in transfer theory.[11] In any event, statistics as applied to the two-country model would give widely different results in these circumstances: North America's marginal propensity to import from other industrial countries in 1948-1960, .019; other industrial countries' *MPM* from North America, 1948-1960, .008; Denmark, 1924-1938, *MPM* = .73; Norway, same time period, *MPM* = .67.[12] One may plausibly conclude that each transfer would have to be studied on its own; generalizations can mean little.

TRANSFER UNDER KEYNESIAN ASSUMPTIONS

In the classical model, with a constant level of output, the problem of transfer is one of cutting the amount consumed in the payer and raising the consumption and imports of the receiver. But after the Keynesian revolution the transfer problem was recast into a typical Keynesian setting, where employment is not necessarily full and where output can expand without an increase in the domestic price level.[13] To concentrate on the national income aspects, assume that exchange rates and internal rates of interest are fixed by domestic policy. A deficit in the balance of payments is financed

[10] Mundell, *American Economic Review*, L, p. 80.

[11] Kindleberger, *The Terms of Trade, A European Case Study*, pp. 124–25.

[12] The first two figures come from Jacques J. Polak and Rudolf R. Rhomberg, "Economic Instability in an International Setting," *American Economic Review Papers and Proceedings*, LII, No. 2 (May 1962), reprinted in American Economic Association, *Readings in Business Cycles* (Homewood, Ill.: Richard D. Irwin, Inc., 1965) together with an appendix not included in the original publication. The statistics quoted are on p. 590 of the latter. The last two figures come from Jacques J. Polak, *An International Economic System* (Chicago: University of Chicago Press, 1953), table facing p. 156.

[13] Lloyd Metzler, "The Transfer Problem Reconsidered," *Journal of Political Economy*, L, No. 3 (June 1942), 397–414.

by a movement of reserves without any corrective mechanism other than income changes being involved.

Suppose that country 1 undertakes a transfer of foreign aid to country 2. The accumulation of the funds in country 1 will have an impact on the amount spent for home goods and for imports, as in the classical model, but in the Keynesian model some of the impact will be felt by savings. Similarly, in country 2 the receipt of funds will influence the spending on home goods, imports, and savings. It is the combination of direct impact effects and induced changes in imports that leads to the real transfer; and if the transfer is not completed by income changes, subsequent changes in the terms of trade via exchange rate changes are called for in this model.

These generalizations can be made more precise with the help of a model such as the following.[14] In its most general form, the model consists of writing the changes in the two countries' national incomes and in country 1's balance of payments as the sum of autonomous changes in home and foreign demand and the induced changes in these same two categories, as:

$$dY_1 = dH_1 + MPH_1 \, dY_1 + dM_2 + MPM_2 \, dY_2$$
$$dY_2 = dH_2 + MPH_2 \, dY_2 + dM_1 + MPM_1 \, dY_1 \qquad \text{(21-4)}$$
$$dB_1 = dM_2 + MPM_2 \, dY_2 - dM_1 - MPM_1 \, dY_1 - T.$$

The symbols have these meanings: dY_1, dY_2, and dB_1 are the changes in the national incomes and in the paying country's balance of payments. dH_1 and dH_2 are autonomous changes in the demand for each country's own products; they are autonomous, of course, in the sense of being caused by something other than a change in national incomes. dM_1 is an autonomous change in the demand for imports in country 1; it therefore is a change in the demand for the exports of country 2 and appears in the equation for country 2's income. A similar interpretation is to be given to dM_2. The MPH's are the marginal propensities to spend on home products and may include marginal propensities to invest or to spend on the part of governments as well as the marginal propensity to consume. The MPM's are the marginal propensities to import, and T is the amount of the transfer. We assume that all marginal propensities are positive.

To find the effects of the transfer, one approach is to first determine its initial impact on home spending, imports, and savings, and substitute these for the autonomous changes in Eqs. (21-4). As a convenient definition, let MPH' be the fraction of the transfer that affects home spending, MPM' the fraction that changes the demand for imports, and MPS' the fractional impact on savings. Of course, $MPM' + MPH' + MPS' = 1$, since the funds raised will have to come out of one of these categories; and in the receiving country, the funds spent will go into one of these. In the following

[14] Reprinted from Harry Johnson, "Economic Trade and Economic Growth," *Journal of Political Economy*, University of Chicago Press, © Copyright 1956, LXIV, 217–21.

equations, the impact on home spending is given by $(1 - MPM' - MPS')T$, rather than by the equivalent $(MPH')T$.

It is now possible to change Eqs. **(21-4)** to relate them to the transfer:

$$dY_1 = (1 - MPM_1' - MPS_1')(-T) + (1 - MPM_1 - MPS_1)\, dY_1$$
$$+ (MPM_2')T + MPM_2\, dY_2$$
$$dY_2 = (1 - MPM_2' - MPS_2')T + (1 - MPM_2 - MPS_2)\, dY_2 \qquad \textbf{(21-5)}$$
$$- (MPM_1')T + MPM_1\, dY_1$$
$$dB_1 = (MPM_2')T + MPM_2\, dY_2 + (MPM_1')T - MPM_1\, dY_1 - T.$$

It is a straightforward if tedious bit of algebra to solve this three-equation system to see what has happened to country 1's balance of payments. If dB_1 is zero, the income changes have fully completed the transfer; if it is negative, the transfer is incompletely accomplished; and if positive, it has been more than handled. The solution can be expressed in this form:

$$dB_1 = \left(MPM_1' + MPM_2' - \frac{MPM_1}{MPS_1} MPS_1' - \frac{MPM_2}{MPS_2} MPS_2' - 1 \right)$$
$$\times \frac{MPS_1 MPS_2 T}{MPS_1 MPS_2 + MPS_1 MPM_2 + MPS_2 MPM_1}. \qquad \textbf{(21-6)}$$

Since the right-hand fraction is positive, the effect of the transfer on the balance of payments depends on whether the sum of the first two terms in the parentheses are larger or smaller than the sum of the last three. Any of the three possibilities for the sign of dB_1—positive, zero, or negative—could arise. A priori arguments on the transfer problem are as impossible in the Keynesian case as in the classical. More assumptions are needed if more definite theoretical results are desired.

One such assumption that is ready at hand is that used in the classical model, that the transfer is raised by an income tax in country 1 and distributed as a subsidy in country 2. Then $MPM' = MPM$ and $MPS' = MPS$ for both countries. Making these substitutions in Eq. **(21-6)** gives a simple result:

$$dB_1 = - \frac{MPS_1 MPS_2 T}{MPS_1 MPS_2 + MPS_1 MPM_2 + MPS_2 MPM_1}. \qquad \textbf{(21-7)}$$

The income changes in this case are an insufficient transfer mechanism, since the minus sign means that the balance of payments will be in deficit. To complete the transfer, the terms of trade will have to change—presumably through a depreciation by the paying country, since the less-than-full-employment assumption would indicate that expansions of output would leave prices unchanged.

Additional cases were considered by Metzler in his famous analysis of the transfer problem (see footnote 13). One of these is the possibility of one of the countries being stable but the other "unstable in isolation." That is, the latter has a negative marginal propensity to save, which makes it unstable because a small rise in income reduces saving, which leads to a still larger rise, without any end to the process. Applying the income tax-subsidy finance assumption, Eq. **(21-7)** tells us that a negative MPS for one country makes $dB_1 > 0$, so that the transfer will be more than accomplished. However, normally we do not expect to find negative MPS's, so this case should be rather rare.

It is more interesting to experiment with different sorts of financing practices that could be followed. It is by no means necessary for the paying country to raise the funds for the transfer by an income tax; the government might print money, borrow newly created money from the banks, ask for donations from the citizens, sell off stockpiles of copper or outmoded fighter planes, or sell bonds. The receiving country's government has a variety of courses open to it, too; for example, it can pay off debts with the transfer or save it for a rainy day rather than distributing it as a subsidy or remitting other taxes. For example, suppose that the paying government prints the money it needs for the transfer. There will be no impact on spending from the process of financing the transfer, so that $MPM_1' = MPS_1' = 0$. If we keep the assumption that $MPM_2' = MPM_2$ and that $MPS_2' = MPS_2$, Eq. **(21-7)** still applies. The transfer cannot be effected solely through income changes. Similarly, if the government of country 2 hoards the transfer proceeds, so that $MPM_2' = MPS_2' = 0$, Eq. **(21-7)** is relevant as long as $MPM_1' = MPM_1$ and $MPS_1' = MPS_1$. The transfer again would not be complete. And finally, if we combine both cases so that $MPM_i' = MPS_i' = 0$ ($i = 1, 2$), Eq. **(21-7)** is again the relevant one. It is suggested, in fact, that this latter case is the one applicable to German reparations problems of the 1920's, since the German economy was not deflated and the receivers used the funds to pay debts, which did not give any initial impact on spending.[15]

THE OPTIMUM AMOUNT OF FOREIGN INVESTMENT

Private foreign investment has often received a bad press. In Latin America it is "dollar imperialism"; in Canada it is nationalism and concern for the power that U.S. businesses have in deciding what to do with Canadian resources; in France the objection is that U.S. companies are so much bigger than French ones that they may remain untouched by the techniques of control of funds with which France administers its economic plan and just plain nationalism.[16]

[15] See the discussion in Kindleberger, *International Economics* (3rd ed.), p. 375.
[16] Harry G. Johnson, *The Canadian Quandary: Economic Problems and Policies;* Kindleberger, "European Integration and the International Corporation," in *Europe and the Dollar*.

There is, as well, some recently developed theory that questions the results of uncontrolled private investment—but the theory leads to the conclusion that uncontrolled investment is likely to be excessive from the point of view of the interests of the lending country, and that the borrower is likely to gain from it! This is quite the reverse of the popular criticism.

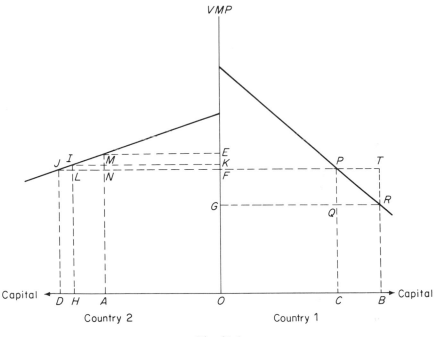

Fig. 21-1

One of the theoretical models explores the consequences of the assumption of diminishing marginal productivity of capital. Suppose there are the usual two countries, competition, and labor as the other factor of production, with country 1 the lender and country 2 the borrower. The capital inflow into country 2 may be into its export industry or its import-competing sector as far as this model goes; all that matters is that the value of the marginal product of capital falls as more is invested. Finally, for simplicity, assume that each country has a fixed fund that may be invested; country 2 will invest all its funds at home, but country 1 has the option between home and foreign investment. The transfer problem is assumed to be solved here.

A geometrical version of the argument is contained in Fig. 21-1.[17] Country 1 initially has *OB* of capital, which is all invested at home with

[17] This is a modification of the diagram in Kemp, *The Pure Theory of International Trade*, p. 199.

a marginal return of OG. Country 2's capital stock of OA yields OE as the value of the marginal product; and in order to maximize their returns, investors in country 1 shift $CB = AD$ of capital into country 2. The yield in both countries is equalized with returns of OF. Why is this said to be excessive from the point of view of country 1? The answer lies in the fact that the total product is the area under the value of marginal product (VMP) curve, and that this total product is split up into the rectangle formed by the value of marginal product and the total amount of capital, going to capitalists, and the triangle under the curve and above the interest rectangle, going to wage-earners. Using this fact, consider what would happen if foreign investment had, in fact, been a little smaller, for example, AH. If investment then increased by HD, an amount equal to the rectangle $ILMN$ would be transferred from country 1's capitalists to country 2's workers. In addition the workers gain the little triangle JIL, but this is not a transfer from profits to wages. In this sense, foreign investment to the point where the marginal product is equalized in both countries is excessive from country 1's viewpoint.

But a similar argument leads to the conclusion that complete stoppage of foreign investment also causes a loss to country 1. Suppose that investment abroad is prohibited and that CB of capital is repatriated. Home production would increase by $CPRB$, but overseas income would be cut by $DAJN = CBPT$. The difference is a loss to country 1 of the little triangle PTR. So there must be an optimum amount of foreign investment, someplace between the amount that equalizes the rates of return in the two countries and no foreign investment at all. Kemp, in an advanced mathematical analysis, shows that the optimum amount can be provided by a tax on the overseas investment income of country 1, the rate of the tax being a function of the ratio of foreign capital to total home and foreign capital in country 2 and the elasticity of country 2's marginal product curve.[18] It should be noted that the control of U.S. capital exports by guidelines, with their balance-of-payments motivation and their detailed administrative character, is unlikely to have any relation to the optimum as defined in this section.

A rather different line of thought also leads to the conclusion that the borrowers gain at the expense of the lenders in international capital flows; this argument depends on the institutional facts of life concerning taxes.[19] Typically, governments give persons with incomes from abroad credit for taxes paid to the foreign country. The resident of country 1, for example,

[18] Kemp, *The Pure Theory of Foreign Trade*, pp. 192–200. An important reference for this analysis is also G. D. A. MacDougall, "The Benefits and Costs of Private Investment from Abroad: A Theoretical Approach," *Economic Record*, XXXVI, No. 1 (March 1960), 13–35.

[19] In addition to the references in footnote 18, see Donald A. Wells, "Economic Analysis of Attitudes of Host Countries toward Direct Private Investment," and Paul B. Simpson, "Foreign Investment and the National Economic Advantage: A Theoretical Analysis," both in *U.S. Private and Government Investment Abroad*, ed. Raymond F. Mikesell (Eugene: University of Oregon Books, 1962).

may face a domestic tax rate of 50 per cent on his income, but have to pay 35 per cent to the government of country 2 for income earned there. Under a double-taxation agreement, he would apply the 35 per cent in country 1 and only have to pay an additional 15 per cent. Thus the investor (risks aside) has no reason to distinguish between investment at home and abroad. For the country, however, the transaction results in a loss of 35 per cent of the total profits, which is transferred to the borrower.[20]

Finally, there is the argument against foreign investment that in the event of confiscation or default the foreign country still has the real capital, whereas if the capital had been invested at home and a similar event occurred, the home country would have the real capital. The investor, in both cases, loses; it is a question of national rather than personal advantage.[21]

There are many other aspects to international capital flows besides the transfer problem and the optimum amount of foreign investment. For example, there is the question as to how intimately the transfer of technology is bound up with private foreign investment. And there is the interesting proposition that the large international corporation is a peerless instrument for economic integration, tying factor markets together internationally just as domestic corporations tie them together within the boundaries of a country.[22] But the two problems discussed in this chapter have a hallowed place in the literature and come under the heading of things everybody should know.

[20] Johnson, *The Canadian Quandary*, pp. xii–xx, lays great stress on the taxation argument in developing the thesis that Canada should not discriminate against U.S investment. He notes on p. xiv that taxes by U.S. direct investment companies amounted to 16 per cent of the 1957 overall government revenue in Canada.

[21] Kemp, *The Pure Theory of Foreign Trade*, p. 200.

[22] Kindleberger, "European Integration and the International Corporation," in *Europe and the Dollar*.

CHAPTER 22

LIQUIDITY, CONFIDENCE, AND INTERNATIONAL MONETARY REFORM

THE GREAT TRIO of modern international financial problems is adjustment, liquidity, and confidence. The previous chapters have focused on adjustment; it is now time to look at the others. The adjustment problem is fundamental to all varieties of foreign exchange systems, but liquidity and confidence questions vary from one to another so that they cannot be handled without institutional knowledge.

Reserves are needed under fixed exchange systems to finance a disequilibrium while the tools of adjustment are doing their work. Indeed, with very large reserves the need for adjustment may be postponed for years. Rather smaller amounts of reserves are called for in flexible exchange systems, if any, since the authorities would typically intervene in the market only if fluctuations grew excessive.[1] When the total size of the world's reserves is inadequate, it is said that a liquidity problem exists. An individual country may have inadequate reserves even if the world total is sufficient, but that is another matter—underdeveloped countries, for example, prefer to spend their foreign exchange rather than sacrifice the imports, as would be required if an accumulation of reserves is to be built up.

HOW LARGE SHOULD RESERVES BE?

The world's total of reserves at the end of 1966 was some $71.5 billion, excluding Soviet countries and Mainland China. This total was made up of about $41 billion of gold, $24 billion of currencies held as reserves,

[1] This was the case in Canada; Rhomberg notes that the intervention was moderate and was not the major influence in determining quarterly fluctuations. Rhomberg, *Staff Papers*, VII, 439.

and $6.5 billion of IMF positions.[2] Was this enough? Or was there a liquidity problem? The amount of reserves needed depends on things like the value of trade, the size of surpluses and deficits experienced, and the degree of confidence foreigners have in the adjustment policies pursued. While research attempting to pin down these factors is being carried on, it is an extremely difficult question. At an early stage of the investigation, the ratio of reserves to annual imports was widely used, and declines in this ratio from some earlier, "normal" period were regarded as signals of reserve inadequacy.[3] The trouble with this measure is that reserves are needed not only to cope with current account deficits (which may be short or long lasting) but also with capital account deficits and speculative runs. Hence the knowledge that country 1 has reserves sufficient to pay for five months' worth of imports does not help much; depending on the situation, this may be plenty of reserves or it may not.[4]

Recently, more sophisticated models have been developed. One of them suggests that the demand for reserves depends partly on past experience.[5] The experience for many countries, it is claimed, can be summarized in a Markov chain of this form:

$$\Delta R_t = a\,\Delta R_{t-1} + u_t \qquad (0 < a < 1). \tag{22-1}$$

That is, the change in reserves in period t depends on past changes, but these changes exert a diminishing influence over time; and it also depends on a stochastic term, a current disturbance coming from a normally distributed population with some mean and variance that can be estimated. Applied to the data from 14 advanced countries, this hypothesis gave statistical results that were not bad.

But if changes in the amount of reserves can be more or less predicted, then so can the total amount of them demanded. Expressing the demand as a linear function of the influence of past disturbances and the mean and variance of current disturbances gives the demand equation:

$$R_t = b - c\bar{u} + da + e\sigma_u. \tag{22-2}$$

Here b, c, d, and e are coefficients to be estimated from the reserve data; $\bar{u}$ and σ_u are the mean and standard error of the stochastic variable u; and a

[2] International Monetary Fund, *1967 Annual Report*, p. 12.

[3] International Monetary Fund, *International Reserves and Liquidity* (Washington, D.C.: International Monetary Fund, 1958); Robert Triffin, *Gold and the Dollar Crisis* (New Haven: Yale University Press, 1960), pp. 35–46.

[4] Fritz Machlup, "The Need for Monetary Reserves," *Banca Nazionale del Lavoro Quarterly Review*, No. 78 (September 1966), 1–48, has surveyed reserves as a ratio not only to imports but also to trade balance variations, capital outflows, past deficits, domestic money supply, and current liabilities, and finds no indication that time series of ratios or intercountry differences in them can be explained by a "need" for reserves.

[5] Peter B. Kenen and Elinor B. Yudin, "The Demand for International Reserves," *Review of Economics and Statistics*, XLVII, No. 3 (August 1965), 242–50.

is the term from Eq. **(22-1)** showing how fast the influence of past disturbances dies away. Applying this equation to the data from the 14 countries in some cross-sectional analyses again gave a statistical outcome that was not bad. But the model is not designed to cope with the problem of speculative runs, which are one-sided in contrast to the assumption that u_t comes from a random, normally distributed population.[6]

This approach is an attempt to analyze the nature of part of the demand for reserves. A different tack is to try to compute the optimal level of reserves by means of a social cost analysis. If country 1 is faced with an ex ante deficit of $1 billion, its alternatives are to finance it from its reserves, adjust by expenditure-reducing policies, or use expenditure-switching policies—or use all three in some combination. Rationally, it would determine what proportion of the deficit to handle with each approach on the basis of making the marginal cost of each alternative equal. An attempt to formulate this precisely has been made by H. R. Heller.[7] In his model the marginal cost of reserves is the difference between the social rate of return on capital and the return on the capital tied up in reserves, while the marginal cost of adjusting via expenditure-reducing policies depends on the marginal propensity to import[8] and the probability that such a policy will have to be used. This information, together with the past annual changes in reserves, is used to calculate the amount of reserves that will minimize the total cost of adjusting and of holding reserves. As both Heller and his critics point out, this approach, while valuable in breaking away from the naive ratios approach, is only a first step; no one has yet computed marginal costs of switching policies, and the large problems of foreign repercussions, confidence, and key currency countries were not handled.[9]

Finally, although not a statistically implemented model like the preceding ones, there is a theory of the need for reserve that every up-to-date student of international finance should know: the Mrs. Machlup's Wardrobe Theory of Monetary Reserves.[10] Professor Machlup believes that he can understand the behavior of monetary authorities by analogy to the demand for dresses, where there is no valid criterion of need, but simply a desire for a few new ones every year. Monetary authorities, it is said, have a similar

[6] For this and other criticisms see Robert Clower and Richard Lipsey, "The Present State of International Liquidity Theory," *American Economic Review Papers and Proceedings*, LVIII, No. 2 (May 1968), 586–95.

[7] H. R. Heller, "Optimal International Reserves," *Economic Journal*, LXXVI, No. 302 (June 1966), 296–311.

[8] If $MPM = .2$, a $5 billion fall in national income is needed to close a $1 billion deficit in the simple model without international repercussions; while if $MPM = .1$, a $10 billion national income cut is needed. The cost of the latter case is clearly twice as high as the former.

[9] Heller, *Economic Journal*, LXXVI, 309–310; Clower and Lipsey, *American Economic Review*, LVIII, 591–92.

[10] Machlup, *Banca Nazionale del Lavoro Quarterly Review*, No. 78, 25–27.

psychology; and if they do not get their desired increase in reserves, they turn to expenditure-reducing or -switching policies. Machlup is particularly concerned about the trade- and capital-restricting forms of switching policies and declares than an annual increase in world reserves sufficient to avoid use of them is desirable.

Several other authorities have suggested that the best way to approach the question of the adequacy of reserves is to look at the balance-of-payments policies currently being used.[11] If it seems that these are in fact policies that force a number of major countries to operate at less than full employment or to use trade or capital restrictions in order to reduce the size of their deficits, it is argued that this is evidence of a generalized liquidity shortage. Now as we know the United States and the United Kingdom have used both tools; in addition, Canada and France have recently used restrictions, and Japan, Italy, and Germany have used expenditure reductions. The increasing resort to such policies indicates a good likelihood that there is in fact inadequate provision for increasing reserves in the present system, and leads to the question, how are reserves generated in the 1970's?

THE CREATION AND MANAGEMENT OF RESERVES

The answer to that question requires knowing a bit about how today's variety of a fixed exchange rate system works. Since the end of World War II, the world has been on a variant of the gold-exchange standard. That is, gold is regarded as the fundamental balancing item, but it is only four/sevenths of the stock of reserves. Most of the rest is dollars ($15 billion, end of 1966) and pounds ($7 billion worth, end of 1965), with $2 billion of miscellaneous currencies. The sterling component has been fairly stable in size since 1951, but the dollar balances have grown to their present size from $4 billion in 1951.[12] This mixture is called a gold-exchange standard because the currency component—dollars and sterling—is itself based on gold reserves, in international but not in domestic transactions.

This international monetary arrangement, with its heavy reliance on what are called "key currencies," evolved rather than being created. Wartime

---

[11] Gottfried Haberler, *Money in the International Economy* (Cambridge, Mass.: Harvard University Press, 1965), p. 41; Machlup, *Banca Nazionale del Lavoro Quarterly Review*, No. 78, 29–34; Richard N. Cooper, "The Relevance of International Liquidity to Developed Countries," *American Economic Review, Papers and Proceedings*, LVIII, No. 2 (May 1968), 634–35. There is a school of thought that puts much stress on the discipline of the balance of payments as a vital force in containing inflation and that gets upset at the suggestion of increasing reserves because that would erode the discipline. Cooper suggests this view is wrong because the sort of wrong-headed policies that adequate reserves would forestall are those that have to be reversed in a short time rather than long-term anti-inflationary policies.

[12] IMF, *1966 Annual Report*, p. 12.

planning at Bretton Woods, when the International Monetary Fund and the International Bank for Reconstruction and Development were formed, envisioned a much larger role for these agencies. But the initial inactivity of the fund while the United States was providing reconstruction funds and goods, Europe's decision to handle their intra-European payments through the European Payments Union rather than the IMF during the early 1950's, and the dollar shortage during which the dollar was a scarce and highly desired currency set the stage for widespread use of the dollar.[13] In the case of sterling, large short-term sterling debts were created during the course of the war, and these remained as a means of payment, rather circumscribed by sterling area controls but gradually loosened up as reconstruction proceeded.

The basic international reserves are thus gold, dollars, and sterling. The International Monetary Fund functions in this setting to make more reserves available to its members on a limited basis. As already explained, each member has a quota; the total quotas in 1966 were about $21 billion. The members may borrow—technically, purchase other currencies with an obligation to repurchase their own currency at a later time—up to 125 per cent of each individual's quota. The right to borrow is regarded as automatic for the first 25 per cent of the quota (the gold tranche), or whatever amount is needed to bring IMF holdings of the currency up to 100 per cent of the quota. Beyond that, access to the fund may be conditional on compliance with various policies deemed desirable by the fund, such as sound fiscal and monetary policy or dropping the use of multiple exchange rates.[14]

The fund's operations have been enlarged over the years by changes in their practices. The first nine years of its life did not see as much as $1 billion of outstanding drawings in any one year, an indication of its relative inactivity. But then the fund dropped the requirement that not more than 25 per cent of the quota could be used in a year, it developed the practice of standby arrangements, where purchases can be arranged in advance and then used only if needed; quotas were enlarged several times; the United States began to make drawings for the first time. As a result, outstanding drawings have gone up in recent years to nearly $5 billion in 1966, with $.5 billion of standby arrangements in force.

Even with the rise in IMF activity in international finance, many steps affecting international reserves take place outside the fund. The previously described U.S. operations in the forward exchange market, the sale of

[13] Harry G. Johnson, *The World Economy at the Crossroads* (Oxford: Clarendon Press, 1965), pp. 22–24.

[14] This practice, fairly common in underdeveloped countries, means that different exchange rates are set on various classes of exports and imports. This has the effect of selective depreciation, since higher rates can be set on exports with inelastic demands and on imports not urgently needed. The multiple exchange rate system is often used as a form of taxation.

inconvertible bonds, and the swap operations described in the footnote[15] are one type of event. Another is the rescue operation that has sometimes been mounted when a country's reserves are rapidly being exhausted to meet speculative capital outflows. In 1962 Canada borrowed more than $1 billion, $300 million from the IMF and the rest from the United Kingdom and the United States. Italy suffered a speculative attack in 1964 and met it with nearly $1 billion of borrowed currency, mostly from the United States and the IMF. The most spectacular rescue was the speedy mobilization of $3 billion of assorted funds in addition to $1 billion from the IMF to help England over an exchange crisis in 1964.[16] These emergency funds help curb the speculative outflows by persuading speculators that there is no chance that the currencies will be devalued because of inadequate reserves, even though the balance of payments is in deficit, but they also show that the IMF quotas are inadequate for such operations and that international cooperation is essential if the present system is to continue to work.

The IMF and the informal rescue operation were brought together in the formation in 1962 of the Group of Ten, who signed with the fund an agreement called the General Arrangements to Borrow. Ten industrial countries agreed to lend a total of $6 billion to the IMF if the fund had a short supply of some currency but needed it for stabilization purposes. However, each of the signers kept the right to refuse to lend, so these funds are not at all under the control of the IMF.

CONFIDENCE

It is obvious from this history that there are two elements in the liquidity problem: One is having enough liquidity to handle the ordinary deficits that are bound to come along; the other is rounding up liquidity to meet speculative crises that develop when the first aspect gives trouble.

---

[15] In a swap operation, an agreement is made between the Federal Reserve System and a foreign central bank to exchange currencies for a limited period of time. For example, the Federal Reserve System might need marks to purchase an excess supply of spot dollars being offered for sale by German residents. Under the agreement, the Federal Reserve System would credit the account of the Deutsche Bundesbank with a certain amount of dollars while obtaining a credit of the equivalent amount of marks with the Bundesbank. The Federal Reserve System would then draw marks from this account to purchase the spot dollars. In another case, it might need marks to meet maturing forward contracts to buy dollars. At the end of the specified time the transactions are reversed. In early 1966 there were 12 such arrangements totaling nearly $3 billion. These operations are handy in meeting short-term capital flows that otherwise might result in gold outflows and hence a loss in reserves for the United States. A full description is in the series of articles by Coombs, *Federal Reserve Bulletin*, every six months.

[16] Robert Z. Aliber, *The Future of the Dollar as an International Currency* (New York: Frederick A. Praeger, Inc., 1966), pp. 39–40.

This latter element has been called the confidence problem. A lack of confidence may be a problem for any country, but in today's international monetary system it is particularly important for the reserve currencies. The reason is that, as well as providing more than two/sevenths of the total stock of the world reserves, these key currencies are looked to as the source of future increases in world liquidity unless substantial reforms are adopted. Substantial increases in the amount of gold are unlikely and gold-tranche positions are not a net addition to total reserves. But in the traditional way of looking at it, increasing world reserves by increasing the amount of key currencies held by foreign monetary authorities involves a deficit for the key currency country. If the deficit is persistent so that the supply of that component of world reserves gets large, the ratio of gold reserves to official liabilities for the key currency country is going to get smaller. This may lead to fears and rumors of devaluation in spite of repeated assurances to the contrary and in spite of the rigidity of contemporary exchange rates. As has happened with the United Kingdom and to a smaller degree with the United States, a flight may develop from the reserve currency. If France and Germany sell dollars to the U.S. Treasury for gold, for example, the world total of reserves would be reduced. France and Germany would have the same amount of reserves, in a changed form, but the United States would have fewer reserves. And the loss of gold may further reduce confidence.[17]

The view that confidence depends on the amount of reserves a country has relative to its short-term liabilities is the traditional approach. This has been challenged as being inapplicable to countries performing the reserve currency function, as we saw in Chap. 15. One dissenting view holds that the United States, in particular, functions as a financial intermediary, acquiring long-term foreign assets in exchange for its short-term liabilities, and that the performance of this function should not cause a lack of confidence when it is properly understood. Another version of the misinterpretation thesis is that a reserve currency country is supposed to supply reserves and that only when the supply is excessive from the standpoint of world reserve needs should any question be raised.[18] But there is no doubt that these are still minority views.

History since World War II shows the role of confidence and its relation to the supply of key currencies. Early in the period, when the dollar was scarce, the United States found that it did not have to attempt to adjust

[17] A theoretical approach to this problem is in Peter B. Kenen, "International Liquidity and the Balance of Payments of a Reserve-Currency Country," *Quarterly Journal of Economics*, LXXIV, No. 297 (November 1960), 572–86.

[18] See the references to the works by Kindleberger and Tarshis on this point in Chap. 15. Cf. Robert Triffin, *The Balance of Payments and the Foreign Investment Position of the United States*, Essays in International Finance No. 55 (Princeton, N.J.: International Finance Section, Princeton University, 1966), p. 13, for a brief statistical analysis that leads to the conclusion that the financial intermediary thesis is exaggerated.

the balance of payments by restrictive policies on trade, payments, or the national income; it could run deficits and let the eagerly welcomed dollar balances build up overseas. But when dollar surplus became the order of the day, it was found that the reserve currency function brought pressures in addition to those typically expected for a deficit country. These included inhibitions on devaluation to protect the value of the outstanding dollar balances, and on pursuing domestic policies that official holders of dollars considered inflationary, even in the face of unemployment, lest a wholesale cashing in of dollars for gold occur.[19] Some analysts also claim that the basis for restrictive policies on foreign aid and on commercial transactions and the interest equalization tax and guidelines on foreign investment was the desire to maintain confidence by reducing the supply of dollars rather than the traditional motive of balance-of-payments adjustment.[20]

INTERNATIONAL LIQUIDITY REFORM

Thus the confidence problem has implications both for liquidity, since it may slow down or reverse the growth of reserve currency holdings, and for adjustment, since it may make the adjustment policies of the reserve currency country fit the preconceptions of its creditors. As regards the liquidity problem, it has long been realized that the additions to the reserve stock from newly mined gold or Soviet gold sales would be inadequate—hence the mixture of reserve currency and IMF gold-tranche additions to liquidity. The fact that there are so many crises and balance-of-payments-inspired trade and capital controls shows that the question of liquidity is of immediate importance. If additions to liquidity come from dollars or sterling, the confidence problem will be intensified. If the United States should actually achieve a surplus, liquidity would be reduced. Professor Triffin has been forecasting a long-run shortage of reserves for several years.[21] He was joined in 1964 by the Group of Ten, which suggested that possibly Triffin was right and that study should be made of a new form of reserve asset to supplement existing reserves.[22] The *IMF 1964 Annual Report* also suggested that the present system might give inadequate reserves in coming years. The result of the efforts of these groups was the plan for Special Drawing Rights, reviewed below.

[19] William A. Salant, "The Reserve Currency Role of the Dollar: Blessing or Burden to the United States?" *Review of Economics and Statistics*, XLVI, No. 2 (May 1964), 165–72; and Robert Z. Aliber, "The Costs and Benefits of the U.S. Role as a Reserve Currency Country," *Quarterly Journal of Economics*, LXXVIII (August 1964), 442–56, revised and published as Chap. III of his *The Future of the Dollar as an International Currency*.

[20] James Tobin, "Europe and the Dollar," *Review of Economics and Statistics*, XLVI, No. 2 (May 1964), 123–26.

[21] Robert Triffin, *Gold and the Dollar Crisis*.

[22] "Ministerial Statement of the Group of Ten and Annex Prepared by Deputies," which is reprinted in Robert V. Roosa, *Monetary Reform for the World Economy*.

There was no lack of suggestions for them to evaluate. The spinning of plans for monetary reform has taken on the proportions of an epidemic; Machlup's pamphlet, for example, lists in the neighborhood of 100 publications dealing with schemes for reform, and the growth of articles did not stop in 1964.[23] The major reason for the multitude of plans is a lack of agreement on the fundamental features of a reform.

We have already seen that one outstanding difference in approaches to international monetary arrangements is in the role of exchange rates: fixed rates, flexible rates, or the adjustable peg, which is fixed until further notice. Under the IMF, the basic approach is the adjustable peg, which is supposed to be adjusted when there is a fundamental disequilibrium and after consultation with the fund. Since for major industrial countries, at least, the experience has been that rates are not often adjusted, some plans concentrate on ways to make more use of the exchange rate tool of adjustment. Such is the case, for example, with the idea of widening the "band" within which rates would be allowed to fluctuate around a given parity, and obviously espousal of flexible rates is the extreme limit of this approach.

Other analysts of the monetary system more or less accept the prevailing official attitudes toward exchange rates and concentrate instead on the deficiencies of the gold-exchange standard, its erratic approaches to liquidity, and the dilemmas of the reserve currency countries. These authors are likely to concentrate on some way to replace the gold-exchange standard by introducing a new international form of reserves. Before going into more detail about some of these plans, note that there are other dimensions to reform about which agreement would have to be reached, such as the appropriate volume of reserves to create and under what conditions should they be created. Examples of the questions that come up under the latter point are:

1. Should reserves be created automatically up to some previously arranged limit when a country has a deficit, to give time for adjustment, or should they be created under what the Group of Ten calls "multilateral surveillance"?

2. Should a country whose deficit results from domestic inflation be given access to more reserves, or should the privilege be restricted to continuing deficits arising from real rather than monetary disturbances?[24]

[23] Fritz Machlup, *Plans for Reform of the International Monetary System*, Special Papers in International Economics No. 3 (rev. ed.) (Princeton, N.J.: International Finance Section, Princeton University, 1964). Another good source for description and evaluation of most of the plans is R. G. Hawkins and S. E. Rolfe, *A Critical Survey of Plans for International Monetary Reform*, Bulletin No. 36 of the C. J. Devine Institute of Finance (New York: New York University, 1965). Many of the original presentations of various plans can be found in H. G. Grubel, ed., *World Monetary Reform: Plans and Issues* (Stanford, Calif.: Stanford University Press, 1963).

[24] Questions that monetary reform plans ought to address explicitly but that they often approach only implicitly are raised by R. E. Caves, "International Liquidity: Toward a Home Repair Manual," *Review of Economics and Statistics*, XLVI, No. 2 (May 1964), 173–80, from which the above questions were taken.

Of the large selection of plans, three in particular are worth special attention: the Keynes Plan, for its historical interest; the Triffin Plan, important because of its influence as a questioner of the gold-exchange standard; and Special Drawing Rights, the plan proposed by the IMF.

THE KEYNES PLAN

Early in World War II plans for postwar monetary arrangements were drafted by Harry Dexter White in the U.S. Treasury and John Maynard Keynes in the British Treasury. These alternative schemes were the basis for the Bretton Woods conference, which set up the IMF along the lines of the U.S. proposal. Keynes' plan was much more radical. It involved a new currency unit called Bancor to function along with gold as a reserve, with national currencies not to be used any longer for settlements. Bancor would be obtained by:

1. Selling gold to the Clearing Union, the Keynesian equivalent of the IMF, or
2. Making use of overdraft privileges to cover international deficits.

An overdraft consists of writing a check when there are no funds in the account; when a bank honors an overdraft it creates money. Analogously, the Clearing Union would create Bancor. The IMF does not create money, by contrast; it simply loans out funds from a previously deposited pool of currency, in effect. The Clearing Union would function like an honest-to-goodness bank and, like a bank, could refuse to make loans unless the client had his affairs in order. In this case it was proposed that the bank would have power to enforce changes in exchange rates, tariffs, or domestic policies as a condition for allowing the overdraft. Quotas would be set as to how much Bancor a country could draw, much more liberal quotas than the IMF originally set. Charges on both debtor and creditor balances were suggested to encourage returns to equilibrium; since surplus nations would receive Bancor credits on the books of the Clearing Union whose usefulness would only be to settle some possible future deficit, it was hoped that a charge on them would make the surplus country somewhat more eager to adjust than it often is.[25]

The Keynes Plan ran into opposition because it would have created a strong international monetary organization, impairing national sovereignty; because many deemed it inflationary with its initial $30 billion of quotas, which would increase because they were based on a moving average of trade turnover; and because there were those who preferred foreign exchange

---

[25] J. M. Keynes, "Proposals for an International Clearing Union," Cmd. 6437 (London: Her Majesty's Stationery Office, 1943), reprinted in Grubel, *World Monetary Reform: Plans and Issues.*

controls to multilateral freedom of payments. The plan was apparently based on the model of a world in which the United States ran surpluses because it could or would not achieve full employment, while other countries ran deficits because they did maintain full employment; it was designed to allow them to pursue expansionary policies. The inflationary danger was that perfectly automatic credit creation would also be consistent with a model where the United States maintained full employment and the others pursued inflationary over-full-employment policies. But this could be handled by appropriate discretion on the part of the Clearing Union, which in turn would depend on quotas and voting powers. The benefits would be its contribution to the liquidity and the confidence problems.[26]

THE TRIFFIN PLAN

Professor Triffin made use of Keynes' suggestions when drawing up his famous plan for reform. But he added some new features; in particular, not only would the IMF be able to allow overdrafts in Bancor, which depend on a deficit country taking the initiative, but also it could create Bancor on its own by buying securities in the open markets of any country it wanted to, paying for them by giving Bancor credits. Limits on this process would be set up to prevent inflationary overcreation, but if national actions were not contributing enough to the expansion of liquidity, the IMF would act. Countries could also acquire Bancor by depositing gold, dollars, or sterling with the IMF. Initially 20 per cent of their foreign exchange reserves would have to be exchanged for Bancor, and gradually all of it would be. When that had happened, the liquidity and the confidence problems would be under control.[27] In the discussion of the plan, Professor Johnson suggested that the confidence problem still remained; if the fund did engage in open-market operations, its Bancor liabilities would grow relative to its gold assets, and the countries holding Bancor could exchange 80 per cent of the new Bancor for gold if their confidence was impaired by the low gold ratio of the fund. The plan can be provided with gimmicks to try to cope with this, such as Triffin's subsequent suggestions of high interest rates on holdings of Bancor and raising the required ratio of Bancor holdings to total reserves.[28]

While there would be many operational problems to be solved, such as the best capital markets in which to conduct open-market operations, the

[26] The Keynes Plan was criticized at great length when it was first presented; a more recent summary and criticism is Robert Triffin, *Europe and the Money Muddle*, Yale Studies in Economics: 7 (New Haven: Yale University Press, 1957), pp. 93–109.

[27] Robert Triffin, *Gold and the Dollar Crisis* pp. 102–20.

[28] Harry G. Johnson, "International Liquidity—Problems and Plans," *Malayan Economic Review*, VIII, No. 1 (April 1962), 1–19, reprinted in Grubel, *World Monetary Reform: Plans and Issues;* Robert Triffin, *The World Money Maze: National Currencies in International Payments* (New Haven: Yale University Press, 1966), Chap. IX.

optimum amount of new reserves to create, and so on, these could no doubt be solved if countries were willing to make the plan work. It rests on the premise that there would be more confidence and liquidity with the plan than with the present gold-exchange standard; but this will be true only if the national monetary authorities wish it to be so.

SDR'S

At the moment, the national authorities apparently are not willing to go so far. The plan that won the approval of the governors of the IMF and that subsequently was adopted by the members provides for a new IMF facility called SDR's (Special Drawing Rights). The SDR's are to be kept completely separate from the already existing General Drawing Rights. They will work something like this: Suppose that the IMF has allocated $30 million in SDR's to Spain. If Spain has a balance-of-payments deficit, it can transfer the SDR's to, for example, France, receiving francs in return; and it may then use the francs to support the peseta in the exchange markets. Spain is not required to repurchase the SDR's, as it presently would be if it had used the General Drawing Rights of the IMF. France keeps the SDR's until it in turn has a need for acquiring other currencies to settle a balance-of-payments deficit. Thus by adding SDR's to the accounts of its members, the IMF can create reserves; and these reserves can be transferred from one member to another.

The SDR plan is well hedged with safeguards and restrictions. The plan calls for a basic period (normally five years) during which SDR's will be created at a specified rate and at specified intervals. The length of the basic period, the timing of the creation of new SDR's, their amount, and the rate of their allocation, however, are subject to the approval of an 85 per cent majority of the IMF voting power. Since the EEC members have a total vote of $16\frac{1}{2}$ per cent, they can exercise a veto; and since France is well known to be cool to anything except the old-fashioned gold standard, there is concern that the amount of SDR's may be too limited. There is also a provision that members who vote against the creation of new SDR's may elect not to receive them.

On the side of restrictions on the use of SDR's, they are to be used for meeting balance-of-payments deficits, not for changing the composition of reserves (this is to prevent a run from dollars into SDR's). A country using them is expected to make no more than an average net use of 70 per cent of its allocation, apparently to encourage a "balanced" use of all reserve items, and to use them to buy currencies from countries with surpluses or strong reserve positions. Countries acquiring SDR's from others are protected by a gold value guarantee, a payment of interest, and an upper bound on their obligation to take SDR's of twice as many as their cumulative allocation.

The SDR's represent a slow bit of evolution rather than a mutation in the gold-exchange standard. For one thing, there was much discussion during the negotiations that a precondition for activating the SDR plan was that the United States and the United Kingdom had first to achieve balance-of-payments equilibrium, which could well postpone their creation for some time. It does not establish control over the total amount of liquidity, but only over part, although presumably the amount of SDR's created will vary in rough relationship to the behavior of gold and dollars in relation to the consensus of need. Since the new SDR's are to be distributed according to existing quotas, the criticism has been made that too many of them will go to the advanced countries and not enough to the less-developed ones.[29] This is in spite of the fact that as a percentage of reserves the quotas of LDC's are higher than for the advanced countries, so that the SDR's would raise reserves of the LDC's by a higher percentage.[30]

It is by now apparent that ingenuity can come up with many different solutions for the liquidity and the confidence problems. But it is also true that there is no concensus about the appropriate solution among the academic experts. Meanwhile the official negotiators for monetary reform are struggling to find an acceptable division of control within the basic framework of the present system rather than contemplating fundamental reforms.

It is important not to lose sight of the adjustment problem in contemplating liquidity. The volume of liquidity needed depends on the size and speed of the adjustments that have to be made to achieve balance-of-payments equilibrium; simultaneously, the pressure on a country to adjust depends on the amount of liquidity at its command. And the nature of the adjustment problem also should be considered. Temporary balance-of-payments problems—deficits caused by crop failures, abnormally high inventory accumulation, or other short-run phenomena—give little trouble here. It is entirely appropriate to use international reserves to tide over these deficits and replenish them when the emergency is over. It is the long-run adjustments caused either by changes in comparative advantage, long-run development programs, wartime dislocations, or continued inflations that bring up the issue of the appropriate amount of liquidity. With insufficient liquidity and fixed exchange rates, adjustment pressures can require sacrificing the internal balance goal or the excessive use of controls. Excessive liquidity

[29] See Robert Triffin's testimony in Joint Economic Committee, *New Plan for International Monetary Reserves*, Part 2 (Washington, D.C.: U.S. Government Printing Office, 1967), p. 138.

[30] Alexandre Kafka, "International Liquidity: Its Present Relevance to the Less Developed Countries," *American Economic Review Papers and Proceedings*, LVIII, No. 2 (May 1968), 596–603.

allows postponing the adjustment and has two effects: a transfer of resources from the surplus to the deficit country and the possibility of inflation, since the surplus country's money supply and national income rises while the deficit country is not forced to deflate. Someplace between the two extremes is the appropriate level of reserves. The advocates for reform have in common the belief that the appropriate level requires guidance.

INDEX

Markov chain, 273
Marshall, Alfred, 42, 43, 93, 129n
Marshall-Lerner condition, 229, 231, 245
Marshall Plan, 85
Meade, James, 47, 115–16, 116n, 141
  on balance of payments, 190, 191, 192n, 223
Metzler, Lloyd, 45–47, 45n, 233
  on capital transfers, 267–68
Michaely, Michael, 59n, 75, 232n
Military transactions, 177
Mill, John Stuart, 20
Minhas, B. S., 59
Money:
  balance of payments and, 183, 184, 187, 190, 193
    gold in, 180, 191, 195, 205
    inflation in, 192, 196
    money supply and, 201–5, 207–8, 216, 217, 251, 252
  as convertible currency, 180–81
  gold-standard in, 262, 275, 280, 281, 283, 284
  gold-tranche position in, 180, 181, 183, 185, 187, 276, 278, 279
  international monetary system in, 180–81
    confidence in, 272, 273, 277–79, 282–84
    liquidity problem in, 272, 275, 277–80, 282–85
    reform of, 279–85
    reserves in, 180–82, 191, 193, 197, 205, 208, 217, 239–41, 243, 256, 272–83
  liquidity demand for, 251
  optimum currency areas in, 259–60
  during productivity growth, 148
  tight-money policy in, 193, 214, 215, 219, 254
  See also Balance of payments; Capital; Exchange rates; Interest rates; International Monetary Fund; Savings
Money illusion, 234, 235
Monopolies, 20, 57, 86–92, 117, 167
  in Pareto optimum, 116
  prices affected by, 166
  quotas and, 132–33
  temporary, 88–90
Moroney, John R., 66
Mundell, Robert A., 39n, 40n, 74n, 259
  on spot rate, 242n, 251n–52n
Myint, Hla, 160
Myrdal, Gunnar, 158

Natural resource products, 64, 66
Net national product (NNP), 197–200, 208, 214
New products, 89, 103, 144, 204
Nurske, Ragnar, 102, 192n, 244

Offer curves, 33, 37–49
  defined, 38
  demonstration effect and, 102
  in economic growth, 149, 151, 157
  elasticities of, 39–43, 46, 109, 109n–10n, 111, 120, 263

Offer curves (Cont.)
  income distribution and, 103–6
  in increasing returns, 96–99
  for optimum tariff, 120–21
  tariffs affecting, 44, 223
  trade indifference curves showing, 49
  in transportation costs, 70, 72–73
  See also Demand curves
Ohlin, Bertil, 50n, 52, 66, 262
  See also Heckscher-Ohlin model
Oligopolies, 86, 92, 144
Optimum currency areas, 259–60

Pareto optimum, 115n, 116–17
Pearce, I. F., 232n
Pigou effect, 234, 235
Prebisch, Raúl, 158
Prebisch thesis, 166–68
Price index, 204n, 214, 234, 258
Price levels:
  in balance of payments, 208–10
  in capital transfers, 262, 265
  exchange rates and, 225, 227
  in expenditure-reduction policies, 212–13
Price ratios, 26, 34
  in competitive markets, 7–8, 22, 117
  in increasing returns, 95, 98, 125
  international, 10–11
  in monopolistic factor markets, 90–91
  in offer curves, 37–38, 41
  posttrade, 13
  pretrade, 11, 13
  tariffs affecting, 28, 44, 45, 106, 110-12, 125, 131
  in terms of trade, 109
  in trade indifference curves, 49
  in transformation curves, 22, 26, 27, 48, 83, 117, 162
  in transportation costs, 71–74
Pricing, discriminatory monopoly, see Dumping
Producers' surplus, 129, 129n, 131
Production:
  economic growth affecting, 149–54
  equilibrium of, 53, 91, 94, 96
  factors of, 20–22, 46, 151, 197
    in customs unions, 134
    in developing countries, 159, 161, 162, 165
    in Heckscher-Ohlin model, 50–58, 108
    in input-output equations, 61, 81, 82
  in increasing returns, 94–98
  in monopolistic factor markets, 90–91
  scale of, 143–44, 159
  variable, 47–49
Production functions, 22–25
  in comparative advantage theory, 20
  as different, 59–60
  Edgeworth-Bowley box diagram for, 24–25
  as homogeneous, 50, 59, 59n
    in Heckscher-Ohlin model, 50–51, 54, 55, 60
  population growth affecting, 30–32
  returns to scale of, 92, 104, 151
  technology affecting, 24, 25
  in transformation curves, 20–22, 25

291